CLASS FIVE
CHRONICLES

Things Mother Never Told You 'Bout Whitewater

JEFF BENNETT
Contributing Editor

SWIFTWATER PUBLISHING COMPANY
Portland, Oregon

To all of our parents: It was all done in the studio with stuntmen, mirrors, and tricky camera angles... honest!

Published by Swiftwater Publishing Company, P.O. Box 3031, Portland, Oregon 97208-3031. © 1992 by Jeff Bennett. All rights reserved. No part of this book may be reproduced by any means except as may be expressly permitted by the publisher.

Front Cover: Class V+ "That's Dumb", Upper Kings River, California. Photo by James Thomson/Rapid Shooters. From the *Classic Images* Calendar, which can be purchased through Rapid Shooters, 7221 Hwy 49, Lotus, California 95651. (916) 621-0259

For a pulse-raising Class V video featuring many of the rivers in this book, check out *Blazing Paddles* by Camera One, PO Box 75556, Seattle, WA 98125. (206) 547-5131

Publisher's cataloging in publication data

Bennett, Jeff, 1961-
    Class Five Chronicles: Things Mother Never Told You
    'Bout Whitewater / by Jeff Bennett — 1st. Ed.
    Bibliography: p.
    Includes index.
    1. White-water rafting—Guide-books   2. Rafting (Sports)
    3. Rivers—United States   4. Rivers—United States—Literary
    collections   5. United States—Description and travel
    I. Bennett, Jeff, 1961-   II. Title
    ISBN 0-9629843-3-7
    Library of Congress Catalog Card Number 92-090707

Manufactured in the United States of America
First Edition/First Printing

Printed on Recycled Paper

"If there is ever a Twelve Step program for whitewater addicts, Jeff Bennett should be a founding member.

Class Five Chronicles is less about river running than about adrenaline addiction, about the insatiable need for a Class V whitewater fix, about the exhilerating excitement that follows survival of a 12 foot waterfall.

From Siberia to the South Fork Salmon, from Costa Rican rainforests to the Upper Colorado, Bennett leads us on a madcap, hairball tour through some of the wildest river runs on earth.

Like many of us who run Class V, Bennett may be in denial about the danger, but he's no fool. This chronicle of death-defying whitewater is peopled by expert paddlers, people who know how to escape from the wrath of the rivergods, people who know rivers aren't conquered, only survived.

You'll have a ball with this book. You'll learn a lot about rivers you may think, someday, you'd like to run. But as Bennett warns in the preface, *don't let your mother catch you reading it!*"

— **David Bolling**, river runner, author
and former Executive Director
of Friends of the River

"Looking for the ultimate in whitewater runs? Join a host of world-class paddlers as they eddy hop down some of the finest Class V rivers in four countries. Share in their exciting and seemingly outrageous adventures. Then, if you're qualified, turn to section two and you too can have the same stories to tell."

— **Mary McCurdy**, National Organization
for River Sports

"If you are looking for a peek at the cutting edge of paddlesport today, this is it!"

— **Richard Penny**, author,
The Whitewater Sourcebook

Authors:	Jeff Bennett
	Bob Carlson
	Jim Cassady
	Mike Doyle
	Dave Hammond
	Timothy Hillmer
	Tim Keggerman
	Doc Loomis
	Kevin O'Brien
	James Snyder
Photographers:	Eric Bader
	Jeff Bennett
	Nathan Bilow
	Bryan Cavaness
	Mike Doyle
	Doc Loomis
	Vera Loomis
	Michael Maloney
	Doug Mrva
	Kevin O'Brien
	Therese Peterson
	Kathy Rech
	James Thomson
Editor:	Tonya Shrives
Cover Photo:	James Thomson/Rapid Shooters
Cover Concept:	Jeff Bennett
	Tonya Shrives
Cover Design:	L Grafix

The "DANGER" sign at Cedar Flat welcomes paddlers to Burnt Ranch Gorge on California's Trinity River. (Doc Loomis photo)

A WORD OF CAUTION

This book contains a broad array of rivers, most of which exemplify the extremes in difficulty, unpredictability, and danger. Even though the rivers described herein were *run*, that does not necessarily mean that all of the rivers are regularly considered *runnable*. All of these trips were made by seasoned experts, utilizing the best equipment, and invoking all safety precautions.

This book is not a recommendation to run these rivers. In fact, it would be our recommendation that you *do not* attempt any of these rivers without first talking to people who have paddled them, obtaining all of the information and skills necessary to insure your own safety, and then floating in the company of others who know the rivers described.

Swiftwater Publishing Company and the authors shall have no liability to any person with respect to physical harm, property damage, or other loss or damage caused directly or indirectly by the information contained in this book.

TABLE OF CONTENTS

Section One: Extreme Descents and Misadventures

(Gore Canyon story appears courtesy of Paddler Magazine)
(All stories and photographs without credits are by Jeff Bennett)

Section Two: A Guide To The Rivers

(Taos Box story appears courtesy of Paddler Magazine)

Section Three: Appendices

FOREWARD

Every morning for the past seven days I've marched into the bathroom, flicked on the light, and checked myself out in the mirror. No, I'm not vain or anything. It's just that I keep expecting the big change to come.

You see, last week I flipped for my 67th time. No kidding! This time it was at Last Chance on California's Salmon River, and it was flowing 7,500 cfs! Sure, it's not *all* that bad of a rapid, and sure I've flipped there before... but I always managed to swim to an eddy before getting sucked downriver into this gnarly Class V mess called Freight Train. But that's what made this swim different. You see, I didn't even come close to the eddy. In fact, I don't even recall *trying* for the eddy.

Anyway, there I was, heading for another Class V trashing. But, for some reason, it just didn't seem like that big of a deal. Anyone in their right mind would have been scribbling a will on the arm of their paddle jacket. But I felt right at home... again!

I was sucked down into the watery darkness at the very first ledge, and didn't rediscover daylight until I'd passed through the entire 100-yard mess. And somewhere in the midst of that swim, I experienced an inexplicable sensation. Right behind my ears. I could not have thought about it for more than a second before it suddenly dawned on me... the change was coming! I was finally sprouting gills!

I could hardly believe it myself!

I'm sure that it's the gills that have warped my perspective of whitewater boating. While all of my buddies are getting worked up about things like flips, swims, and wraps, I revel in the tales these experiences impart. With proper preparation and safety precautions, these misadventures make up the part of whitewater that gives the sport an element of risk, danger, and excitement! It's the stuff that great campfire stories are made of! And besides, without some perceived sense of danger and risk, running rivers would be about exciting as a wet game of pinochle.

Now, before we get started, I'm sure that some of you are going to challenge the authenticity of these tales. So, to set the record straight, all of these stories portray actual events and real, live people. Honest! In fact, most of the stories are little more than diaries of some pretty gnarly runs. You know, the typical "what I did last summer" and "no shit, there I was" type of stuff.

However, throughout this book, a couple of names have been changed to protect the guilty. And, where it has occasionally suited me, I have invoked convenient lapses in sanity, aquatic delusions, and poetic license in order to produce more readable versions of the truth. Still, one would need to look no further than the table of contents to see that the rivers and people of *Class Five Chronicles* exist in a larger-than-life world, one step beyond the common realm of Class V paddling. A world that needs no exaggeration.

Well, it's about time to kick off your booties and shed your preconceptions about whitewater. Don't let your mother catch you reading this book, and *flip* a page...

River running will never be the same!

Ned Sickels gets into the action during Camera One's filming of "California Whitewater." He's heading into Class V Freight Train!

ACKNOWLEDGEMENTS

This book is the culmination of years of whitewater travels. Along the way I met many fine people to whom I owe a great deal of gratitude. Without their support and shared love of whitewater, these fine memories would not even exist, and I would not have seen half the rivers spoken about here. There are many other people whose support off the river made this project possible. They also receive my warmest thanks. Some of these people include Mike Bader, Mike Blumm, David Bolling, Bill Bowey, Dan Buckley, Fryar Calhoun, Jim Clements, Bo Colbert, Rick Croft, Bill Cross, Jib Ellison, Jim Foust, Dale Fuller, Rafael Gallo, Carol Hammond, Lars Holbek, Robert Koch, Misha Kolchevnikov, Mark Leder-Adams, Ronnie Leder-Adams, Glenn Lewman, Don McClaran, Dave Mullins, Jack Nelson, Richard Penny, Dave Prange, Julie Prange, Scott Quinn, Jerry Redell, Beth Rundquist, Cindy Scherrer, Steve Scherrer, Val Shaull, Mike "Harpo" Sher, Mike Strickland, Robert Tanner, Grey Wariner, Roger Zbel, Chan Zwanzig, and everybody else credited throughout this book.

I would also like to thank the following manufacturers, retailers, outfitters, and organizations for their contributions to this book, and for keeping me on the water or supplied with top notch gear over the years: Alder Creek Kayak Supply, B & A Distributing, Beyond Limits Adventures, Inc., Boulder Outdoor Center, Canoe Magazine, Carlisle Paddles, Carlson Designs, Cascade Outfitters, Colorado Kayak, The Competitive Advantage, Crested Butte Rafting, Extrasport, Guy Cables Enterprises, Inc., Hy-Tek Helmets, Kokatat, National Organization for River Sports, North American River Runners, The North Face, OS Systems, Pacific River Supply, Paddler Magazine, Patagonia, Perception, Polzel Manufacturing, Power Bars, Precision Rafting Expeditions, Preferred Modes, Project RAFT, Rapid Shooters, REI, Rios Tropicales, Rivr Styx, Sawyer Paddles and Oars, Sierra Designs, Upper Yough Photos, and Whitewater Manufacturing, Inc.

THE UPPER KINGS

"Boatmen seek to find in themselves that grace under pressure that Ernest Hemingway defined as courage. For many it is a religious experience absolutely necessary to their psychological welfare. Then there is the importance of being humbled by forces far stronger than themselves. Only the foolish, or the very novice, talk about 'conquering' rapids; what you really conquer, if only for a moment, is your own insecurity. "

Roderick Nash, The Big Drops

It was one of the most impressive sights a river runner could ever hope to see. Majestic granite cathedrals rising thousands of feet from the valley floor, carving cool grey patterns against a cobalt sky. Only an occasional cloud broke the pattern of geometric perfection, a silvery ripple in a sea of blue. It was a soothing, enchanting, almost hypnotic sight, bearing the depth and timeless clarity of an Ansel Adams photograph. It was damn near perfect. Damn near.

The flaw in this fantasy world of marbled greys and ink blues was that it existed only so long as I continued staring skyward. Up towards the domain of winged creatures. Winged creatures and trail walkers. But down here, travel was all but forbidden. There was nothing soothing. Nothing enchanting, or even mildly hypnotic. Only the Upper Kings River. And mile after mile of Class V whitewater.

From our bouldery perch above the mighty Kings, I turned to Mark Helmus, a veteran of prior Upper Kings' expeditions, and asked what the next half mile of river had in store for us. "Well," he said, "this is a long stretch of Class V rapids leading into the bad stuff."

Class V rapids... *THEN THE BAD STUFF?!* I returned my concentration to the cliffs, envied the birds, and curled my toes deep into my Tevas.

Somewhere above the whispering wind I heard a faint knocking. Kind of like the tic-toc of a grandfather clock, but faster. Tracing the sound I looked downward, only to see my knees beating the steady, staccato rhythm that had been dimpling my eardrums.

"Damn," I thought, "if my dog were doing that, I'd get it wormed!"

I started to sweat. That kind of feeling you get when you've got too much adrenaline and not enough action. Then I had an idea. "Mike. Where's Mike? If I strangle Mike I'll feel better."

Our descent had actually started one week earlier, around Mike Doyle's coffee table. It was June of 1987, and a lot of California rivers had already started drying up. A moderate drought was taking its toll. Not only on the rivers, but on the rafters that depended on them for their sanity. We were looking for a fix. A thrill. Something that'd get us through the season, if it had to.

We started talking about putting together an Upper Kings trip. Maybe get some guides, a few boats, and see what happens. But it was still pretty early in the season for the Kings. Most boaters, sensible boaters anyway, wait until the deep snows of California's Sierra Mountains melt away, leaving just enough water to "safely" raft the Kings.

Mike was standing in the middle of the kitchen, casually pondering the subtle flavorings of the Budweiser that adorned his left hand, while listening intently to the phone in his right hand.

"I guess it's running about 2,700 cfs," Mike said, hanging up the phone.

"What's that mean?" I asked.

Mike looked at me and started to laugh. "I don't know. No one's ever rafted it that high."

I'd heard Mike laugh like that before. Usually before we were hammered in some ugly rapid. He's kind of funny that way. But I was sold. I'd been itching to do the Kings for a long time, and this was my big chance. I cancelled some guiding commitments, bought a new paddle, and got psyched.

Two days later we were banging our way across the mountains in a twelve-man van, cursing the heat, and talking about the river.

The Kings is Class V from the moment you get in your car. The shuttle is one of the longest kidney-jarring mountain rides you'll ever make this side of Peru's Puacartambo River. Plus, there's no way to minimize the agony. Roll up the windows and the California heat will toast your brain. But if you leave the windows down, you'll be spitting dust balls before you're half way to the put-in. I just shut my eyes and dreamed of cool Colorado mountains, Alaskan winters, and beer commercials.

Arriving at Yucca Point, we unpacked our equipment and marvelled at the spectacular canyon dropping away at our feet. Two thousand feet below us, and just upstream of our put-in, the Middle and South Forks of the Kings emerged from huge granite chasms to form the Upper Kings. It was a refreshing backdrop for the two mile hike down to the river, carrying our rafts and all the gear for a two day trip.

Actually, I lucked out during the hike in. I was sharing raft carrying duties with Mike. Or, to be more precise, I was providing Mike with enough emotional support to get him—and the raft—to the bottom of the trail. His 6'7" packhorse of a frame was carrying so much of the weight that it was hardly worth my energy to assist. Anyway, I figured that if God wanted *me* to carry half of that raft, he would have made me 6'7" too.

After rigging the rafts, we made our way down to the first rapid, Butt Hole Surfer, only to find that we had slightly underestimated the river. We dropped over the first ledge into what was supposed to be a Class IV rapid, and instantly found ourselves getting spun sideways. As we dropped precariously into the next hole, a couple of ounces of fear sent a surge of power coursing through our veins. We spun back downstream, pulled hard on the paddles, and made it to the first eddy.

This was not a good sign. If we couldn't handle the easy stuff, what would happen when we got to the hard stuff?

We decided to take it easy, pick the least heroic routes through big rapids, and eddy hop when necessary. This method worked fine, except when there wasn't any easy routes or eddies. Then it was paddle like hell, lean into the drops, and hope for the best.

We picked and paddled our way through the next few miles, exchanging heavyweight blows with giant, boulder-strewn rapids like Grizzly, Nightmare, and The Wall. By the time we'd reached Warp Two and Cassady Falls, just over three miles into the trip, our fun meters were pegged, and our energy levels were low. The mere sight of these two rapids was the last straw. By the time our thirty minute scout was over ("You gonna' run it?" "No, I'm not gonna run it. You gonna' run it?" "I'm not gonna run it." "Hey, let's get Mikey. He'll run anything!"), half the crew had their sleeping bags spread out and dinner on the stove.

By the time the sun hit camp the next morning, a five man crew had assembled to run Warp Two. This ten-foot-high waterfall sent rafts sailing into a Class IV rapid. Then, after 100 yards of whitewater, the river plummeted one more time into a horseshoe shaped cauldron known as Cassady Falls. Though none of us had any desire to run Cassady Falls, Warp Two was too good to pass up.

We paddled the raft round and round the eddy, waiting for the morning's coffee to kick in, and reviewing our game plan one more time. Plan "A" was to come off the bottom of the falls pointing left. That way, we could drive the raft onto a rock and jump out before we were committed to running Cassady Falls. Plan "B" was to grab onto one of about ten throw bags that would hit us if Plan "A" didn't work, and pendulum into shore. Fortunately, Plan "A" worked. The raft pierced the hole at the base of the falls, and surged onto the left bank. We were overjoyed to find ourselves shaking hands with the shore crew and walking around Cassady Falls.

Before the excitement of Warp Two had even worn off, we found ourselves at the lip of another big rapid... That's Dumb.

"I'd say chances are one-in-a-hundred you'll make it through that hole upright."

"Yeah, but what would the consequences be if we flipped?"

"A gnarly swim."

"Yeah, but it's not a killer. I mean, you'd flush right out. How many throw bags do we have?"

"About six, I guess."

"And it'd make a hell of a picture, wouldn't it?"

"Yeah."

"Let's go for it then!"

Unlike any of the other rapids on the Upper Kings, That's Dumb is brutally short, and irresistibly simple. From upstream, the rapid first appears as a horizon line at the far end of a deep emerald green pool. Then, as the river enters the rapid, vertical cliffs and house-sized boulders choke the river down to 30 feet in

An expert paddle team shows how Class V+ "That's Dumb" got its name during the sixth raft descent of California's Upper Kings River. (Photo by James Thomson/Rapid Shooters)

width. At the same time, the Kings plunges ten vertical feet into liquid cotton candy, travelling all too fast in the wrong direction. Strangely, it doesn't even resound with the boisterous roar typical of such drops. Instead, it sounds more like a trout slurping a fly from the surface. A 14,000 pound trout!

That's all there is. Nothing but swift, green water enters and exits the rapid, and no life-threatening hazards exist beyond the grasp of the hole. All you do is pick a line, hit the hole... and hold your breath.

We had good reason to think long and hard about that drop. Everyone on the trip had seen the Cassady and Carlson raft get munched here in the early video version of "California Whitewater." And now the river was even higher. Staring deeper and deeper into the hole, I started to feel like a one-legged man heading into an ass-kicking contest.

By the time the same feelings of doubt had ran its course through our group, only seven paddlers remained optimistic. Much to my surprise, I was one of them. But, the hole seemed plenty survivable, and surely, seven strong paddlers in a big SOTAR could punch through. Led by this collective misconception, we boarded our craft.

With people, cameras, and rescue bags once again scrambling along the rocks, we divvied out the seats and paddled a few times around the eddy. This time, our game plan was to... well... end up downstream... preferably in the boat.

All too fast, someone gave us the thumbs up, and we were on our way. In a flash we were poised at the lip of the drop, staring into a liquid, foamy, orgy of water. In the midst of my excitement, I became a spectator to my own uncertain fate. "They're screwed," I thought, not realizing that "they" included "me." Cynicism overrode any desire I may have had to paddle. In fact, paddling seemed as ridiculous of a notion as sticking your foot out of a rollercoaster to give it a faster push. We were going fast enough.

Suddenly, the crashing jolt of the big hole jarred me back to reality. I dug my paddle deep into the foam and watched the front half of the raft disappear. Then, as if shot from a submarine, our SOTAR's 22-inch tubes soared perfectly skyward like a misguided yellow torpedo. The last thing I remember before joining the crew in a grand swim-along was a rainbow of life jackets streaming through the air like autumn leaves in a windstorm.

Fortunately, I had remembered to keep two hands on the paddle before entering the submarine portion of this adventure. The witch's theme from the Wizard Of Oz soundtrack rang through my head as I rode the paddle through the tornado of deep currents underlying the King's surface. Had the paddle been a broomstick, I would have surely flown back to shore. But that was not an option.

By the time my head popped back into the atmosphere, I had swum past the chorus line of wide eyes and expended throw bags. I turned over on my belly, and swam to an eddy downstream.

Having just experienced one of my finest swims, the remainder of our surface activities seemed almost trivial in comparison. As we approached the entrance to the incomparable canyon between

Rough Creek Falls and Garlic Falls, the more knowledgeable members of our group deemed the river *too high* for safe passage. We jumped out along the left bank, and spent the next half-hour lining, portaging, and paddling the canyon. The award for this achievement was a front row view of Garlic Falls, which plummets one-thousand windblown feet into the Kings River.

Past Garlic Falls, the final sets of Class V rapids—Body Slam, Pyramid and Hand-of-God (so named after Chuck Koteen attributed a successful upside-down run of this rapid to an "unseen hand")—laid down beneath the hearty cheers of our paddlers.

Passing Garnet Dike Campground—the uppermost take-out for Upper Kings trips—we found ourselves paddling blissfully through small Class II rapids. However, our success in the upper canyons had not gone unnoticed. As one of the rafts casually drifted toward the Class III hole at Bonzai, the river gods, hellbent on revenge, lifted their fists one last time, and came down squarely on the unsuspecting crew.

As we pulled the upside down raft and swimmers into an eddy, we smiled, laughed, and praised the river gods. This time, we thought we'd snuck one out. Finally scored a victory against the river. But in the end, it's always a tie. And that's the way it should be.

FIRST DESCENTS OF THE UPPER KINGS
By Jim Cassady

Kayaking was in its infancy in 1960 when Maynard Munger, Roger Paris, and Bryce Whitmore made the first descent of California's Upper Kings River. The most difficult rivers being run by even top kayakers were only Class III and IV, and it would still be another five years before the Tuolumne would first be kayaked.

Maynard Munger was an avid river runner from the nearby city of Fresno. He hiked along the canyon to the top of Garlic Falls and looked 1,000 feet straight down to the majestic Kings River. Over a mile from top to bottom, the Kings forms one of the world's deepest and most forboding canyons. Its lure was insatiable.

Roger Paris was a reknown whitewater racing champion from

France. He had moved to northern California and had quickly become a guru to local kayakers. At the time, kayakers were just starting to wear helmets, and Roger felt that life jackets impeded execution of the eskimo roll. None of the kayakers on the Kings trip took either a helmet or life jacket.

Though the team had planned to complete the 10-mile run in one day, the river proved to be a greater challenge than expected. They spent the first night bivouaced deep in the canyon with nothing more than their early generation neoprene tops for warmth and the canyon night for a blanket. Their innate survival instincts delivered them through the canyon, but they still had to portage 15 or 20 times. It would be another 12 years before any boaters tried the Kings again.

In 1981, Jim Cassady led the first raft descent of the Upper Kings. "We had two Avon rafts—the best equipment available at the time—with one rigged as an oar boat and the other set up for paddling. Even with a top notch team, the going wasn't easy. It took us three days (though we only planned two) to make it through the canyon, the second day covering less than two miles. We ran one raft at a time, with the crew from the other raft stationed downstream of the rapids with throw ropes to pull us into tiny eddies. The bathtub design of these early rafts had to go!"

No rafters tried the Upper Kings again until 1984 when Cassady returned to the river using his newly-designed self-bailers. Now, dozens of kayakers and rafters go down the Upper Kings every year.

GORE CANYON
"THE RIVER OF FEAR"
By Timothy Hillmer

> *"...I had been thrown out of the boat in a rapid where I spent some time tumbling underwater in nature's frigid spin-and-rinse cycle.... My life had not passed before my eyes, but somewhere in the middle of the third rapid, cartwheeling along ass over teakettle, caroming off rocks, the phrase 'holy shit, this is serious' began running through my mind."*

> *Tim Cahill,* A Wolverine is Eating My Leg

Butterflies in the stomach; a sixth sense foretells that today my luck will vanish like a beacon in the fog. Call it paranoia or call it honest fear; this is what any rafter, canoeist or kayaker feels before running a Class VI rapid for the first time. An atheist in a world inhabited by river gods.

And this is how I feel now as I stand at the top of Colorado's Gore Canyon Rapid on the upper Colorado River. It is the challenge of confronting the unexpected, much the way a blind man might face a day of travelling across unfamiliar terrain. No matter how many rivers I run, no matter how well I train, there is always a fear that perhaps these skills are not enough. My nerve trembles. Failure lurks.

I am here with an exploratory team from the Boulder Outdoor Center (BOC), a Colorado-based rafting company. Only two weeks earlier, the BOC made the first successful paddle raft descent of Gore Canyon without portage. We have returned to attempt it again, only this time at a lower and more technical water level of 1,500 cfs.

For two years I have listened to other boaters tell vivid horror stories about this brief six-mile run. In Doug Wheat's excellent book, *The Floater's Guide to Colorado*, he begins and ends his description of Gore Canyon with these words of caution: "If you are looking for an enjoyable raft or kayak run, Gore Canyon is not for you... it is not recommended." And in *Rivers of the Southwest* by Fletcher Anderson and Ann Hopkinson, the authors describe their horrifying kayak descent of the Gore at 10,000 cfs, one in which Ms. Hopkinson was nearly killed after being pinned by an undercut rock. As their guidebook simply states: "Gore Canyon is the most difficult paddlable whitewater in the Colorado River...Ill-informed rafters have twice attempted this run. Both attempts failed dramatically in the first mile."

Gore Rapid roars on. Located only a mile into the canyon, it is the first real challenge of the trip. I watch now as Eric Bader, the 25-year-old owner of the Boulder Outdoor Center, heads back upstream to make the first attempt on Gore Rapid in an open canoe. I do not question his skills, merely his sanity. Only two hours earlier, I had watched him unload his green Perception HD-1 canoe at our put-in west of Kremmling, Colorado. Next to our self-bailing rafts, his boat looked like a dehydrated nightcrawler. But I realized that no one is better suited to attempt this than Eric, a veteran of over 15 kayak descents of Gore Canyon. As he passes my safety position on his way upstream, I smile and send a psychic sign of the cross his way. Go in peace, my friend, and paddle like hell.

I am doubtful of his chances of success as I wait below, safety-bag in hand. A canoe is a canoe and this rapid is a meatgrinder no matter what vessel challenges it. My gory meditation is broken by a shout and I look up to see Eric paddling into the first drop. His entrance is pinpoint precise, perhaps made easier by the narrowness of his canoe. He surfs the inside curve of a pillow then drops straight into the maelstrom. Like a scalpel in a landslide, he slices through the main hole, pauses on the boil surging upstream of the undercut rock, then slides like an eel around it, carefully slithering through the remaining obstacle course. It is a flawless run and Eric paddles into the eddy, smiling like a little kid splashing in a bathtub.

Our crew hikes upstream to raft it. Brian Brodeur, a veteran guide for the BOC, will captain. We studiously scout the entrance drop, then climb into our Riken self-bailer and head out. I feel pumped up and ready; it's full speed ahead.

We approach the rapid with an upstream ferry, carefully maneuvering across the river and through a Class III rock garden directly above the entrance drop. We pivot around a boulder, spin, and charge toward the first turn. Our boat slides agonizingly into a rock just left of the chute, then hangs at the lip of the falls. Then we are in it. My body arches out into the cascade, reaching for current. The moment flashes by as our boat plows into the hole, stops with a sledgehammer blow, then rises perilously up like a drunken tightrope dancer pointing at the sky. I am slammed backward out of the raft, thrust into a huge reversal and surrounded by a violent whirl of green and white. Like being shot out of a rocket silo, I am flushed away and under. I pop up, gasp for air, then am yanked down again.

No mercy. I am aware of my feet downstream, of being hit by a barrage of rocks and straining to break the green surface and swim left. It is a mad, topsy-turvy waterslide of a ride as I try to swim and cover up for protection. Suddenly I see a throwrope and latch onto the line. I feel my battered weight swing into the slim eddy with a pendulum motion. I see Eric smiling above me. I rest in the shallows on a rock, spitting out water and coughing. I probe for a bruised knee, give thanks for the shore under my booties, and curse Gore Rapid.

I was not the lone swimmer. After talking to Eric, I learned that Kim, a strong paddler from Steamboat Springs, Colorado, had also popped out of the raft and had somehow managed to pull herself out on a rock. The boat and remaining crew nearly capsized in the hole, but were mercifully spit out into the current where they wedged upon a boulder. After paddling over to retrieve Kim, they proceeded to slide their way down the remainder of the rapid. Our second crew, in an oarboat rowed by Gene Dennis, wisely decides to portage after witnessing our folly. Their self-bailing SOTAR is hoisted up the talus-laden slope with ropes, then carried around by way of the railroad tracks high above the run.

I am exhausted from my swim, but Gore Canyon shows little compassion for my plight. The river does not let up. The bottom section of the half-mile Gore Rapid consists of two Class IV+ boulder gardens, then a violent, six-foot drop over a mass of razor-sharp rock. We proceed with caution. All boats negotiate the final falls without mishap, then spill into a beautiful jade pool. It is our first chance to look back, take a deep breath and be aware of the immense canyon we float. In contrast to the relentless rapids, the high rust-colored walls rise peacefully on either side like slabs of gleaming bronze. Isolated magnificence in the heart of the 11,000-foot Gore Mountain Range. To rest in the pool at the bottom of this gorge almost makes my harrowing swim worthwhile. We are here where few have been, all believers in a world of river gods. With our sense of adventure renewed, we plunge ahead.

The pace is furious as we paddle through uncountable and unnamed Class IV and V rapids. We stop two miles past Gore Rapid on river left to scout Tunnel Falls. As I move along the shore I am greeted by a roar from beyond the horizon line. What I see upon moving closer forces me to doubt my purpose here. It is breathtaking, as if the entire riverbed had been smashed away with earthquake force to create a 12-foot curtain of froth and power. It is also terrifying; the illustrated textbook example of a keeper. As I study the waterfall, I spy a possible run on the far left where the river makes a slight turn and pours over and off a rock slab jutting out from shore. Here the reversal is less violent and almost forgiving, but it contains a corkscrew turn with zero room for error. To not pirouette to the right at the brink of the falls would mean floating sideways or backwards over the drop, into the jaws of the dragon. May the river gods be with us.

We set up safety lines along the shore for Eric, then watch as he sneaks down on river left with his canoe. He drawstrokes around an annoying rock and approaches the brink of the falls. He hangs on the inside bend of the turn. Amazingly, like some cosmic daredevil, he is smiling as he plummets down. His green canoe bucks up violently, then slips past the boiling foam of the main falls. I am envious of the ease he exhibits. I dream of narrow rafts and winged lifejackets. Paddle or fly.

Our crew returns to the raft in silence. We will follow Eric's route and hope that our wide boat can squeeze down the narrow chute. Lifejackets are cinched tight. Helmets adjusted and snapped on. The wind howls upstream.

We hug the left shore and slide through the rocky upper section. I draw left, trying to keep our raft away from the main current tugging toward the falls. As we approach the horizon line, I feel panic set in. Instead of turning right and into the corkscrew bend, we plow head-on into a rock knifing out from shore, bounce off, spin, and slide over Tunnel Falls backwards.

Falling. Like ripping down a rollercoaster blindfolded and out of control. I feel the boat surge up on its side and cover me in a shadow as I am enveloped by the dark veil of the falls. My body is sucked down and under. Then, like being shot out of a cannon, I am hurled downstream underwater. I pull myself out of the river just above the next rapid and kneel prayerfully in the shallows. On the opposite side I count heads and see that our paddle crew is safe. Even our upside down raft has been pulled to safety. Eric paddles up in his canoe to check on me. Feeling humiliated and stunned, I wave OK, get a throwbag from him and head upstream to set up safety for Gene Dennis' oarboat.

I perch alone on a truck-size boulder near the mouth of Tunnel Falls. The wind whips up the constricted canyon and I must brace against a rock or be blown from my position. I try to forget my exhaustion and fear. In times such as these it is best to trust one's past history acquired from running other Class V rivers. Don't think; react. Go with the flow. Forget the dragons.

I hear a shout from across the river and see the second boat approaching. Gene Dennis is rowing while Ivan Schmitt, another Steamboat guide, paddles up front. As they draw close to the main drop, I see Gene is having trouble with his oars in the narrow channel, bumping and scraping them against rock. He is momentarily popped out of his rowing seat as Ivan continues to paddle. Their boat approaches the falls backward, then attempts to pivot around and forward. With sickening familiarity, I see their raft ricochet off the shore, whirl helplessly around, and dive head on into the horrible mouth of the main falls. Ivan is buried in a torrent of water as the raft flips. Gene is sent flying through the air with one hand clasping an oar, like a flailing acrobat who has missed his trapeze.

Red throwbags arc out across the water, aimed at the bobbing heads of the swimmers. Ivan and Gene each snag a line and are quickly reeled in. Eric helps nose the flipped boat over to shore with his canoe. I pause momentarily and gaze at Tunnel Falls, thankful that no one had been sucked back into the killer reversal.

With the afternoon fading and the canyon bathed in shadow,

I rejoin my dazed paddle crew and we push on. Passing hurriedly through a series of minor rapids, we stop to scout Toilet Bowl, a river-wide ledge hole. It was here, nearly three years ago, that Eric almost drowned while attempting to rescue a fellow kayaker trapped in the reversal.

As we reach the scouting point to study the drop, we suddenly see Eric in his canoe hurrying along the river's left side, attempting to sneak down a rocky slot which hugs the shore and avoids the hole. We scramble for throwbags as his canoe successfully squeezes through the boatwide cavity, then overturns and is sucked back into the reversal. Eric somehow jettisons from his boat at the last second and swims to shore. We watch in horror as the green HD-1 is battered and tossed like driftwood in the power of the hydraulic. Eric scrambles up to our perch, wet and out of breath.

"No way was I going back into that hole," he says.

Throughout the 15 minutes that the canoe recirculates in Toilet Bowl, I push out of my mind any thought of what this killer hole would have done to my friend. I only give thanks he is alive and next to me on shore.

A decision is made to line the rafts around Toilet Bowl, and we do so, using carabiners and thick climbing ropes. Suddenly the canoe pops out of the reversal and is sent downstream unmanned. We give chase with Eric now paddling in our raft, and run the last major rapid of the day, Kirshbaum, in the wheat-gold light of sunset. We hoot and holler through each wave, paddling in unison. Finally we catch up to the canoe below Kirshbaum, where it has miraculously lodged intact between two rocks.

As we float the remainder of the run down to the take-out at Pumphouse Beach, I look around and see the tired faces of our crew, exhausted by Gore Rapid, Tunnel Falls and the innumerable rapids between. We are together here in the twilight, a small procession heading home. I think of ancient ships at dusk returning from distant lands with their holds full of gold, silver and spices. I think of the early explorers I studied as a child—Balboa, Cabrillo and Drake—those who discovered new worlds and returned home to the welcome of kings and queens.

There will be no royal welcome or feast at our take-out. Din-

Gene Dennis delicately feathers his oar to give his passenger a better view of Tunnel Falls in the Gore Canyon section of the Colorado River. (Photo by Doug Mrva, Boulder Outdoor Center)

ner will consist of leftover lunchmeat and a few cookies eaten as we pack our gear in the dark and wait for the shuttle vehicle to return.

I only know that come next summer, I will once again be scouting Tunnel Falls and perhaps plotting a new route over this 12-foot abyss. I know that at night I shall dream of current, of rivers, of a beautiful wave endlessly curling back, repeating the sharp cycle of water and motion and return. I know I am a river runner, as far from any historical limelight as Pizarro was from discovering Eldorado. But I have learned that within myself, a landscape has been surveyed and charted, a dark continent explored.

(Special thanks to *Paddler,* which first published this story.)

THE RUSSELL FORK
By Dave Hammond

*"I couldn't believe my eyes. The banner across Highway 80
at Elkhorn City, Kentucky, read, 'Welcome Whitewater Sports-
men.' ...The greeting banner was a refreshing change from the
hostile reception often received by paddlers who venture into new
territory. In Appalachia the locals are wary of outsiders,
especially when they dress like alien gladiators and prefer
jousting with rapids to Sunday religion. "*

David Brown, River Runner Magazine

Where does a river junkie in need of a pre-Winter fix go after the Army Corp of Engineers cuts off the water supply on the Gauley River? For this river junkie, it was off to Kentucky's notorious Russell Fork. In October of 1987, this was the closest Class V north of the equator capable of heading off the impending winter whitewater withdrawal.

For several years I had heard of the annual fall pilgramage to the Russell Fork, but had never been able to fit its short two-weekend season into my busy river schedule. Finally, after a few phone calls about river flows and logistics, my chance had come. I loaded my van with gear and bodies and headed south from West Virginia.

Joining me were Steve Campbell of The Rivermen—a commercial outfitter on the New and Gauley Rivers credited with many tough river descents—and a half dozen of his guides looking for some end-of-the-season excitement.

The Russell Fork, as it is known in whitewater circles, is actually a tributary of the Levisa Fork of the Big Sandy River, which eventually flows into the Ohio. It drains a small area of rugged mountains in the coal mining country of east central Kentucky and the extreme western slopes of Virginia's Appalachian Mountains. The run begins in Virginia on the Pound River just below John W. Flanagan Reservoir before entering the Russell Fork downstream in the spectacular gorge which highlights Breaks Interstate Park.

We had decided to reach the Russell Fork a day early in order to scout what we could prior to Saturday's release of 1,350 cfs into the streambed. When we arrived Friday, we found a flow of about 100 cfs and hiked downriver via the railroad tracks that conveniently paralleled the entire run.

It didn't take long before we had abandoned the railroad tracks and headed to the very bottom of the canyon for a closer look. In the midst of our rockhopping and scouting, the river revealed an increasingly steep gradient, numerous house-sized boulders, and some of the ugliest undercut rocks and ledges any of us had ever seen.

With the sobering images of the Russel Fork's waterless rapids under our hats, and our imaginations running wild, we adjourned to camp for a night of restless sleep.

Arriving at the put-in the next morning we discovered that we were not alone in our quest. At least two dozen rafts and more than fifty kayakers had shown up with the same idea. We rigged our two rafts quickly and waited for the siren which would signal the water release and an impromptu LeMans style start.

We raced down the Pound through a blur of good Class II-III rapids. Then, shortly after entering the Russell Fork, we came to the first of the Russell Fork's big drops, Tower Falls. This big Class IV+ drop was named for towering cliffs on river left. To run it, you enter a narrow slot against the left wall before dropping into a six-foot falls and narrowly avoiding a car-sized pillow on the right.

There is an eight-foot by ten-foot wide flat rock above Tower Falls that provides a scouting platform for boaters. When we arrived at the rapid there were six or eight boats and kayakers perched precariously along every square inch of the rock. As each new arrival tried to paddle himself onto the rock, he'd collide with ankles, feet, or the heaps of equipment littering it. The collisions usually sent a paddle or kayak off the rock and into the maelstrom below. Having quickly picked our own line, Steve and I successfully negotiated our rafts through the debris and slid over the final sticky drops.

After Tower Falls we decided to abandon scouting in an effort to stay ahead of the circus. We motored downstream through continuous Class IV rapids like Twist and Shout to the next mandatory scout, Triple Drop. This *big* Class V rapid has three drops of six, eight, and ten feet. Our previous day's efforts picking out landmarks above major rapids like Triple Drop had been a wasted effort. The long line of rafts, kayakers, and boaters cluttering the banks for one hundred yards above the big horizon line left no doubt where we were. We squeezed our boats onto the shore and hiked downstream in time to see a major rescue event taking place.

The first drop of Triple Drop contains a riverwide hole with six to eight feet of water greedily washing back into its maw. Good kayakers would punch the hole and continue downstream, while the bad ones would surf, windowshade, or just pray until making their eventual exit from their boats. Swimmers were immediately bombarded with throw bags from their shorebound angels. Some unlucky swimmers missed the ropes and continued downriver for an ugly ride through the last two drops. These anctics fueled reports of broken boats and bones throughout the day.

We watched more than a half-dozen swims—sometimes as many as three at a time—before we got in the raft and shoved off.

Our larger rafts easily ran the first drop, allowing us just enough time to set up for the second drop, an eight-foot tongue terminating in a boat-filling hole. A distance of about thirty-feet allowed us to clear the water from our eyes and choose which side of the final drop to run. Plan A involved taking a line through a vicious sluice against the right wall, while Plan B involved following a line over the steep ten-foot vertical on the left. Both rafts opted for Plan B, missed a nasty horn half-way down the drop that had gnarled some other boats, and floated free of the falls unscathed.

Our next stop was El Horrendo, the biggest and most infamous rapid on the run. Most of the hoard of boaters were still upstream, allowing us time and space to make a thorough scout.

El Horrendo starts with a sticky diagonal drop of about six feet which, once it lets go, wants to shoot boats over some steep and shallow ledges far left. Our goal was to punch the hole above the main drop and execute a 45 degree turn in order to stay right. This would line us up for the *horrendous* twelve-foot drop that high-

A pair of rafters take Tom Love's Shredder through El Horrendo on the Russell Fork. (Photo by Therese Peterson, Upper Yough Photos)

lighted the rapid. Coming into the rapid, we gave it a sphincter factor of nine, but downgraded it to an eight after our flawless runs.

Leaving behind El Horrendo, we carved our way through another mile of complex Class IV and IV+ rapids, made a clean run through the infamous S-Turn, and arrived at Climax, the Russell Fork's awesome grand finale rapid.

Stopping for our last scout of the day, we found the river having one last laugh with some unfortunate open boaters. The first canoeist was thrashed over a turbulent lefthand drop and narrowly avoided an imminent decapitation on a huge midstream rock. The second canoeist selected a rightside trashing, where the river kicked through and over a twelve-foot ledge. We learned from their mistakes and completed our own clean runs—Steve's raft to the left, and my raft to the right.

We left Climax and headed toward a take-out that the locals had graciously bulldozed the day before. Floating the final stretch of river, we couldn't help but wonder what all the hype and horror stories had been about. This run was *a piece of cake.*

The next morning arrived bright and sunny, with colorful fall foliage bursting in a rainbow of oranges, reds and golds throughout the rugged gorge. Though we had conquered the river the day before, this was to be our day to tame it.

By the time Steve and his buddies returned from a morning mountain bike ride we were heading for a late start. So, we used a lower put-in just a short distance above Tower Falls. As we hit the river we noticed an obvious lack of boaters. The ranks had been thinned by about two-thirds from the previous day's crowd, but we attributed the low paddler population to injuries, attrition, and some common sense.

Still feeling cocky from the previous day's successes, we approached Tower Falls one hundred yards behind a group of three kayakers. We ran the top slot only to find one of the kayakers glued in the sticky hole at the bottom of the rapid. Our furious backpaddling only slightly slowed our inevitable collision. We bulldozed the kayaker with only a hint of momentum, then found ourselves surfing the hole.

I barely had time to take my next breath before getting sucked out of the raft with one of the other paddlers. I recycled a couple of times, got spit out downstream of the raft, and surfaced just in time for a little kayaker's revenge. I had just taken my first breath when, KABOOM, I was blindsided by the unmanned waterlogged kayak and dashed against a rock downstream. I got my wind back, reached the raft, and headed downriver.

After hitting nearly every rock in the slalom-like Twist and Shout just above Triple Drop, we found ourselves too far right to eddy out. Still feeling that we had the upper hand we went over the first drop way too far right and started our second surf of the day. Some adrenaline-induced paddling pulled us free, barely dodging the hydraulic bullets that had claimed so many paddlers the day before.

Yet to be fully humbled, we took a long lunch at El Horrendo, basking in the sun on the house-sized rock that forms the right wall of this ominous drop. Still not realizing that the river had us directly in its sights, we finished lunch, got back in our rafts, and drifted up over the first ledge. Our lackadaisical paddling resulted in a quick ninety degree turn, a millisecond sidesurf, and a warpspeed flip. With my sphincter meter now fully pegged, I clawed my way to the surface and found my beautiful raft surfing with me in the hole. I made a desperate grab for the floor lacing and miraculously pulled myself onto the overturned raft.

I ran the remaining twelve-foot drop glued to the bottom of the flipped boat and emerged unscathed in an eddywide yardsale of equipment, bodies, and my own obedient paddle. I grabbed my paddle just in time for the fourth unwelcome surf of the day.

A couple of minutes and two throw ropes later, I was on the shore cleaning out my shorts with the rest of my mangled crew. Suffering from a severe whitewater overdose, we managed to blunder our way to the take-out, where I swore (albeit, momentarily) that I had had enough whitewater to last me until next Spring. Driving up from the take-out, an imaginary scoreboard lit up the road: DAVE 1, RUSSELL FORK 1.

There will be a grudge match next year!

NORTH FORK OF THE PAYETTE

"Rock-strewn and white with foam, the Payette dropped away, thundering down-canyon like a herd of mustangs after a whiff of King Kong. The effect was debilitating.... When the situation comes to this, there are only two known cures. The first is to see that your return address is on every stitch of paddling gear, then get in the boat and run. The second is to see that every stitch is safely packed, then get in the car and drive away. "

> Don Banducci, in Greg Moore's and Don
> McClaren's Idaho Whitewater

I had seen runs like the North Fork of the Payette before. Usually from a safe distance. Like from my living room couch, watching National Geographic specials or the Wide World of Sports. But this time was different. I was standing right on the North Fork's banks, nervously sizing up a Class V cataract called Jacob's Ladder, and digging deep for some inspirational words to pump up my paddle crew.

Six years of anticipation had preceded this moment. And now, all that time had solidified behind me, its weight compressing my adrenaline-charged body between the pipedreams of old, and the cold, wet rush of reality before me. My own proclamations that we were going to make a pioneering paddle raft descent of the North Fork of the Payette had grown into a deranged psychological bulldozer, pushing my reluctant body along the rocks while my eyes searched for a path of deliverance through the raging maelstrom. Though the thought of portaging the entire mess had yet to cross my mind, I found the thought of actually running Jacob's Ladder physically disconcerting.

Turning my body upstream, I began the slow trek back to the vacant raft. My gait was slow and deliberate, as though I were traversing the rim of some great crevasse. And I savored each step, revelling in the sensation of my Teva's compressing between rock and flesh, and hoping like hell I'd savor the same sensations when the day was over.

If there was any consolation in the moment, it was in the fact that I was not alone. A team of expert paddlers—made up of Dave

Prange, Doc Loomis, Jim Clements, Bryan Cavaness, and Scott Quinn—had joined me, and had already dragged me successfully through the first half of the run without mishap. But now the team was following my shoreline trail back to the raft like the Seven Dwarfs on valium.

Here we go again!

My trip down the North Fork of the Payette had actually started all the way back in 1984, while standing elbow to elbow with a room full of Patagonia-clad adventurers. It was the second night of an adventure film festival, and the next movie on the projector was entitled "A Breath of Whitewater."

This timeless film featured an all-star cast of kayakers, and brought light to the "Mt. Everest of whitewater"...the North Fork of the Payette.

I sat, mesmerized by the endless series of cascades crashing across the screen, and wondering what it would be like if *I* were in one of those kayaks. It didn't take long before, more than anything I'd ever felt about rivers before, I wanted to do *that*. I wanted to do the North Fork of the Payette.

After the show I turned to Ron Reynier, a hot kayaker from White Salmon, Washington, and told him that I was going to run the North Fork.

"Good," he said, not making any effort to hide his amusement and doubt.

"Really, I am."

Ron's reply was tainted, perhaps, by his knowledge that I couldn't yet roll a kayak. Heck, I could hardly yank a sprayskirt over the cockpit before I was in serious danger of flipping. But my confidence remained intact. I *was* going to run the North Fork. It'd just take a little time to acquire the necessary skills.

While I worked on my kayaking skills, the North Fork faded from my memory, becoming less important as other Western rivers beckoned my exploration. But, by late 1988, I again found myself watching North Fork footage. This time I was joined by Dave Prange and Steve Scherrer, watching a new video in a Sandy, Oregon whitewater shop called Alder Creek Kayak Supply.

Watching the video, I was immediately amazed by how far back the limits of whitewater had been pushed. Instead of the usual gang of expert kayakers, Alan Hamilton, Kris Walker, and others were making their way downriver on large catarafts. I couldn't help but envy these inflatable boaters as they made their early descents of the North Fork. But I couldn't thank them enough for tossing me the invitation I'd long been waiting for: they said that the North Fork of the Payette had yet to be run top-to-bottom in a paddle raft.

I immediately looked at Dave, only to find he was one step ahead of me. "Let's go!" he said. And that was all it took.

Our first trip to the North Fork of the Payette ended in utter failure. It was Labor Day weekend, 1989, and our long road trip from Portland, Oregon was made with one car, three boats, and about nine different personalities.

All of the planning that had gone into the trip had stirred up a frenzy of egotistical conversation around camp. Though that suited the paddlers just fine, it was taking its toll on the support team and holiday river cruisers. Before long, it became obvious that our plans were going to have to be compromised to save some good friendships.

We managed to squeeze in a little bit of scouting, and one trip down the lower five miles of the North Fork before tempers started to unwind, and new plans were made for trips down the Class III+ Cabarton section of the North Fork, and the Class II+ to III Main Payette run. We spent the next two days running the easy sections, pouting around camp, and eating sack lunches at rest stops.

It wasn't until late Summer, 1990, when we arrived at Smith's Ferry with a new crew, ready to capitalize upon our original plans.

The first day of our second trip began with more scouting and memorizing routes through all of the biggest rapids. It was the first time many of the crew members had seen the entire river, and the endless cavalcade of froth paralleling State Highway 55 seemed nearly indecipherable. Rather than try to memorize and run the entire 15-mile run in one shot, we decided to first run the lower third, from Swinging Bridge down to the town of Banks.

We carried our 14-foot SOTAR down to the water, and wedged our six pairs of feet deep into the foot-scoops. As paddle captain, it was my responsibility to give the pre-river chat. I

The first paddle raft descent of Jacob's Ladder, North Fork Payette. (Photo by Vera Loomis)

looked at my veteran crew, and felt hopelessly devoid of words. What do you say when you're about to enter six miles of continuous Class IV and V whitewater? "Don't screw up," I muttered. "Oh, and don't even *think* about falling out!" My brilliant words evoked a couple of confused looks from the team as I nosed the bow out into the current.

At first, the North Fork toyed with us. The nerve-wracking sight of the last rapids of the upper run loomed over our shoulders as we slid through a series of otherwise straightforward drops. But the river rarely exceeded Class III, providing us a cordial introduction to the trip.

The North Fork is not a wide river—often 25 to 30 yards across—but it is rocky and steep. Along its 15-mile course, the river drops an average of 112 feet per mile. And, during the construction of Highway 55, the profusion of boulders that were blasted away from the riverside cliffs found their way into the river bed. Add to these factors the narrowing of the river by man-made piles of rip-rap along the highway, and you can imagine what happens. The water shoots out of the valley near Smith's Ferry like a watermelon seed from a pair of wet fingers. Heading towards Screaming Left Turn, we were about to witness this unique phenomenon firsthand.

Gazing downstream, the river looked like a bank to bank display of spuming fountains. In the middle, a rocky island divided the current into two twisting channels, forcing some decisive maneuvers in confusing hydraulics. We slid toward the rocks, then cranked a hard left turn to pull ourselves into the cleaner of the two routes. The raft shook like a motorcyclist crossing railroad ties, but held fast in the current. Near the end of the channel, the raft blasted through a sharp ledge-hole, then settled back into a long series of lively Class III waves.

We had hardly begun to celebrate our run through Screaming Left Turn when the North Fork reared up again. This time, Jaws One dropped off to the right into an ominous looking hole. Again, we spun the raft to meet the hole straight on and pulled through the foam unscathed.

By the time we arrived at the final rapids above Banks—Juicer and Crunch—it had become obvious our crew stood a solid chance of surviving the upper run. Though the rapids looked no less threatening than when we first got there, our experience on the lower section led us to believe that the water moved through the drops so fast that there was not enough power to flip our weighty raft. We began testing our theory by hitting holes straight on, rather than avoiding them, and by taking tougher routes through the rapids. By the time we floated under the final bridge and onto the sandy beach at Banks, we were elated. Synchronized and psyched up, our crew was ready to try the upper put-in at Smith's Ferry. But it was not to be. Dusk sucked away any hope of running the upper river that day. Still, we were able to return to camp knowing that day two would put us at the top of the run.

As morning broke on the second day, we quickly devoured stacks of hotcakes and eggs, then took off upriver to rescout the upper run. Most of our time was spent a short distance from camp, scouting two of the river's tougher rapids—Jacob's Ladder and Golf Course. Together, these two rapids form such a blistering display of whitewater fireworks, that even the best kayakers often find themselves shouldering their boats, and stumbling weak-kneed down the road.

But, even without Jacob's Ladder and Golf Course, the upper section was awe-inspiring. Much of the action was non-stop and thoroughly abusive. After an hour or so, we finally resigned ourselves to the notion that scouting was a useless endeavor on a river this continuous.

We were met at the put-in by a small crowd of kayakers, representing paddling communities from all corners of the United States. In the calm pool below the parking area, Alan Hamilton and Dave Mullins rigged their catarafts, getting ready to tackle the run "the easy way." And out in the middle of the river, a couple of "crazies" practiced surfing their two-man kayak—a Topolino Duo—before heading downstream for another North Fork *first*.

We let the kayakers migrate downstream before boarding our raft. Finally, we looked up at our support crew, gave the thumb's up, and floated off to battle.

We were little more than a few minutes into the run when the North Fork disappeared over the first of many horizon lines. The first rapid, Steepness, drop-kicked us through a series of soft holes as the river plunged 15 feet in about 30 yards. We emerged downstream soaked, but smiling. As if to conceal our victory, the river whisked us downstream, around the bend, and into a new parade of rapids.

Gradually, we picked our way down the rapids of the upper section. At times, our imaginations would play games with us. We'd paddle furiously for the bank, thinking we were at the lip of one of the big rapids. At other times, we bombed unwittingly through rapids that we would have otherwise preferred to have scouted. At one point—at the brink of a pulse-raising rapid known as Nutcracker—some of the crew had had their limit of excitement. A near mutiny unfurled on the banks above the rapid which resulted in a very short walk around Nutcracker's crux move. Still, everything else in Nutcracker was run. And with each passing mile, a singular question began echoing louder and louder in the back of our minds: *"Where the heck is Jacob's Ladder?!"*

There are few words in the dictionary suitable to describe Jacob's Ladder. At least none that I could print without being castigated by the censors. So, I defer to the imaginations of Dennis Whitehouse and Bob Walker, both of Kentucky, whose shared biblical visions of winged kayakers flittering among the stairsteps to heaven ended with the rapid's naming. Even today, whether standing on the shore getting ready to run Jacob's Ladder, or sitting in a boat staring into the gut of the rapid, it is a religious experience.

We were standing before our own day of whitewater judgment, respectfully quiet. A few yards away, Jacob's Ladder defied our attempts to find a safe route for a paddle raft. In less than 100 yards, the river dropped more than 30 feet. A couple of huge holes in the top half of the rapid absorbed much of the current, and threatened to flip any boat that drifted too close. Near the end of the rapid, the river plunged six vertical feet into an ugly recirculating hole. And in the midst of the major obstacles, the river twisted and rolled, like a serpent trying to devour itself.

We lined up on the top of the rapid, positioning ourselves for a left-side route around the big holes. But in the blink of an eye, we were being sucked toward the center of the rapid. Dave Prange, a powerful, long-armed paddler, threw out a huge draw stroke from the left side of the raft and dragged the five remaining crew members into the refuge of an eddy half way down the rapid. We slid to a halt upon a steep, barely submerged ledge, and reevaluated our game plan.

By now we had avoided the worst hazards of the top half of Jacob's Ladder. We just needed to hold a straight line through the remaining hydraulics to position ourselves for the final falls. We pushed out of the eddy and spun the bow downstream. A series of powerful strokes sped us across the surface and onto the lip of the final drop. With G-force, the raft snapped downward, whipping our bodies through unhuman contortions. I pinned my hope on my footcups, and held on with my toes for all I was worth. Before my body had finished passing through its first plane of motion, the raft snapped back skyward, and surrounded our grateful hides like an enormous PVC catcher's mitt.

Our momentum carried us deep into the next rapid—Golf Course—where a junkyard of VW-sized boulders, and sharp drops battered our tired raft about. Our remaining energies were expended straightening and restraightening the raft each time the river would swat it to the side. But our efforts again proved successful. The final few yards of river above Swinging Bridge were among the most jubilant and rewarding I'd ever experienced.

We finished off the run that day, this time collapsing on the now familiar take-out at Banks.

We never did find out whether we were truly the first team to take a paddle raft down the North Fork of the Payette, but I knew that I had pioneered a path deeper into my own soul than I'd ever gone before. The North Fork was a pinnacle of sorts, the brass ring of my whitewater career. The years of anticipation had paid off, and now it was time to pass the baton to a new generation of paddlers.

I'll see rivers like the North Fork of the Payette again. But I won't mind one bit if it's just from the comfort of my living room couch!

ZEN AND THE ART OF RAFT REPAIR

"...Reality is the leading cause of stress amongst those in touch with it.... As a lifestyle, I find it too confining. "

Lily Tomlin and Jane Wagner, The Search For Signs of Intelligent Life in the Universe

Raft repair is truly an artform. The well-seasoned raft gives us insight into the mental makeup of the raft's owner, and preserves confidence in our meager craft many years after its initial manufacture.

Now, we all know that there are those times when you're just going to pour shore adhesive on a tube and hammer down a patch with the nearest rock. But, the gracefully aged raft does not have tell-tale amateur glue marks radiating from its hypalon bandaids like so many squashed starfish. The carefully applied patch has been glued to perfection, bevelled at the edges, and rolled until nary a molecule of oxygen remains affixed to the interior surfaces.

Learning to become this proficient at raft repair is easier than most people think. This proficiency begins with an understanding of raft materials, adhesive solutions, and proper application techniques.

At the outset, it is important to note that the various glues and solvents used in patching rafts can be extremely hazardous to your health. I don't expect anybody to be mixing up toluene highballs after a tough day at the office, but continuous inhalation of toluene or MEK vapors can lead to disintegration of vital nerve endings and brain cells. They can cause headaches, memory loss, and, uhm, *dain bramage.*

OK, wait, where was I? Oh! Before commencing your project, be sure to find a well ventilated area to work in. Now, this is the ole "do what I say, not what I do" addage.

Why, just last week I had to repair two tubes and a couple of foot straps. Typical end-of-the-season stuff. Since it was raining pretty hard outside, I had to do all of the work in my shed.

What a tin box! Not only is there no circulation in that shed—especially with the doors shut—it gets pretty damn warm. Hot!

Whew!

Now...where was I? Oh! By the time I got done patching the second tube, I had to glue my feet to the floor to keep from floating away. Really, man. I was, like, pinned up against the ceiling. My sister had to come and get me down.

But, in so far as that brain damage stuff goes, I don't think it had, uhm, uhm....

What was I talking about?

The cumulative harmful effects of raft solvent vapors can strike at any moment!

UPPER PACUARE RIVER

"...River running introduces something new: the drama of being somewhere you manifestly don't belong, of balancing on that razor's edge where you're neither out of control nor even really in control, of playing with forces so much greater than your own that you just can't win—and then, at least temporarily, winning when you stop fighting the river for a moment and becoming part of it."

Lito Tejada-Flores, Wildwater: The Sierra Club Guide
to Kayaking and Whitewater Boating

What a face! My good friend Dave Prange looked like one of those love-sick spouses you see hanging around airplane terminals. It was the same look you get from a basset hound. I felt kind of sorry for him. Well, almost. OK, I guess I really didn't give a rip!

I was too wrapped up in the excitement of our forthcoming raft trip down the upper section of Costa Rica's Pacuare River. While Dave was in our Reventazon riverside camp, nursing his digestive system through the final stages of Costa Rican Revenge, we'd be bouncing off ledges and crashing holes in one of the world's most beautiful canyons. I waved goodbye, then turned to join our Australian buddies, loaded the van, and headed out.

It was only 7:00 in the morning. More than a few hours before my usual waking time, but long after my last meal. Our van bounced along Costa Rica's muddy highways like a drunken steer. While Dave's pepto-bismol coated stomach simmered and brewed at the Reventazon camp, my own stomach began making those all too common "feed me" noises. You know, the one's that sound like a backed up sink unclogging itself. Food—as always—became my top priority.

As we rounded another bumpy corner into a quaint Costa Rican village, Andy stopped the van in front of a Central American version of a mini-mart. A pair of friendly eyes peered from the store's pastel hollow.

I stepped up to the counter, and began talking. "Ola. Buenos dias, amigos." That was it. I'd exhausted my entire Spanish

45

vocabulary. Sensing some sort of forthcoming reply, I quickly bailed out of my front step position and let Piwi Spears do the talking.

"Uno pan y uno Coca Cola."

"What's pan?" I asked.

"Bread," replied Piwi.

Mmmm. Bread and coke for breakfast. Considering that a big loaf of fresh baked bread and a coke cost less than fifty cents, it sounded great. I practiced a bit, and made the same request. "Uno pan y uno Coca Cola."

Expecting a silent passage of food, I almost fell over when "amigos" hit me with a long, lightning fast, barrage of Spanish — complete with machine gun rolls of r's and other ethnic consonants. Being an ignorant gringo, I got the same feeling I get when my computer goes beserk. I had no idea what to do. Fortunately, the shopowner was only pulling my leg. We all laughed at my expense and bid farewell. Soon, we were again rolling toward the put-in.

While our van rocked and bounced along the muddy Costa Rican byways, I found my thoughts lost in the dreamy haze of dripping greenery and rugged hillsides. Everywhere we looked, hills rose abruptly from narrow valleys, disappearing into a misty blanket of clouds. Only the brown slash of road in front of us broke up the thick cloak of exotic vegetation and deep green coffee plantations.

"Here we are..." said Piwi. The fact that we were *somewhere* was enough of a surprise for me. "...this is the put-in."

We were just upstream of a short steel bridge about five miles above Bajo Pacuare. But, since my attention had been focused on the scenery, I hadn't the foggiest idea how we got there. Accordingly, I was shocked when ten minutes after our arrival a little blue rental car came skittering up the muddy road in our direction.

"Hey, Jeff, that looks like your mom's car!"

"No way."

"Yeah, it's your mom."

My mother had joined the entourage of rafters for the 1991 Costa Rica Rally—one of the early world competitions for whitewater rafting. Having lingered in camp a minute too long, she was cornered by Dave and talked into driving him to the put-in. The passenger door swung open and Dave's big smiling face moved skyward.

"You didn't think I'd let you guys have all the fun, did ya?"

Dave had figured that the agony of missing a great run, and of having to listen to everyone talk about it, would far exceed anything his stomach could inflict upon him. We thanked my mom for the help, tossed Dave a paddle, and headed for the bank.

Making our way through the first small rapids, lines from Michael Mayfield's and Rafael Gallo's *The Rivers of Costa Rica* started scrolling across the horizon as if on a giant, imaginary movie screen. Their Upper Pacuare River description starts with a Class V, VI rating, then settles into more palatable prose: "This seldom run section of the Pacuare is one of the world's great whitewater treasures, but its length, difficulty, and isolation preclude all but the most determined and skilled paddlers from attempting it." Although "determined" and "skilled" probably fit our group, we were guilty of a serious imbalance. What we made up for in brawn, we all but lacked in brains. But perhaps these were the perfect components of an Upper Pacuare paddle team.

A small wave snuck up and smacked the bow, drenching me back into reality. I could now see a junkyard of boulders fifty yards downstream. Then, turning my head downwards, I was surprised to see my knuckles turning a whiter shade of pale. Obviously, the oncoming rush of endorphines had already made its way down my arms and into my fingers, imparting a grip that would frighten a boa constrictor.

The first few rapids on the Upper Pacuare really aren't all that bad. Intimidating boulder fields quickly reveal friendly sluices that provide bouncy, liquid Disney rides past massive brown heaps of boat-grabbing rocks. Our confidence fed upon itself as we powered the raft from eddy to eddy, taking the cleanest lines around holes and over steep drops. Even the toucans flying overhead seemed to dip a wing in admiration of our expertise as we glided casually into deeper necks of the gorge.

This fresh feeling of relaxation allowed us to enjoy the magnificence of the Pacuare River Gorge. Giant blue morpho butterflies traced neon flights across the dark background of unbroken jungle. Further skyward, colorful birds danced erratically across the canyon tops. And from somewhere far beyond the banks, eerie National Geographic sounds echoed from tree to tree, giving us the feeling that we really were *out there*.

I felt like we had been tossed into a Road Runner cartoon. The kind where the Wiley Coyote paints a scene, and the Road Runner streaks through safely. Only this time, the scene was a tropical paradise, the kind you see on post cards, and the road was a Class V river right through the middle of it.

Piwi shouted to us, "This is where it *really* starts getting good!"

The canyon walls clamped shut, leaving a narrow corridor through which the river disappeared. Undercut car and truck-sized rocks whipped the river into a frothy mess that seemed to gradually blend at the surface with the falling rain.

Piwi paddled his kayak quickly toward our boat before we reached the lip of the first drop. "It could be different," he said, "the earthquake really shook up a lot of stuff in these canyons. This is Hydraulic Blood. But don't let the name shake you up."

The earthquake Piwi was referring to had hit Costa Rica many months earlier. Although much of the country had recovered from its devastating effects, this section of river was not commonly paddled, and the canyon walls were still unstable. It would be easy to drop into a rapid, only to find some Class V move that wasn't there last week. It seemed like a fine reason to scout.

Just as my foot was about to hit the bank, Simon paddled his kayak into the eddy. "When you're up on the bank," he said, smiling, "watch out for snakes. I've heard some people say they tend to show up around here." Great, I thought. It's *only* a Class V rapid, but it's a *Class VI* scout! I stepped gingerly, tip-toeing from the top of one boulder to the next, finally stopping at a spot that could be guarded against any legless intruder.

The more adventurous members of our team made a slippery, clinging traverse along a steep cliff to scout the left side of Hydraulic Blood. When they got back, they gave a wide-eyed "looks *fine*." Like when soap opera doctors tell grieving wives their husbands will be fine: "He's *fine* Mrs. Smith." "I want the

"Hydraulic Blood," Upper Pacuare River, Costa Rica.

truth, please tell me, Doctor." "He's *fine*. He lost two arms, a leg, and his head, but he'll be just *fine*."

Piwi went first, expertly darting from eddy to eddy in his nimble kayak, until he finally disappeared over the last—and biggest—drops.

"Looks easy," joked Mike. Yeah, sure.

Next, it was our time to go. Knowing that we would not be able to eddy hop, we picked the cleanest line through the upper ledges, hoping to buy time to pick our moves above the final ledges.

The strategy worked. We bounced through a couple of two-foot drops, and arrived at the biggest moves intact. "BACK PADDLE!" yelled Mike. "DRAW RIGHT!" We stuck the boat square on top of the cleanest line available, rode the surge, and prepared for the final drop.

"FORWARD!" The river had saved the best for last. After 75 yards of impressive boulder gardens, the floor dropped out from beneath the Pacuare and the current descended steeply into a twisting ramp/hole combination. With no place to go but down, our raft plunged six feet into the frothing hole, and blasted out the far side intact.

"WOW!" I exclaimed, "what a rapid!" Then, as if to mock my private celebration, Harpo and Steve Scherrer followed in their kayaks, bobbing above the waves and holes with the ease of a couple of kids riding on a merry-go-around.

Still, this was to be the whitewater high point of the trip. Downstream, another big rapid tossed an enticing lure to an unsuspecting paddler. Fortunately, Piwi knew better, and warned us that "Jumping Bobo Falls" was off limits. What used to be a wild ride, terminating in a Class V+ ten-foot waterfall, is now a deadend pile of behemoth boulders. The rapid got its name from the curious fish which migrate up the falls to reproduce. But "Bobo," in my grade school, also meant "stupid." And that is exactly what someone would have to be to run this gargantuan garbage disposal.

Soon the canyon opened up, and the rapids became tame. The intensity of the upper canyons was replaced by a soothing rhythm of Class II and III rapids. My mind began to wander as the endorphines faded away. So soothing were the jungle, rain, and exotic sounds, that I was almost too far lost in a daydream to notice that we had reached the take-out.

We ditched our boats a couple of miles downstream of San Martin and began climbing a muddy road in search of our shuttle driver. We did not know whether the road into the canyon would even be passable, and were not surprised when the van was nowhere to be found. Fortunately, four-wheel drive trucks had been shuttling commercial passengers to the river for a run down the Lower Pacuare, and one of the drivers was able to inform us that our van was waiting at the top of the hill... two miles away. We sweet-talked our way into a ride out of the canyon, thereby avoiding a long trudge through the ankle deep mud.

By the time our group rolled back into camp, we had little to say. The Pacuare had been a spectacular run. The combination of Class V whitewater and exotic rainforests was surreal—bigger than life.

To me, our silence was a sign of respect—an acknowledgement that rivers sometimes reveal too much for something as insignificant as a human to comprehend in a single day.

THE GRAND CANYON

"It is against regulations to swim in the Colorado River in the Grand Canyon. But they tell me that every now and then someone swims through a medium-sized rapid to see what it's like. As far as I know, no one has ever attempted to duplicate our swim—certainly no one has succeeded. And now, I guess, no one would be allowed to try. Not that we set out to make some sort of record; it really was just a cheap vacation that got a little out of hand."

Bill Beer, We Swam the Grand Canyon

The Grand Canyon. Having said those three words—*The Grand Canyon*—what visions come to your mind? Sidehikes to Deer Creek Falls? Lunchbreaks at Red Wall Cavern? Or do you conjure images of huge waves, and rapids like Granite, Crystal, and Lava Falls?

Chances are, whether you've run the Colorado River through the Grand Canyon or not, you've heard about the Grand Canyon experience. Stories of hair-raising flips at Lava Falls, peaceful drifting among spectacular, timeless rock corridors, and endless nights of world class camping. The Grand Canyon mystique permeates every facet of modern river running, leaving few of us untouched.

Legends have been borne on the massive waves of the Colorado River, and strong men have perished under the weight of its relentless currents. Even contemporary travellers—nestled among the comforts of hypalon tubing, welded steel frames, and aluminum shafted oars—display heartfelt respect for the awesome power of the Colorado River. The Colorado's rapids are forces to be reckoned with. Rowed, portaged, or lined. But never swam. Or, are they?

The story begins with Bill Beer and John Daggett—two young men set upon the adventure of a lifetime—standing above the raging maelstrom at Soap Creek Rapid. Both men are trying to decide who should have the honor of going through the rapid first.

At first blush, the scene looked little different than on many other Grand Canyon trips. 7,300 cubic feet per second of unbridled whitewater moved past their feet with all the subtlety of a derailed freight train. Scouting was a mandatory precursor to survival. A line would be chosen, and the walk back to the top of the rapid would begin.

The only difference was that, this time, their walk upstream would not lead them back to a boat. There would be no reliance upon the massive flotation usually provided by modern rafts. Instead, the courageous pair would step right into the river above the rapid, towing their drybags behind them, and swim the Grand Canyon.

I first heard about this adventure from an old Grand Canyon guide, and later read about it in Bill Beer's book, <u>We Swam the Grand Canyon: The True Story of a Cheap Vacation That Got a Little Out of Hand</u>. So remarkable was Beer's tale that I felt it necessary that we modern adventurers share a moment of humility while bowing to the courage and audacity displayed by Beer's and Daggett's accomplishment.

By April of 1955, few more than 200 adventurers had descended the Grand Canyon. Those that had survived the run were heroes of sorts. Venerated river pioneers. But to Bill Beer and John Daggett, the pioneers' heroism was self-inflated, and certainly not worthy of the praise bestowed upon these early river travellers.

During a small get-together, Bill and John made their disdain known to their friends. They belittled the rivermen's accomplishments. But, instead of stopping with merely mocking the river runners, John Daggett took the conversation one step further. Knowing full well that neither he nor Bill had enough money to purchase a raft, John said that they could—and would—swim the Colorado.

It was a bold idea, to say the least. It had only been 86 years since John Wesley Powell's historic 1869 descent, and only 17 years since the first boaters had run all of the rapids without portaging. Plus, neither had ever seen the Colorado before.

But, as the idea grew, Bill and John spent time at the library, studying maps, and reading old chronicles from prior expeditions. They also wrote to the gauge at Lee's Ferry for water levels and temperatures for different times of the year.

As they continued their research, many of their problems

Granite Rapid in the Grand Canyon. Is this any kind of place to be swimming?! (Photo by Doc Loomis)

became immediately apparent. Since there was no Glen Canyon Dam in those days (hallelujah!), peak flows exceeded twenty times the volume of low flows. Lake Mead, at the end of the Canyon, appeared on the map to be 50 to 60 miles long with no take-out. And, finally, the water would be numbingly cold for swimmers on an extended trip.

Any doubts about pulling off the trip were shorn when John announced at a party their plans to swim the Colorado. They now had to live up to their proclamation, and prove to themselves it could be done.

Though the information from the Lee's Ferry Gauging Station told them that warmer water would await them in August, Bill and John pressed toward their April launch date for fear of losing momentum. They instantly set out to obtain the necessary gear to sustain their body heat in the chilly Spring waters, and to keep their gear dry while floating downstream.

Since neither could afford wet suits, they purchased rubber shirts for $15 a piece from a local dive shop, and completed their outfit with woolen long-johns. Rubber World War II radio boxes were purchased for 89 cents a piece, and were crammed full with sleeping bags, cooking gear, and 24 days' worth of food. They even brought along a movie camera given to them by a Hollywood film maker. Ironically, the film for the camera cost more than a raft would have!

Before departing for their "vacation," Bill and John were interviewed by local TV stations and the Los Angeles Times. The pair made them promise, however, that news of their trip would not be publicized until they were on the river. That way, it would be too late to stop them.

They then wrote their wills and headed toward Lee's Ferry.

Their first encounter with the Colorado was at Needles, California. John jumped from the car and tested the water. He proclaimed it too cold for swimming, but was reminded by Bill that they had the rubber shirts and long-johns to keep them warm.

Their next stop was Pierce Ferry... a small, nowhere type of place that they had spotted on the maps while searching for a possible take-out. There, they made camp for the night. Once, they were awakened by the startling blast of an atom bomb exploding thirty miles away at a Nevada test site! But by morning things were looking better. John walked north from camp and found the river two miles away.

Along their route from Pierce Ferry to the Lee's Ferry put-in, Bill and John stopped along the South Rim to catch a tourist's view of the Canyon, then finished the day's travel at Lee's Ferry.

By morning their gear was double-wrapped in plastic and shoved into the obese rubber boxes. Before entering the river a little pre-trip footage was shot of a nearby sign, which read, "No swimming in the Colorado." They then donned their gear, carried their gear-laden boxes to the water (the boxes now weighed 85 pounds each!), and swam into the river. Back on the shore, Dave—their trusty shuttle driver—took a few more movies before waving farewell.

The river, having heard nothing about their grand scheme, bid them a most discourteous welcome. Their first day on the river was fraught with windy blasts of sand and water, leaking boxes, wet maps, and soaking wet camera gear. Even as they made their first night's camp at Six Mile Wash, the river gods hissed and snarled, lifting sand and ashes from their campfire and spewing it all over their gear. The only way they could see their way along the beach, and protect their eyes from the fire's cinders, was to wear their diving masks in camp!

Their first taste of whitewater came at Badger Creek Rapid. Rather than test the main current, John and Bill tried to slip along the bank in the slower, shallower parts of the rapid. This miniature adventure quickly taught them to avoid the shallows, thus avoiding the bruising effects of fast currents and hard boulders.

As John and Bill made their way into Marble Canyon, the immensity of their experience began making a lasting impression. Despite the cold, and the subtle paranoia of what lurked downstream, each man took time to appreciate the majestic beauty that has made the Grand Canyon so famous. They also began to learn more about river hydrology as they made their way downriver.

They learned to run rapids feet first, and were able to pick out safer routes down big, glassy tongues and around nasty holes. Still, John met a huge, undercut rock in President Harding face first. After a brief bout with the sharp rock, he emerged cut severely on his head and on his hand. Though the injuries were not too severe, it was a quick and harsh reminder of the river's power, and of how far they were from the nearest hospital.

Soon after drifting into the Grand Canyon itself, John and Bill pulled over for a rest just below Tanner Rapid. Looking at the horizon from their camp, they could see the Desert View Tower on the South Rim. They talked of hiking out the Bright Angel Trail, 18 miles downstream, to resupply their soaked food cache, and to acquire some much needed repair materials.

After some lunch, they got back in the water and swam to their next camp below Unkar Rapid. There, they found out that they had left their coffee upstream, and decided that it was now imperative that they resupply at the South Rim.

The next morning marked the one week anniversary of their put-in date. It also marked the day they ran the second biggest rapid on the Colorado... Hance Rapid (Crystal was not a very large rapid in 1955). After some considerable procrastination, and with much trepidation, they made their way into the heart of the current and swam into the rapid. The river proved to be very forgiving, and released them unscathed.

Downstream, they cached their gear behind some rocks and made their way from the Kaibab Suspension Bridge onto the Kaibab Trail. One of the first men to come down the trail recognized the duo, and informed them that rangers were looking for them. This was their biggest concern—that the rangers would stop them from completing their trip.

At Bright Angel Lodge, high atop the South Rim, they noticed a local newspaper, in which the headline read, "FEAR PAIR LOST IN COLORADO SWIM TRY." Excited by the newspaper reports, their success thus far, and the hope of complete success, John and Bill began talking to the locals about their trip. But their unbridled chatter passed the ears of the rangers, who then cornered John and Bill and held them for a short while in an effort to dissuade them from the trip. Despite threats of jail time, the pair convinced the rangers that they should be allowed to finish the trip so that hoards of daredevils wouldn't arrive trying to complete the

The Grand Canyon. (Photo by Doc Loomis)

trip themselves.

Their philosophy worked. The rangers released the pair, and even gave them some helpful hints about the next major rapids... Horn Creek Rapid, Hermit Rapid, and Lava Falls.

By day 20, the river had risen to 14,000 cfs. Standing on the right bank above Lava Falls—where the Colorado drops 37 feet through an incredible cataract—John and Bill peered into the river with enormous respect. "At first sight," Bill said in his book, "Lava Falls seemed to deserve its ugly reputation. On second sight, it still deserved it."

They procrastinated endlessly—as modern river runners still do—before entering the rapid. They talked of possible lines, threw driftwood in the currents only to watch it disappear, emptied their full bladders, and ate lunch. Finally, Bill grabbed his bags and entered the river.

With John filming from a rocky perch on the right shore, Bill entered the rapid. Though he had picked out a clean line while scouting, the rapid's entrance was nearly invisible from water level. He missed a clean tongue and slipped off the brink 20 feet too far to the left. In the next few seconds he cartwheeled through holes, over waves, past rocks, and into the safe haven of an eddy downstream of Lava Falls.

Next, John swam the rapid while Bill took pictures with a 35mm camera. When they rejoined, they agreed that Lava was the worst rapid on the river, but not quite so life threatening as people had made it out to be. They even had enough wit left about them to talk about doing it again... some time.

Twenty-five days into the trip, they found themselves drifting through unfamiliar territory. They had not bought the last strip map for the lower canyon because they could not afford it. They were also down to one can of peaches between them, and were worried that their rations would run out before the end of the trip.

Finally, passing around another bend, they spotted people waving to them from the banks near Pierce Ferry. As they drew closer, they noticed that there were three people, one of whom was quickly snapping pictures while the others beckoned Bill and John to shore. The group turned out to include Bill and Buzz Belknap, and a ranger sent there to await their arrival. By twilight, Bill

Belknap had directed them to the mud flat landing at Pierce Ferry. There they exited the river, and entered the legends of river runners.

The full story of Beer's and Daggett's adventure makes for excellent reading! I highly recommend Bill Beer's book, <u>We Swam the Grand Canyon, The True Story of a Cheap Vacation That Got a Little Out of Hand</u>. *It's available through the Mountaineers.*

TUMWATER CANYON

*"As the river forced its way through the chute, it compressed
from some fifty feet wide to fifteen. Then it exploded through the
chute like gas exiting a carburetor, spilled over a short
waterfall, and at the bottom built a "keeper"....*

*'It is a killer,' Chmielinski said when we had finished
scouting the run.*

I knew the correct rejoinder: 'No problem.'

*Then I let fly with an act of urination so wildly out of
proportion to my liquid intake for the day that I felt my face
begin to pucker. "*

Joe Kane, Running the Amazon

As if our group were connected by some sort of subliminal
strand of consciousness, or trained by the same Pavlovian
master, we responded unanimously to the sight before us.
Our entire team stepped over the guardrail and answered the call
of nature until the "urge to purge" subsided.

Though we managed to lower our level of internal hydration,
our acts did nothing to pacify the morning's nervous excitement.

Having established a pretty good system for judging the
classification of a rapid by the number of paddlers that have to go
to the bathroom, it was obvious that the section of whitewater
thundering past our bouldery perch was Class V.

And who could argue? The Wall—the first and gnarliest of the
major rapids in Washington's Tumwater Canyon—explodes
through a quarter mile long cavalcade of keeper holes, intimidating
ledges, and exploding waves. We had driven six hours to see this
rapid, and unless one of us had enough humility to fake an attack
of appendicitis, we were destined to run it later that afternoon.

This section of Washington's Wenatchee River—between
Tumwater Campground and the town of Leavenworth—did not
receive much attention from rafters before the advent of self-bailers
and catarafts. An awe-inspiring high water descent by Ole Hougan
and Pete Karp in the mid-1970's did nothing to diminish the river's
dastardly image. The run was done at outrageously high flows
using standard-floor rafts. TV cameras were on the scene to
capture the descent for a Seattle TV station.

The footage they obtained showed just how little control a rafter has when fastened to the surface of an enormous, powerful, and angry river. At one point, one of the oarsmen was catapulted from his seat between the oars, and over the front of the raft. Luckily, he managed to grab the bowline before going completely out of the boat. With the raft surfing nearly vertically in a huge hole, he had to climb back up the frame to a highside position until the boat finally bucked free.

Though the run barely crept over the threshold of success, it fortified the status of Tumwater Canyon as a mystical endeavor reserved for those on the lunatic fringe.

Over the last ten years, Tumwater Canyon has reluctantly assumed a more friendly persona. Part of that change is due to the fact that rafters now run the river at lower, more reasonable water levels. The other part of the change is due to big advances in equipment design and techniques.

Most of the Wenatchee's biggest rapids are over 100 yards long, with big holes and ledges dotting their entire length. Self-bailing rafts and catarafts allow oarsmen or paddle teams to maintain control at the end of the rapids, where they would have otherwise been wallowing downriver at the mercy of the river gods.

So, what exactly is Tumwater Canyon? This steep section of the Wenatchee River flows between the rugged granite heights of Tumwater Mountain and Icicle Ridge. Three major Class V rapids, one runnable twelve-foot dam, and a bevy of smaller rapids rip and tear at the river as it makes its way toward Exit Rapid (Class VI) and the Icicle Creek confluence. With Stevens Pass Highway paralleling the North bank, rafters are afforded an easy scouting opportunity before they run any of the major drops, and an easy retreat if the rapids prove to be too much. The highway also provides great access to prime photographic locations for the camera-carrying members of the group.

Between Tumwater's more infamous rapids, the Wenatchee River offers plenty of peaceful paddling. As it passes beneath the Highway 2 Bridge at the beginning of the canyon, the Wenatchee tip toes toward the steeper sections like a sneaky child.

Soon, Class II and III rapids frolic among the surface, giving occasional ill-advised tourists little indication of the enormous surprises downstream. One Class III-IV rapid highlights the upper section of the canyon before the river again pools out at the usual Tumwater put-in—a small roadside turn-out. Just a few river minutes downstream of this put-in, the sneaky kid throws a tantrum.

It was later that afternoon, when I found myself face to face with the tantrum thrower, right in the middle of Tumwater's biggest rapid... The Wall. Though I had spent a good portion of the morning scouting the rapid, half way into this mess I began looking for all of the landmarks I thought I'd familiarized myself with during the scout. As these vanished from view, my desire to confront a pissed off river quickly dried up. I flashed a "beam me up, Scotty" look toward our road crew, but the river kept drawing us closer to the lip of yet another series of huge ledge holes. Something had to be done.

I snapped back into action, bellowing tyrannical screams and paddle commands ("PANIC! PANIC! GOOD!! OK, NOW FLAIL!!!"). My crew somehow responded in an eloquently choreographed parade of forward strokes, drawing the raft along the only feasible lines through minefields of hazards. The river bound into huge fists of green and white water—pushing us one moment and pulling us the next—and slammed our raft through each successive hole with incredible speed. Since I'd long lost any hope of finishing The Wall upright, each successive hole took on a new meaning: "Good, that's another ten yards I won't have to swim."

Then came the whiteout!

All I felt was a blast of water... like taking a drink from a firehose. A new surge of adrenaline coursed through my brain, closely followed by crisis strategies. High siding seemed like the best idea, which I did. But, then again, drinking a cold brew in Leavenworth seemed like a better idea... only, Scotty had dropped the transporter, and I couldn't get there fast enough.

Soon, I noticed that the hole's locomotive roar was becoming friendlier. Almost human. Once I squeezed the last quart of whitewater out of my eyelids, the true source of the commotion became apparent. The roar was coming from my exhuberant crew,

Foam and fury: Dave Mullins exiting "The Wall" in Tumwater Canyon, Wenatchee River, Washington. (Photo by Bryan Cavaness)

screaming with joy and high-fiving paddles in the easy water below The Wall. We'd done it. Upright! Well, I'll be....

The Wall was the toughest rapid we had to deal with in Tumwater Canyon, and a teacher of Tumwater's powerful secrets. Lessons learned in its big holes and powerful waves became strategies to be applied in the canyon's other rapids.

But, despite our successful descent, we were still students of the river. All we truly learned was that no single strategy carries with it any guarantees in Tumwater Canyon. Sometimes, it takes just a little luck to break the grasp of a big keeper, or to make the final move around a hair-raising ledgehole.

Later that day we found ourselves in Leavenworth, hovering over those beers I'd craved at The Wall. Rather than the usual post-river elation that follows most big descents, our table was church quiet. Only the sounds of bobbing adam's apples and clinking glasses broke the silence.

I found myself transfixed, staring deeply into the foam on my beer. My mind began replaying rapids like an old nickelodeon. Soon I was back at The Wall, teetering above the final hole. I twitched in my chair as the raft repeated its surge skyward, twisted, and hung at the lip of the final curler.

But this time I didn't have to highside. The desparation was gone. I fast forwarded my way back to town and rejoined reality.

Across from me, Doc Loomis slowly emerged from his own liquid dream state. His tired eyes began to crease as a grin spread wide across his face.

We were thinking the same thought. No doubt about it.

"Hell of a river," said Doc. "Hell of a river."

THE CHEAT RIVER
By James Snyder

"The amount of time you spend looking at a hole is directly proportional to the amount of time you're going to spend surfing that hole."

Harpo

Hero stories... you've probably heard a million of them. Usually they're about someone else, some hot-shot river guru with lots of money and exotic plane tickets. But this time it's about your's truly—Jim Snyder.

My story is set against West Virginia's incredible Cheat River, where I sat in my kayak at the bottom of Beech Run Rapid, before the Great Flood of '85. The gauge was reading 1.65 feet, the highest level we allow unguided rafts on the river. And, at that level, the worst hole on the entire Cheat River lurked at the end of this rapid.

Now, the hole at Beech Run Rapid isn't really all that big by most paddler's standards—it's only a low pourover about eighteen inches high—but it is sealed off on all sides by deadend currents. A bona fide textbook keeper, designed by the river gods to be the exact shape of a four-man raft. The hole curls in at the outer edges, and forms a huge, liquid catcher's mitt at its midsection. Rafts stick to the watery mitt like ants to a sucker. And, once they've lost their momentum, rafters can spend fifteen or twenty minutes gyrating and surging in the hole, rarely bursting beyond its powerful round shoulders without some extra assistance. Still, the odds of getting out of the hole increase as the next raft upstream lines up for its ride. You see, it's only a one boat hole, so the new boat just provides fresh meat as it knocks the used raft free.

Beech Run Rapid has such a nasty reputation that everyone else on the river tends to pull up to shore, hang out there, and watch the entertainment. But, even with the obvious hazards, raft guides are hard pressed to avoid the hole. Since almost every trip sends some unsuspecting crew into the hole, we always post a guide nearby to pick up the pieces... which was exactly my job that day.

Earlier in the trip I had paddled ahead of my raft trip so that I could be in position at the hole when it arrived. As I paddled to the hole, I couldn't help but notice that the trip ahead of ours had already succumbed to the usual river-borne problems. But by the time I arrived, all of the *pusher* rafts had run by, and the last raft was inextricably entwined in the hole's sticky web.

One survivor was left in the raft—a fine looking female about twenty-five years old.

The raft beneath her weary body had been bucking so violently that she had finally resigned herself to the safety of the floor. On the shore an irritated guide shouted "PADDLE HARD" as she stirred the hole with her paddle. I was the only one in a kayak, and knew that my group would soon be lining up for their ride through the hole. I quickly appraised the situation, and felt that it was time to respond to her distress in some classic manner. After all, I had a heck of a shorebound audience, and all the makings of a seasoned veteran. At least *I* knew what to do.

With astonishing deftness, I paddled to the raft from the downstream side and pulled myself into it. Then, I carefully placed my paddle into my kayak and gave it a shove toward safety.

"Let me have that paddle, and I'll get us out," I declared to my new found admirer. She glanced back at me, exhausted, and gladly relinquished the helm.

It was now my job to pendulum the little raft back and forth across the hole until it grabbed enough current to float free of its prison. The only problem I had was with the paddle. This boat's original owner held to the inane theory that rafts stay out of trouble on their own, and that any major river dilemma is necessarily caused by the passengers. In an attempt, I guess, to counteract the passenger's input to his or her own fate, the outfitter issues little flexible toy paddles. I mean, you couldn't smack a wiffle ball with one of these paddles. With my tremendous guide-type muscles, I quickly twisted the paddle into a pretzel while my tired partner rested in the bottom of the raft. Frustrated, I paused in the middle of our whitewater rodeo and reevaluated my grand rescue plans.

At this point, the story took a significant turn. In fact, the raft spun 180 degrees, sending me onto the lowside of the raft, which was now nestled deep in the trough of the hole. When I stood to get a better position on the downstream tube, the raft bucked and sent me flying feet first between the falls of the hole, and the raft itself.

Now on the way out of the raft, I reached to grab a tube and pull myself back aboard. But, instead of making a fittingly heroic self-rescue, I ended up getting my arm caught between the side rope and the raft. It was one of those entanglements Slim Ray and Charlie Walbridge lecture about. The reason why loose ropes don't belong on rafts.

I couldn't believe it. There I was, snagged in the rope while the falls crashed down on my head and shoulders with incredible force. Even with my free hand on the rope, I couldn't lift myself high enough to get my lips to the surface, or to get some air into my lungs. And to add insult to injury, my raft partner had now taken up camp on the downstream tube, preventing the raft from flipping and surfing free.

I was hating life. Hating those flimsy toy paddles. Hating the innocent woman, the hole, the raft, and my little weanie arms. The situation remained deathly static, giving me plenty of time to realize that, more that anything, I wanted out of the water. Fast! Still, the lady wouldn't move, the raft wouldn't turn, and my arm wouldn't come free. I struggled inches below the surface, enraptured in a singular desire to breath. This underwater world was for scuba divers. Jacques Cousteau. Not for river heroes. Not for Jim Snyder.

I peered skyward through the falls, hoping for a change. And just above me I could see the woman peering down, watching me drown beneath the falling water. This kind of stuff never happened to Superman, Aquaman, and all the other superheroes. Maybe I needed to go back to hero training school.

Finally, as things could get no worse, my luck began to change.

In a moment of glory, *my* newfound hero stretched across the raft, reached deep into the water, and planted a firm grasp beneath my armpit. Her weary arms pulled and pulled as the falls fought hard to defeat her struggle. The tug-of-war seemed to last forever, but she would not give in. I contributed by laying there, suspended

Maximum air time in "Big Nasty" on West Virginia's Cheat River. (Photo by Kevin O'Brien)

between time and water. Above, her grip strengthened, inching my weary body upward, until, in an instant of incredible determination, she leaned into a final, explosive thrust.

Blasting free of the water, my body launched into a rainbow arc across the raft. The torque we created blew the boat straight downstream, free of the hole. I laid in the bottom of the raft exhaustedly admiring my partner as she stared benevolently down upon me.

As my body's desire to heave and gasp slowly subsided, I took a few more sweet breaths, looked up at her, and said "I think you saved my life."

"I think I did," she replied, flashing one of the kindest grins ever to work its way into my memory.

She and her trip paddled away soon after depositing me on the shore. I was never to learn her name or see her again. She had intrepidly shattered the lines of the sexes with her chivalry and valor, leaving me sitting on the bank forever in her debt.

Even today she has my eternal debt and gratitude. She's *my* hero!

BLACK CANYON OF THE GUNNISON
By Tim Keggerman

"The Black Canyon of the Gunnison... is a paragon of river sculpted chasms.... For several miles it plunges down a 240-foot-per-mile grade, by far the steepest for a large river in the Southern Rocky Mountains. It races over falls, under piles of house-sized boulders, and through menacing cataracts.... Rafts... are dangerous and impractical. "

Doug Wheat, The Floater's Guide to Colorado

With the rivers of Colorado drying up, our Summer guiding season was coming to an end. It was the time of year which river guides neither look forward to, nor know how to handle when it arrives. I turned to one of my fellow guides at Crested Butte Rafting and began talking. By the time our conversation was complete, we both had decided that we were ripe for some high adventure, and that the Black Canyon section of the Gunnison River was the call.

The Black Canyon of the Gunnison is considered Colorado's number one scare water. In a twelve-mile stretch, the Gunnison River tears its way through the depths of a 2,000 foot deep gorge, containing the highest cliffs in Colorado. Upstream, Crystal Dam provides dam-released flows, leaving enough water in the river for paddling late into the Summer.

The Black Canyon's history is as deep as the gorge itself, with heroic feats and boat-smashing failures fueling nearly mythical tales of grandiose proportions.

We were keen to the river's warnings, and picked a strong crew of expert boaters, including Aaron Lypps, Kris Pogoloff, and myself. Since this would be an extraordinary trip, we decided that it would be nice to invite a couple of top-notch photographers whom we knew, Nathan Bilow and Garry Sprung. Garry Sprung is known affectionately to us as "Gnerps." These guys were hot behind the lenses, but lacked in scare adventure experience—their inexperience would haunt us later in the trip.

It was Friday, and all of us had the next week off. We called the Black Canyon National Monument office to get the needed permission to enter the canyon and were told to sign in at the park office. After gathering our gear, we packed the van and loaded in.

Gnerps and Bilow drove Gnerp's truck from Crested Butte, over Kebler Pass to Hotchkiss, and downriver to where the North Fork of the Gunnison and the Main Gunnison converged. This was to be our take-out. There, we left Gnerp's truck and proceeded on with our shuttle.

Our river trip was to cover a total distance of 30 miles, so we figured that, at the most, it would take us three days and two nights to complete the descent... well, we hoped it'd be *no more* than three days.

We put in at the East Portal near the southeast end of Black Canyon National Monument. I read from Doug Wheat's guidebook, The Floater's Guide to Colorado, that this trip was for crazies only, and was *not* recommended to be run. Plus, the guidebook recommended flows of *less* than 500 cfs for safety... today it was running at 2,000 cfs!

We turned to Bilow and Gnerps and advised them that they might want to change their minds. The high water level was a perfect reason not to take the trip. Heck, *we* were scared ourselves, and if they had any second thoughts, now was the time to speak up. Once we were in the canyon, it would take nothing less than extreme angle rock climbing to get out. Rad stuff!

After loading the raft with food and gear, we embarked at 3:30 with Bilow and Gnerps still aboard. The run began with sweet, easy Class III rapids for about the first three miles. When we came to our first Class VI rapid, we headed to shore. There, we set up camp under a beautiful full moon and stars that hung like crystal chandeliers amidst the towering canyon walls and tall, ragged spires. Earth's most awesome canyon caressed all of our thoughts.

The next morning arose bright and sunny. We had scouted the drop below camp the night before and decided we would walk around it. That made me sleep easier. But by morning light, I could see a way to get a thrill by taking my kayak through the incredible drop. I helped carry the raft to a safe launch site, then toted my kayak to the rock cliff next to the fifteen-foot cascade. There, Aaron helped launch me into the massive four-foot boils,

15 feet below. I did a perfect tail stand in the middle of the next drop, and eddied out with the raft.

Now, feeling the adrenaline surge like the river, I knew we were in for an incredible adventure.

The next few miles were fun. Big Class IV rapids building into Class V's and getting hairier and hairier. We were having a ball.

After having a close call at one of the rapids, we decided we ought to scout the next drop. It was a huge, angry rapid, with a twelve-foot tongue leading into an exploding monster hole on the left, then fanning through a ten-foot lead into a river-wide keeper. This one was pushing the envelope for us, and we all knew it. My first thought was that we ought to walk around it. But, as I looked deeper into the rapid, my balls began to grow as my brain began to shrink. We were paddling perfectly, and I knew that there would be plenty of rapids to walk downstream. This one had a line. When Kris mentioned that he wanted to go for it, I seized the opportunity. "Why not?" I said, "that's what we're here for!"

I lead the way through the drops in my kayak, using the "stay close and keep an eye on each other" technique for safety. Well, that worked most of the time. But this time I entered just left of center at the end of a pool, and carved off the top of the tongue. BOOF! I slid to such a soft landing that I nearly forgot about the next drop. Water mounded up around me in three to four-foot boils and slowed my boat's launch off the next drop. I powered right at the crest of a huge surge, slid bow down over a ten-foot falls, and promptly back-endoed into a keeper hole. *Damn!*

I had struck up an impatient conversation with God while the river busily worked me over. I rocked upside down, and began setting my paddle when, in a flash of panic, I remembered that the raft was right behind me. I rolled up, still in the hole, only to see the figure of the twelve-foot raft falling ten vertical feet directly on top of me. Hastily, I flipped back over just in time for the raft to hit me on the hull and power me out of the hole. YEAH!

I rolled up just downstream feeling better, until I looked over my shoulder to see the raft stuck in the same keeper hole. Bummer! Kris was washed out of the boat right away as the raft spun in the hole. Meanwhile, Aaron clung desparately to the gear to prevent it from being jerked free by the river.

Paddling where rafts don't belong... the Black Canyon of the Gunnison. (Photo by Nathan Bilow)

I quickly paddled over to Kris and pulled him to shore right above another ten-foot drop, then eddied out in the last available micro-eddy, which was so small Kris had to hold my bow so that I could get out of the boat. I was no sooner out of my boat before Bilow and Gnerps came floating toward the drop fearfully embracing each other. Kris and I started yelling, "SWIM!! SWIM!!" as I raced to grab my throw bag.

We quickly pulled Bilow and Gnerps to shore, then ran upstream to see how Aaron was doing. What a sight to behold! There he sat in the hole, riding the raft's outside tube like a wild bronc'. I threw him the rope and handed my end to Kris so that he could pull him in while I raced back to my kayak going after the gear floating loose from the raft. After deciding not to run the next drop, I scrambled to put in below it and scouted downstream while watching our gear and food floating away. In the midst of the rainbow of gear floating by, the camera equipment caught my eye. I paddled out and struggled to save what I could, but the gear turned out to be too heavy for me to save in the Class V+ water.

That's when I started to get scared. No food, no cameras... I restored my composure and snagged three paddles. Kris still had his in his hand, so we'd have enough to complete the trip.

The next mile of canyon contained continuous Class VI cataracts. It was easy to talk everyone into a portage fest. We ran what we could, but walked almost everything. It was truly rocky mountain hair water at its extreme. Mandatory eddies, treacherous carries, gnarly poison ivy, and no escape from the remoteness. I loved it! The hard work—lots of hard work, I should say—revived our confidence, and restored our cheer.

One mile downstream and four hours later, we came to another tough portage around a twelve-foot waterfall. Beneath the falls, a glassy pool ended with what seemed to be the river's end. Beyond that pool, the river seemed to explode into five miles of fifty-degree tilts, undercut flumes, and unimaginable rapids. It was unreal! Like nothing you could ever imagine. Whitewater fantasy land, or maybe even a step beyond.

We set up camp and spread out the remainder of our supplies. Dinner was slight... a spoonful of top ramen and peanut butter served on a stick. As the sun sank beyond the canyon tops, we retired to our second night's sleep. Laying there, I tallied our losses: one first aid kit ($100), one pump ($50), two paddles ($30), food ($30)... oh, and some camera gear *($4,000!!)*. Still, we had gained one of the most exciting days of our lives.

I laid there staring at the narrow crease of sky adorning the gap in the canyon walls. Crossing the starlit sky, I could see a satellite moving up the canyon. I felt humbled, small and childlike.

The next morning, sun again shook us from our sleep. I ate the last apple and took a hike downstream to scout a route for our portage. We decided to carry up away from the huge mounds of house-sized undercut boulders, and seek paths along the very foot of the 2,000-foot cliffs.

Even in the midst of our struggle, the scenery was captivating. Shear polished canyon walls dazzled the eye. Painted Wall loomed above, Colorado's premier climbing wall. Bald eagles soared.

There was a feeling of magic in the air. High adventure!

The carry was brutal! A portage from Hell! It took us eight hours to reach the first beach. The calm pool looked so sweet. And it was sweet, but short.

The rapids that followed proved to be too much, and our next carry was the scariest of all. A narrow ledge led to a dead end box canyon. We struggled with our equipment, concentrating hard on every foot step. The trail ended just below a monster hole, where I did a rock launch back into the river. We all cheered Kris as he fell into the river on the last hairy move and survived.

We had made it through the Black Canyon, and were now in the Class III and IV rapids of the Upper Gunnison Gorge. The last drop roared behind us as a huge grey cloud swelled and bellowed in front of us. A storm was setting in. It started getting dark, quick, so we made camp at the next beach. By the time we got around to building a fire it had already begun spitting rain.

Thank God for plentiful firewood. It was a nasty thunderstorm, with high winds and blowing rain. We used the raft as a wind break and kept a huge blaze roaring. We did what we could to dry our stuff out, and ate our last dinner... water and ramen spice (our noodles were gone). We were getting used to adversity to the max. The fire called for complete teamwork, and we all did what needed to be done. Though our dinner was meager and our camp primal, our meal seemed to be a celebration feast at the end of what felt like a three-day storm.

Our final morning was cloudy and cold. Fourteen mile long Gunnison Gorge entertained us with Class III rapids interspersed with lots of long pools. A flock of 15 bald eagles followed us most of the way down the rest of the run. I begin to feel that this trip was one blessed by the Big Spirit. These eagles were messengers of peace.

We arrived at the North Fork confluence at 12 noon. Unlike other trips, there was no sitting around, no braggardly reflecting upon the trip. There'd be time for that later.

This time we could only think of one thing... *FOOD!*

We packed up our gear and made a bee line for the nearest burger stand.

ENDLESS SUMMER
"RIVER BOARDING AROUND THE WORLD"
By Bob Carlson

"Wild rivers are earth's renegades, defying gravity, dancing to their own tunes, resisting the authority of humans, always chipping away, and eventually always winning. And wild rivers bring out the renegade in us, enticing us to leave behind all that we've been taught and to let ourselves surrender to their special symphony."

Richard Bangs, Whitewater Adventure

I was in Costa Rica, ten days into the two week Project Raft Peace Rally/Rain Forest Festival, sleeping in the mud and trying to kick a dysentary hangover when I got a message from my brother Bill back in the states. "Bob Carlson, call brother about Gauley Festival," the wrinkled paper said.

This message had mercifully interrupted a nightmare I was having about a river-wide hole on the Upper Pacuare that recycled me five times the day before. I was having to dismount my board, reach into the falls, and swim out the bottom, over and over again. For some reason the phrase "the cheese, the cheese, beware the cheese!" had been playing in my head as I tumbled underwater in my dreams.

Just two days earlier I had body boarded the Peralta section of the Reventazon River with my buddies from Rescue 3, Eric Martin and Barry Edwards. This run is like 18 miles of Lava Falls-sized waves jammed in a Tuolumne/Gauley-sized river. The next day we did the Upper Pacuare, which was like the Russell Fork followed immediately by Cherry Creek, stuck in the jungle, during a monsoon.

Now, I love whitewater body boarding, and hardly go down rivers any other way any more. But, I guess I just can't do it two days in a row with dysentary, because on the way back from the Pacuare, I started barfing out the windows of Peter-from-New-Zealand's brand new Ford van. Well, mostly out the windows. They say I hit the air conditioning ducts once or twice too.

So, you could say that after reaching my personal whitewater maximum just a day earlier, I was in no mood to begin planning a 6,000 mile round-trip weekend jaunt to the Gauley Festival, which started three days after I got back from Costa Rica. But, I didn't want to disappoint my brother Bill, and this would be a chance to show that East Coast squirt crowd what *real* low-volume boating was all about.

So, carefully weighing all my options and attempting to make a sound business decision with my face still down in the mud, I decided to go.

The next day, feeling much better, I hitched a ride with Carol Hammond from Beyond Limits into downtown Turrialba, clambered upstairs to the Rios Tropicales office, got an English-speaking operator, and phoned my bro', collect, at work.

"Collect! At work!" he exclaimed, "Do you know how embarrassing that is?!!"

"Sorry, dude, no credit card," I apologized. "What's the Gauley deal?" I inquired.

"The deal is I got a frequent flyer ticket to West Virginia, free hotel for one day, free camping for two nights, free car for four days, and it's already arranged so all you gotta do is get a ticket from Betsy." My sister Betsy is a travel agent, and accumulates more frequent flyer miles than some airline pilots. I merely had to buy her coupon made out to B. Carlson.

"No prob," I said. "We be shreddin' on the Gauley! Iron Ring, here we come!"

"See ya Dude!" We both exclaimed as we hung up. Within seconds, a wave of anticipatory euphoria swept over me as I rushed next door to the bathroom to barf up another quesadilla.

A week later I was back in California completely beat. I slept 'till Tuesday with a raging swimmers ear that made the world sound like a giant echo chamber. I got my sister's ticket on Wednesday for $350.00, packed Thursday night, and started flying out to the Gauley with my brother Friday morning. He was all excited to get there, but I was kind of mellowed out. An airplane cabin was seeming more like home to me than my apartment.

As our plane crossed over the Grand Canyon, I began thinking about an earlier bodyboarding trip back East.

Two years earlier I had travelled to the Nantahala Outdoor Center at the 1990 Project RAFT rally and done a bunch of surfing with my buddy Jim Cassady at Nantahala Falls. But, when we tried to go downriver on the Chattooga, we had gotten busted by the BLM, the State Police, and the Forest Service. It seems that the previous year some French guys on Hydrospeeds had tried to go downriver and gotten beat up... by the river I mean.

Still, Moustache—the French guy who created the sport of Hydrospeeding—deserves some credit for his contributions to river swimming.

In France, Moustache is a master promoter. There are huge base camps in the Alps dedicated entirely to Hydrospeeding trips. It's the macho bungee-jumping type of European thing to do. He's been doing it for like 10 years, and taken thousands downriver. If you haven't seen one, the Hydrospeed itself is kind of a forty-pound roto-molded half-a-kayak/motorcycle-fairing thing with a keel and two handles. In comparison, my ethafoam boards are five-pound, flexible, multiposition boards, directly evolved from Morrey boogie boards. The Carlson River Boards surf like crazy and are customized for Swiftwater Rescue.

Anyway, the Sheriff's exact words were, "If I let you guys go downriver, then the very next thing is we're going to get every damn fool with a six-pack and kickboard from K-Mart trying to go down here and breaking their necks. I'm not about to let that happen. And, if you try to go down the river, I might just give you a ticket, but my friend here from the State Police is going to follow you and put you in jail."

I tried to explain that we were the safe and sane ambassadors of a high-tech cutting edge new sport, but the Sheriff didn't buy it. I said my boards were four inch thick ethafoam, and you can't get ethafoam at K-Mart. But he said drunks don't know that.

I said I had a hard enough time convincing professional river guides that river boarding was safe as rafting or kayaking, so why did he think the general public was going to swarm downstream like lemmings just because they saw me and Cass' go down river once in full body armor? He said, "I don't care about that, I deem this NOT a suitable water craft and you can NOT go down."

Rather than create an intrastate/international incident, we went down the Nolichucky instead. It was too bad for them because we could have rescued a bunch of pregnant swimmers at the bottom of Bull Sluice if they had let us.

But, back to the Gauley.

We bounced through Chicago O'Hare, caught a feeder flight to Charleston, rented a car and jetted two hours south into West Virginia arriving at the North American River Runners campground at Friday midnight.

It was freezing in camp. We grabbed a beer and a spot by the fire with Charlie from Carolina who had met me in Costa Rica the week before. There we conceived a bold plan: If it was going to be this freezing tomorrow, we'd call everything off.

We woke at the crack of dawn, dew on our tents thick enough to make break-the-drought headlines in California, and looked around.

At the picnic hut next to us there was a hotel-style buffet banquet with coffee, orange juice, toast, sausage, bacon, grits, muffins, hot cocoa and three kinds of eggs. The nice lady cook/hostess asked us if we were in the 6, 7, 8 or 9 o'clock group, because if it was the 6 o'clock group we'd better get our food fast because the bus was leaving.

I replied, "No, I think we were the 1 o'clock group, maybe the NO o'clock group if it didn't start warming up any faster."

The NARR camp was huge. All the buildings and camps at Beaver Point on the South Fork of the American could have fit on their property with room for several Greyhounds left over. Full busses were leaving every fifteen minutes and some busses were cut in half to make flatbed decks on the back to carry rafts stacked ten high. It was like Squaw Valley on a weekend.

Our host Donny Hudspeth introduced us to Chris the squirt boater who could guide us down river. We grabbed food, jumped in a car, and headed through the green hills of West Virginia to the huge Summersville dam at the put-in.

At Summersville Dam three tubes were working, sending three, twenty-foot wide jets 120 feet straight out in a horizontal torrent that exploded thirty feet high when it hit the river.

That was the put-in, right beside ground zero. Not inside the explosion of course, but right beside it in a granite-size eddy that fed you directly INTO the explosion if you could cross the three-foot-high eddy fence right side up.

But people thought nothing of it. Commercial boats filled with combination row/paddle rigs and 10 or 12 people each were stacked up a quarter-mile deep along the asphalt boat ramp, each boat receiving a custom last minute safety talk from the guide before being whistled onto water by a uniformed State Policeman. One boat every five minutes, just like clockwork. And you'd better be ready when your whistle blew—they put 40,000 people down the Gauley in four weeks of the season in an average year. It is amazing.

Wanting to avoid the incipient stampede of the commercial cattle chute we snuck down the rocky embankment off the parking lot, plopped our boards in the water, and took off with Chris the squirt boater leading the way.

Now "Chris the squirt boater" is kind of a misnomer, not because he wasn't in a squirt boat, but because everybody was. I'd never seen so many tiny, glittery kayaks in my life, blasting and mystery moving and back endering and surfing constantly.

I don't kayak anymore because I dislodged my shoulder six times in one roll a long time ago, and I can't fit in a squirt boat because my knees would squirt blood. But the nonstop 360's these guys were doing on waves made me really see the point—squirting is fun!

I was wondering what they were thinking of me while I was watching them. Bill and I had been aceing all the named drops and punching all the holes we couldn't miss. But we ran so fast there was no time to impress anybody. We sort of looked like two guys walking down the sidewalk, even though it was pretty big whitewater. So I said to Bill, "Dude, let's show these guys how to surf!"

We busted an eddy full of boaters and got in line. Bill caught the breaker, got up to his knees, and waved to the crowd. I dove in, knee rode for a little bit, and then spun the board underneath me so I could ride backwards. Then we wove around each other like jets in a dog fight, then front endered out.

I thought we were pretty hot, but all we got from the crowd was a couple of smirks and one guy that said, "Hmmm, looks like fun." So, rather than try to figure out the enigma-wrapped-in-a-mystery that is the mind of the East coast boater—whose living God of squirt is Jeff Snyder—Bill and I decided to avoid the hard sell and the status contests and just have a bunch of fun.

And that's what we were doing when, without warning, these squirt dudes caught up to me and Bill and started asking all these questions like, "How long you been doing that?" "How much do they cost?" "Lemme me see that thing!" "Didn't I read about you guys in AWA?" and "You guys did Cherry Creek on that thing?!" All the while, wearing sort of a puzzled what's-going-on-here? kind of look on their faces.

It seems that while just messing around, Bill and I had surfed into a supposedly *unsurfable* hole like we had been shredding there all our lives. Just goes to show ya—sometimes you do the most when you try the least. I still wish I knew where it was that we did whatever it was that we did when we did it!

The rest of the day went like that... having a great time, meeting new people, and getting great PR for the new sport of river boarding.

Then we came to Pillow Rock, a nice big rapid where the whole river plows into a sheer rock wall on the left, making a 100-foot long, six-foot thick pillow boil that funnels everything onto a Volkswagon-size rock. The choice run is down the middle, skirting some center holes and paddling furiously away from the pillow, missing the Volkswagen and plopping into the eddy on the right.

We stood there for about 45 minutes, watching the carnage. A couple of boats would have perfect runs, and then for some reason, boat after boat would plow into the pillow doing the most hideous splatting 360's over and over on the rock wall. I mean you could hear these boats scraping and crunching and thunking upside down 'till "Smack!", they'd hit the Volkswagon, and "Plunk!", they'd land perfectly upright in the boulder eddy.

Then—without exception—these boaters would pump their fist and shout in the universal victory gesture that translates, "Yo' dudes! I really kicked butt there!" I guess this was the crazy squirt boaters' idea of maximum underwater fun. And they thought *we* were crazy!

We were wondering if the whole day was going to go this way

Bob Carlson, Jim Cassady and Paul McHugh shreddin' on their river boards. (Photo by Michael Maloney, San Francisco Chronicle)

when these two C-1ers showed up. These guys kind of floated over the center holes. They had paddles as big as snow shovels and seemed to pop their whole boat right out of the water at will. I remembered one of them sailing into the center hole and doing a one-armed pressup on his huge paddle right on the breaker of the hole just long enough to "kerplop" into the eddy higher than any of the hundred previous boaters. He had shown us the true line through Pillow Rock.

Then Bill and I went, taking this way conservative line as close to the center holes as we could get. I thought I went right, but I got swept center and kicked off the Volkswagen underwater with my flippers, but generally caught the eddy respectably high. When we got into the crowd, I asked if anyone knew who those C-1 guys were because they sure looked smooth to me. One of them said, "That's John Lugbill." John Lugbill, only the best C-1 guy in America, and I didn't even recognize him. Boy was I embarrassed!

Then, Lugbill himself paddles up and says, "Hey, you're the guys in AWA!" I said, "Yup." Then he grins big and says, "Gonna surf that hole?"

"That hole" was a hideous, steep, deep shallow-bottomed vortex between the volkswagon and the pillow wall.

"Well, I love surfing, but I don't do holes on a dare," I said, trying to be a good ambassador for my sport. Later that day I was regretting not running "that hole"—it did seem runnable at the time. But later that year I found out "that hole" is famous for breaking kayaks in half. No wonder Lugbill was chuckling.

So we leave Pillow Rock, cake Lost Paddle and Tumble Home, and make our way down to Iron Ring, a sluice falls with a strainer tree stuck in a hold on the right and a raft-snagging mid falls rock/hole on the left. We run it no prob', and are hanging out in the eddy considering a second run when we see a squirt boat and a couple of inflatable kayaks come through. The squirt dude was way under volume. I mean, isn't your *sternum* supposed to be above water most of the time? The foam bottom IK guy seemed too in control somehow, and was feeding back into the falls for some pop-ups when Chris said, "That's Roger Zweibel in the micro squirt and Jeff Snyder in the IK. You guys should meet each other."

Well it was the famous Snyder—the man who invented squirt; the man who swims rapids with a weightbelt because his wetsuit gave too much flotation; the man who broke his neck three months earlier and was out here today product testing an Atillas foam floor kayak.

Jeff said he'd heard of us in AWA and said to come on out to Friendsville sometime to swim the Upper Youghiogheny. I said great, and maybe you should start guiding Carlson River Board trips out here on the Gauley. We both took each others' suggestions under consideration.

So we left Iron Ring, ran the rest of the river, and came to the take-out... a Class V hike 1,000 feet up slippery, shaley Panther Creek. It looked just like Snuffy Smith country. Our boards didn't weigh much so we figured, "Hike out? Piece of cake."

So, how come half-way up the hill we were getting passed by kids with canoes on their heads? It was either the American Triathalon/C-1 team going by, or our wetsuits with the inside knee pads were binding our legs and holding us back. Or it could have been old age and a loathing of running. In retrospect I am sure it was the Olympic C-1 team. How lucky we were to meet all these superstars just by chance!

The Gauley Festival was that night. There was lots of beer, gear, chicken and hairball videos. I even ran into a girl I knew from California.

The put-in the next day was a reverse Panther Creek descent down to Five Boat Hole, the greatest surfing place on the Gauley.

Five Boat Hole is a river-wide ramp/hole about a foot deep with a three-foot high v-shaped wave at the bottom and big feeder eddies on both sides. We knew this was going to be a great place. Bill and I nudged our noses into the entrance curler and "zzzzipp!" slammed into the middle of the "V". It was so stable and easy it was amazing. We flew our bodies so it looked like magic. We knee rode in tandom. I did spinners with the board. The eddy audience cheered and Blackwater Video recorded it all. Remind me to pay them for my copy of the tape someday.

We continued on. The lower Gauley has big drops but more flatwater and much better camping than the upper. And it has Ledges... a sequence of five slabs of shale on river left that make five perfect peaked, clean, steep surfing waves, and great lunch spots to boot. We had to stop. There, by coincidence, was Charlie and his buddies from North Carolina. So we mooched lunch in exchange for letting them try our boards.

This turned out to be a real kick. Every kayaker at that lunch spot got out of his boat and tried our boards. One guy turned out to be a stunt water skier and began kneeriding his first time up. The crowd went nuts!

After an hour and a half of fun at the Ledges we thanked our hosts for lunch and continued on around the corner, looking foward to Sweets Falls, Hell Hole and the rest. But as we turned the bend we stumbled upon a commercial raft rescue in progress.

"Great, another sales opportunity," I thought. The raft was just outside throwbag distance so I swam to a tiny boulder midway between the shore and wrap, dragged my board up on the rock, received a line from shore, coupled it to a second bag, relayed it to the wrapped raft, and swam on.

It was a semi-routine rescue but it turned out to be an hour well spent because the Safety Director of the AWA, Charlie

Walbridge, just happened to be observing the whole thing. What luck! I had been trying to get my stuff in his catalogue for two years. He agreed the boards looked interesting and paddled off with a smile.

We swam on, caked Sweets Falls, and surfed a bunch there because the French guys did it last year. Punched Hell Hole without knowing what it was even though we'd been warned about it. Mooched a ride on a raft till the end, hitched back to the put-in, tossed all our gear in the tiny rent-a-car and began driving to Charlottesville.

When we got home Monday night, we figured the whole trip cost us $500—car, meals, hotel, and airfare for two guys included. And we just checked our boards right through baggage like a suit case.

How simple can you get?! This was Bruce Brown/Endless Summer type/Round the World Wave Chasing at its finest... and cheapest. We felt like kings and promised ourselves to do it again.

We are even planning our own video now. Send your recommendations for the world's finest standing waves to Carlson Designs, 143 Tewksbury Ave., Point Richmond, CA 94801.

CHERRY CREEK

"It was like a dream come true. To our amazement, we found that we were able to run one after another of these fearsome chutes and drops. The rapids that later became Mushroom, Lewis' Leap, and Flat Rock Falls caused us the most hesitation. (At the time, we referred to them as Numbers One, Two, and Three.) But we made it every time, and at the bottom of the rapid we'd just look at each other and laugh. We could hardly believe we were really doing it. "

Marty McDonnell, as quoted in California Whitewater, by Jim Cassady and Fryar Calhoun

The Cherry Creek section of the Upper Tuolumne River is the seventh wonder of California's whitewater world. A design in perfection, laid out across a deep, v-shaped Sierra valley as if the river gods themselves were taking up Class V boating.

In some ways, Cherry Creek is not much different than other classic Class V California rivers like the Upper Kings, or Forks of the Kern. There are long pool-drop rapids, chock full of car and van-sized boulders, and just enough time between rapids to rejoice in victory, or to regroup and collect gear. But in other ways, Cherry Creek is much more of a boater's river — access is easier, more information is available, and dam released flows provide predictable water levels and longer boating seasons.

My introduction to Cherry Creek came from the front of a 14-foot SOTAR, cohabited by Tom Dallinger, Rick Croft, Jim Foust, and Dawn Martin. From the back tube, Mike Doyle alternated between casual enjoyment of the canyon's solitude, and blaring, staccato drill sergeant commands.

I walked away from my introductory run duly impressed. As a first timer, Cherry Creek seemed to descend through its valley with all the subtlety of Godzilla making his way through Tokyo. Even today, I can shut my eyes and feel the same rush of uncertainty any boater feels when dropping off a Class V falls, and the disconcerting vertigo experienced when being sucked out of partially wrapped rafts.

But, it was my second run down Cherry Creek that leads me back to the typewriter, sharing again ridiculous adventures that skate the edge of the lunatic fringe.

It was the Summer of '87, the peak of California's drought season. I had been travelling up and down the state, connecting guiding gigs or renting out inflatable kayaks to pot-bellied weekend warriors on the Lower Stanislaus. By mid-Summer, much of the water that nourished our wallets, carefree lifestyles, and mental stability had slipped westward, mixing with the salty waters of the Pacific. We were starting to feel like lost sailors in reverse — stuck on dry land, looking for water.

The more desperate we became, the more outlandish our plans became. There was talk of clandestine runs down the Grand Canyon of the Yellowstone, trips into the hinterlands of Canada, and dreamy chats of Chile and Peru. But in the end, our next adventure laid in our own backyards. An inflatable kayak descent down Cherry Creek.

At first, an inflatable kayak descent seemed absurd. Cherry Creek was no place for these tiny "wannabe" river boats. But there was always the possibility of portaging unmanagable rapids, and long days of sunshine if we had to portage the whole damn thing. It was this extra margin of comfort and safety that pushed Mike Doyle, Rick Croft, and myself toward the put-in, and kept our pulses in check while paddling into the first set of rapids.

As my body slowly melted into the rhythm of the kayak, my mind slipped back to my freshman years of rafting. On an earlier— and much easier—trip, I had stood upon a cliff, shoulder to shoulder with a couple of veteran boaters. The confusing display of twisting currents, foam, and rock at our feet had me completely bewildered. "How are we gonna' run *that*?" I asked one of my colleagues. "*Just go with the flow,*" he replied.

I must've heard that same phrase a thousand times over the years. And often, it carried with it almost prophetic sense. But now, just two miles into our nine mile run, I realized that I'd found a river where going with the flow was all but out of the question.

We were in our first serious rapid—Corkscrew—and all of the current was going exactly where we didn't want to be. "Going

*Jeff Bennett in Class V Mushroom Rapid on the Cherry Creek
section of California's Upper Tuolumne River. (Mike Doyle photo)*

with the flow" in Corkscrew would've wrapped our boats like
hypalon bandaids around some fossilized dinosaur's toe. So, we
chose the least hazardous routes, shucking and jiving across the
current, and paddling like hell for clean slots and soft landings.

In the next mile we became more attuned to the personalities
of our IK's. Their usefulness extended far beyond simple glory
boating. When our route-finding techniques failed us, we could
easily step out of the craft, up onto a rock, and back into the river
on the other side. When the river was too far below a portage
route, the IK's became a big pillow to jump into, and when the
water was too deep to step into between distant boulders, the IK's
became tiny land bridges.

One of the most useful aspects of these craft was as balloon
armor. Since staying aboard a tiny inflatable boat in a boulder
strewn river while plummeting toward the Pacific at 105 feet per
mile wasn't always easy, we devised new techniques to preserve
our hides. The second our IK's would flip, we'd pull them in front
of us like a catcher's vest to cushion the rocks, and climb onto the
flipped craft even while dropping down steep chutes. It was an

adequate safety measure, and a sure-fire way to ward off rocks, major dunkings, and gnarly bruises.

We'd perfected these techniques by the time we arrived at Mushroom Rapid. This Class V behemoth is one of the Upper Tuolumne's legendary drops. In the first 50 yards, the river drops 30 vertical feet as it tumbles through a series of sharp ledges and big holes, ending with an unnerving plunge toward a severely undercut rock. The consequences of a flip or a swim would be *unthinkable*... which is *exactly* what I was thinking as I approached the drop.

With Mike and his camera poised on the left bank, I jammed myself into my boat, took a deep breath, and reached for the current with my paddle. In a moment I was bouncing through the first series of ledges, inching my way toward Mushroom's heart-pounding finale. The kayak steadfastly bucked through each hole, leaving me squarely set for the last drop. Then, like a kid on a carnival ride, I felt my stomach stay in one place while the rest of me hurled downward with eye-watering speed. Before my mind even processed the blur of spray and wind, the rapid was over. I'd avoided the undercut rock, paddled into the eddy above the next drop, and sat there, pinching myself to see if it was real. Soon, Mike and Rick sat in the eddy next to me, pinching themselves, and smiling with the intensity of some lucky lottery winner.

Downstream, the Upper Tuolumne grew steeper by the yard. The familiar routine of running pool-drop rapids gave way to survival paddling in drop-drop rapids, and friendly gatherings in the safe harbor of eddies became an event sorely missed. Within a half-mile of Mushroom, we were in the Miracle Mile. This section of the river drops over 200 feet in a single mile, leaving kayaks pointed perpetually downhill as they slide through a barrage of Class IV and V drops.

About 6.5 miles into the trip, the Tuolumne disappeared over another horizon line as Lewis' Leap stepped into the chorus line of awe-inspiring rapids. This time, Mike went first, lining up on a central chute and dropping four feet onto a barely submerged rock. A few determined paddle strokes drove his kayak in a zig-zag pattern through the next few small drops, and set him up for the final leap. Mike spun to the right, paddled hard, and leaned back.

From my vantage point, all I could see was the tail of his boat snap skywards, followed by an utter disappearance of anything but water. By the time I jumped onto a boulder to see what had happened, Mike paddled away from the rapid with his paddle spinning in a victory twirl.

"No big deal," I thought, as I boarded my IK. "Follow Mike's line and you'll be fine." I duplicated his every stroke, entering the chute straight as an arrow, curving around the submerged rock, and driving headlong toward the falls. But Mike was bigger than me, and stronger. My strokes weren't what his were, and I wasn't able to get my boat set straight in time for the last drop.

The river blasted open like a big trap door, leaving me hovering two feet above my rapidly escaping kayak. "Balloon armor," I thought. "Balloon armor!" I reached for my boat and bellyflopped onto the vacant floor. *Thwack.* The boat slapped the water like a giant beaver tail, my extra weight acting to amplify the sound. I rode the rapid out like that, sprawled across the floor of the boat with my fingernails deeply embedded in anything grippable. It was an amusing scene to say the least.

Lewis' Leap marked the summit of our Upper Tuolumne adventure. Just downstream, Flat Rock Falls contained a severely undercut boulder, which attracted water—and anything floating on it—like a huge, morbid funnel. We chose the only sane route, scurrying along the right bank with our boats in tow.

When we arrived at Lumsden Falls, our elation nearly rose to a narcotic level. We began talking of inflatable kayak descents down its 30-foot staircase. But the closer we got to the edge of the falls, the more sensible we became.

We left Lumsden Falls behind—something to talk about at the next campfire—and floated to our take-out at Lumsden Bridge Campground. Before our kayaks were even rolled up and in the back of the truck, talk started to fly of new rivers. We'd found a new form of amusement and a world of adventures beckoned.

RUSSIA: GLASNOST AND FAST BOATS
By Doc Loomis
(As told to Jeff Bennett)

"The trembling ashes of a mighty fir swayed gently as its flame danced to an unending procession of laughter and song. Late into the night, brilliant constellations presided over the raucous chorus. Somewhere in the distant heavens, a mythological God chuckled in delight... Chuya, Nantahala '90... now only fond memories tucked snugly inside our hearts, these rallies from yesterday, have sparked the dreams of tomorrows realities. "

Project RAFT

F lipping through the pages of your favorite whitewater catalog it would be easy to perceive whitewater rafting as something purely American. As home grown as Huck Finn, John Wesley Powell or Nathaniel Galloway. Yet thousands of miles away, the Russians developed a love of whitewater which nearly surpasses our own in terms of national popularity.

In 1979, Misha Kolchevnikov tapped into his nations's love of rafting, and organized the first Chuya Rally. For Misha, the Chuya Rally was to be rafting's answer to kayak slalom competitions—an opportunity to match skills against those of other river runners, and an opportunity to share their sport with friends.

Only eighteen rafts arrived at the Chuya River in 1979, the first year of the competition. But, by 1988 the Rally had grown to 88 rafts from 22 Soviet cities.

In 1989, the Soviet Union was undergoing a massive political transition. One that eventually lead to the demise of the Soviet Union, and the installation of the Commonwealth of Soviet States. As Mikhail Gorbachev rolled in the age of *glasnost* and international cooperation, American rafters began to join Russians on rivers like the Katun and Chulishman.

In 1989, with support from the Soviet Peace Fund, the Chuya Rally opened its doors to teams from the United States, Great Britain, Australia, and other countries around the world. 200 team members from 13 countries gathered on the banks of Siberia's icy

Chuya River for the 10th annual Chuya Rally. This international rafting community fused ideas, concepts, and their love of rivers, igniting a revolution in the sport of whitewater rafting.

By 1991, the United States had hosted "Nantahala '90, an International Peace Camp and River Rally," and Costa Rica had hosted "Costa Rica '91, A Tropical Rainforest Festival." The new raft designs and specialized equipment that appeared at these races closely mimicked the Russian designs proven so successful at the Chuya Rally. By 1992, the popularity of catarafting—even paddle-catting—had exploded in the United States.

Doc Loomis competed in all three of the early rallies, and shared his thoughts and memories with me for this interview. Doc is a legendary figure in Pacific Northwest rafting circles, and has an unparalleled number of first raft descents to his name. He gives credit to the Russian rafters—whose zeal for rafting goes beyond high-tech boats and comfortable gear—for much of his present passion for river exploration.

J: Doc, you've been to all three of the big rallies so far... the Chuya Rally in '89, Nantahala '90, and Costa Rica '91. What differences have you seen between these festivals?

D: I don't think there are any big differences. Maybe in the slalom courses or the particular events, but the rallies themselves are pretty similar from year to year. Costa Rica had some awesome whitewater. It was warm, and at least on the downriver race on the Reventazon, we were doing whitewater that people would've paid an outfitter $100 to paddle. Same deal on the Lower Pacuare... it was a world class environment that was just a pleasure to be in. At the Nantahala, we got to run a lot of different rivers. Rivers that I'd long heard about but never seen. Plus, many of the world's top paddlers were there. It was incredible. But, the Chuya Rally was extraordinary in that it was the first international rafting rally to bring together rafters from all over the world.

J: Tell me a little bit about how you got to the Chuya Rally site.

D: Well, to start, the Soviet Peace Fund sponsored the entire event. From the moment our feet hit Russian soil, we were treated as guests. Everything was provided for us. It was an incredibly warm feeling. The Chuya River itself is in Siberia, probably about 100 miles north of the Mongolian border. So, since we flew into Moscow, we had a long way to go to get to the Chuya. After our first night in Moscow, we returned to the airport and flew five hours to the Siberian city of Barnaul. When we got there, it was freezing. There was still snow on the ground. Next, we got on some busses for an eight hour ride to Gorn-altaisk.

J: Where?

D: Gorn-altaisk.

J: OK. Spell that for me.

D: Ha, ha, ha... sure!

J: OK, where'd you go next?

D: Well, after a night in Gorn-altaisk, it was back aboard the busses for another day-long trip to the Chuya. This is where our trek started becoming real interesting. At one point, after we had been travelling mile after mile of dirt roads, we hit a hill heading up to a high pass. Up until then, each bus driver knew his place in the caravan. But, when we hit that hill, all of the faster buses began overtaking the slower buses. It was a one-lane road with steep drop-offs in places. At the other end of this road, the police were stopping all oncoming traffic so we could have drag races up the hills. Then, going down the other side of this pass, the buses started jockeying back into their normal positions. They were barrelling downhill as fast as they could go, and it was really pretty scary. A Class VI road trip to a Class III river.

J: Did your gear travel with you?

D: From the time we got to Moscow, everyone travelled together, and there were something like three semis pulling double trailers full of luggage. Each one of us was responsible for carrying our own luggage, getting it through the airports, getting it weighed, getting it on the airplane, etc. And, this happened anytime we stopped at someplace new. Add to that the language barrier, and you can see what it would be like.

J: How about rafting gear, what did you bring?

D: I was one of the few westerners to bring his own boat. I mean, there were other westerners there with boats, but I brought an oar-cat to compare it to paddle-cats. I couldn't believe that the paddle-cats would be any better in the gates than the oar-cats.

J: Did you pass many villages along the way?

D: Yes, once we were out of Gorn-altaisk, we passed by some very rustic villages. Many of the homes were made from rough-hewn logs, much the same as our homes would have been 100 years ago. Horse drawn carts shared the roads with us, and many people used horses as their sole source of transportation.

J: What was the camp like when you got there?

D: The Chuya River camp was huge. The river itself had about a foot of ice along the bank, but camp was pretty decent. There were tent communities set up for each team, and country flags flying above the tents. One of the neat things were the big yurts... big siberian versions of teepees. They were perfectly suited to the terrain, really roomy and warm.

J: Where were the people from?

D: Well, there were boaters from all over Asia, and plenty of people who had come just to see the events. It was amazing. By the time everyone moved into camp, the grounds looked like acres of giant fabric mole hills.

J: What did you think about the Russian boats when you first saw them?

D: I was amazed. Truly amazed. As you know, they use two kinds of boats there: plohts and catarafts. Every one of them resembled the other, but none of them were alike. Every boat was constructed different, constructed with whatever timbers, tubing, twine, or bags they could get their hands on. Most of the tubes were giant bags that held plastic bags full of air. Their ingenuity was incredible.

J: How'd they go about constructing their rafts?

D: Well, their main tool is a short, broad head axe. Everybody seems to have one. They can carve anything with one of those. They knew just what to do, and how to do it fast when it came time to carve up a new piece of a frame, or a new oar. Still, many of the Russians were already in camp when we arrived, and had done most of the hard wood work on their boats before we got there.

J: The plohts must've weighed a ton.

D: Heck, yeah. I mean, their frames were made out of half of the nearby trees.

J: Tell me more about the catarafts, the paddles, oars, and all.

D: They used a lot of cats. Especially four-man cats. Those boats worked really well too. The crew members carry these big aluminum blades with them for the oars. Kind of like big stop signs. Then, they'd carve an oar from a tree when they got to the river. If they're doing a tough river and hit a portage, they'll scrap the oar, carry the blade downriver, and carve a new oar out of a tree near the end of the portage.

J: What about spares?

D: Well, I saw one guy that must have been worried that his paddle would sink. He had this kind of "paddle float" on his paddle. It was like a balloon that went around the shaft.

J: What other kinds of boats were there?

D: Some looked like they were commercially built. I mean, once in a while, two would look pretty much alike. But, one boat was nothing like the others. It was two huge innertube-like donuts, with molded plastic seats and a frame holding it all together. The paddlers seat-belted themselves into it, and had the bystanders roll them into the river. As I was watching this thing go, I thought "Man, I want to try that." But, there was about 500 other people thinking the same thing. They packed that boat back and forth up the river many times so that new people could try it out.

J: What about their personal gear?

D: All of it was home-made. Whatever they had or wore on the river, they made with their own hands. Every life jacket was different, and just depended on its creator's imagination. One life jacket looked like a guy strapped a whole airline seat around him. Another looked like it was made out of a kid's school backpack. Another just looked like a big pillow with shoulder straps. It was real interesting. Plus, they didn't have wetsuits, or any of the stuff we take for granted.

J: They sound a bit crazy.

D: Yeah, well, when you figure that the river came right off the ice, and that they were out there in the elements, they were really hearty people. I had a lot of respect for them. In fact, just being around those people changed my whole attitude on boating. I mean, they didn't know the meaning of the word "adversity." They saw something they wanted to do, and just did it!

A Russian "ploht" competing in the 1989 Chuya Rally. (Photo by Doc Loomis)

J: They'd probably get pretty excited about boating over here.

D: They'd probably pack into canyons where we'd never think of taking rafts. They'd spend a few days going a few miles on incredibly difficult rivers. I think they're more determined than we are.

J: How cold was it there?

D: Well, at night, it got down to about zero.

J: You mean like zero degrees fahrenheit?

D: Yeah. It was really cold.

J: How 'bout during the day.

D: Once in a while it'd get warm enough to take off your shirt, but, not too much. I guess I didn't expect it to be quite as cold as it was, so I was probably a little unprepared. The first night, I tried to sleep like I usually do, just stripped down to my shorts. But, my sleeping bag was not *that* good. The next night, everything I had was on my body. And, once I figured out what I could layer to stay warm, I never came out of them. Fortunately, it didn't rain that much.

J: Let's talk about the race a bit. Tell me about the events.

D: There was a Class III slalom with kayaks, two man paddle-cat teams, four man paddle-cat teams, and plohts. There was also an orienteering event, and a Class V slalom at Begemot (Hippopotamus) Rapid. The slalom course was a boulder-strewn Class III course, with about 1,000 cfs flowing through it. The gates were pretty tough in places. The so-called Class V slalom was on another Class III section, with one steep drop. But, I saw pictures of the course at higher water, and the big drop could hammer one of those big plohts.

J: How'd you do in the events?

D: Well, I tried to compete in the Class V slalom with an oar-rigged cataraft, and couldn't hold a candle to the paddle-cats. I knew nothing about paddle-cats before I went over there, and I didn't think there was any way a paddle-cat could out perform an oar-cat in a slalom. But, I was wrong. It was a really tight and technical course. You could hardly get an oar in the water to make a move, but the paddlers could go full speed at the next gate.

J: What did the U.S. teams use in the ploht classes?

D: Since the ploht class absorbed just about any boat that wasn't a paddle cat, we got to run a self-bailing raft with five people in it. But, again, the Russian plohts kicked our butts with their finesse and maneuverability since they could run these narrow, technical courses without eight feet of oars sticking out the sides of the boat.

J: What else was in a ploht class?

D: Anything controlled by the sweep boat method.

J: What about the river rescue event?

D: There were four boaters in a raft or paddle cat, one of which was on a rock in the river. And, there was a kayaker. There were ten on a team. The object was kind of to save the swimmer, then negotiate the first gate, then flip the raft, get it through another gate while on the upside down raft, then be rescued by the rest of the team. Meanwhile, the kayaker had to negotiate a couple of gates too. The swimmer starts in the middle of the river on a rock, with a judge on the rock next to him. When the starter says "GO!", the judge throws the swimmer off the rock. I mean, this was *cold* water, and no one wanted to swim. So, that was the judge's job... to make sure the swimmer swam.

J: How'd your team do?

D: Well, you see, we had to pick up the swimmer, then go through a gate upside up, then through another gate upside down. We used a cataraft, and thought we had a cool plan. We were going to head into this little eddy and flip the cat so it wouldn't get away from us. Well, we flipped it, but I got under the boat and it came right down on top of me. When I tried to get up, I found myself caught between a tube and the frame. Then, when I finally got unstuck, I hurried up onto the tube with the rest of the crew. Only problem was, I was facing one way, and the rest of my crew was facing the other way. Man, what a mess.

J: I heard they use a little different rescue system than plain ole' throw bags.

D: Oh, yeah. They have "human throw ropes." These guys were wearing harnesses tied to a long piece of rope. A guy on the shore held the other end of the rope, and one other guy usually helped as part of this three-man rescue team. They'd just dive into the river with the rope attached to them and grab people, boats, whatever. It worked really well.

J: Let's get back into the camp scene. Tell me more about the people, the food, and all.

D: One night I went into one of the yurts, and they gave me coffee—I think it was coffee—and a bowl of meat. It was really neat. Everything was taken care of from the time we got there. Then we'd get potatoes, bread, some huge slabs of something like thuringer, caviar, stuff like that.

J: Caviar?!

D: Yeah, but I can't say that I was too into that stuff. Even though it's expensive in the U.S., you couldn't get me to eat it.

J: How were you treated by the locals?

D: It wasn't like Costa Rica. Many locals had come to see the event, and looked upon us curiously, but did not stare, or ask for autographs, or anything. But all of the paddlers and competitors were extremely friendly. There was a common interest in rafting, a common bond that brought us all together instantly. They recognized us as rafters, not foreigners, and welcomed us with open arms. It was incredible because we'd grown up hearing that the KGB watched you, and that people were thrown in cars and sent to Siberian work camps. But, there was none of that. Each night, they had dancers, jugglers, and other performers entertain us. It was all fascinating, and the people were wonderful.

J: What did you do after the event?

D: Well, I joined up with a team that was going to float down the Chuya and onto the Katun. I got on a big ploht with some Russians, and let them try my cat. It was a big river, with a couple of rocks. Basically, it was the type of run where I'd let my PVC boat slip over rocks without worrying. But, they spent a lot of time maneuvering around rocks so they wouldn't pop the tender bags supporting the ploht. They kind of got on me for not paddling, but they were real nice about it.

J: How was the Katun River?

D: Well, we never made it. We camped on the Chuya the first day, but when we woke up in the morning, it had sleeted hard. I stuck my head out of my tent, saw all that ice on my wet suit, and said "no thanks!" I got a picture of another guy holding his frozen wet suit straight out from his body like a board. There was a road right there, so the bus found us and picked us up.

J: As we talked early, you said you've been to the Nantahala and Costa Rica Rallies. Has the Russian's gear changed since the first event?

D: Yeah. A lot. At the Costa Rica Rally, a few Russians showed up with Extrasport lifejackets, used Carlisle paddles, and paddled a self-bailing raft. Also, their cats had more aluminum and high-tech materials. There was definitely a western influence in the Russian designs, and a Russian influence showing up in some of the western designs.

J: Before we wrap this up, what was the biggest impact the Chuya Rally had on you?

D: That's very hard to explain. You just felt extremely honored to be able to even get a chance to go over there. You may not have liked the food, or the cold weather, but they truly had their arms out and were giving us their very best. They were so far behind us developmentally, but their enthusiasm was irrepressible. They taught me to look beyond my gear, beyond the technology, and to look at the river as my source of joy. It really changed me.

SOUTH FORK OF THE SALMON RIVER
By Jim Cassady

"Whitewater is the summit—the peak—of river running and it is unlike anything else in the world of sports. Shooting rapids is a one-shot deal, the muzzleloader of water sports. Unlike fishing, where you can reel in and try another cast, or rock climbing, where you can rappel down and try another route, whitewater requires that you get it right the first time. There is no reeling back, ...no reloading. You scout, plan, plan again and go. "

Jeff Rennicke, River Days

It had been raining hard in the area for several days as we drove into the Idaho mountains in early June of 1985. There was a layer of fresh snow coating the pass as we bounced along Forest Service roads leading toward the Secesh River—a major tributary of the South Fork Salmon. As we descended into the South Fork watershed, every creek we passed was raging. The road along the Secesh revealed a river which was filled to the top of its banks.

We were getting nervous. High water is not the best condition for making a first descent.

A few days earlier I had received a call from Rocky Rossi. Rocky wanted to film the first raft descent of the South Fork Salmon... or so he said. I figured he was just like the other kayakers, wanting rafters to carry his gear. In fact, kayakers had been plying the South Fork since the early 1970's, but maybe they had just now found a team to carry their gear. Earlier attempts at raft descents had been made, but not successfully. Rocky said it would take three days to make the entire 60 mile float—38 of which would be on the South Fork Salmon, the rest floating on the Main Salmon to reach the take-out at Vinegar Creek.

I knew that the South Fork was considered too difficult to raft. This reputation starkly contrasted from its sister river to the east, the Middle Fork of the Salmon, which has been deemed the ultimate wilderness rafting trip. I scanned the topos and found a few stretches dropping away at 80 feet per mile, but the overall gradient was only 50 feet per mile. Nothing too scary yet.

Idaho's South Fork Salmon River is one of America's ultimate wilderness trips. (Photo by Doc Loomis)

Rocky had told us to bring a 12-foot SOTAR. But, as I foundout more about the river, I realized that early June was peak runoff season. A 14-foot SOTAR would let us carry our camping gear and food, and give us a fighting chance against the stampede of liquid Idaho snow that would be heading downstream about the same time we would arrive at the put-in.

I made the necessary calls to put together a crack paddle boat team. First there was Joe Willie Jones, a former Georgia football player whom I considered to be one of the strongest paddlers around. (Rolling an open canoe was child's play for Joe Willie.) Then, there was Renee Goddard, an experienced SOBEK guide who had participated in the first raft descent of the Watut River in Papua New Guinea. Larry Busby, a veteran Class V California raft guide, also accepted an invitation. The final slot should go to some media person. Some trip organizers fill the media slot with someone unskilled in the ways of rafting, but I recruited David Bolling, a highly-skilled river runner, and a fine human being.

By the time we reached the South Fork put-in, the gauge registered 5.5 feet, which meant an estimated water level of about 6,000 cfs. We hiked along the river downstream from the end of the road. Our first glimpse of the South Fork revealed a beautiful, deep granite canyon carved through the thick central Idaho forest. David Bolling described the sight for the July 1986 issue of *River Runner* as a "...swollen green current threading a path through a wonderland of sculpted rock and pristine pine." Don McClaren, in his book *Idaho Whitewater*, called the South Fork "one of the best whitewater rivers in the world."

The canyon was extra spectacular shrouded in mist and rain. We were mesmerized. But, we could still reason well enough to agree that it was runnable. We returned to the put-in and began carefully rigging our boat. Soon, we were on the river, testing our skills and teamwork in an easy piece of water. Our well-matched paddling abilities fed our confidence. The crew worked in fine-tuned precision, catching even the smallest of eddies with ease.

Now, you're probably expecting the blood-and-guts tales to begin. You've heard them before: "I spit out my teeth after they were ripped from my jaw after we were hurtled over a 20-foot waterfall." "While being maytagged in the hole for an eternity, my life flashed before my eyes. I apologized to all of the girlfriends I had turned into shuttle bunnies." "The force of the hole sucked my lifejacket off my back and crammed it up my ass."

Well, this tale is one of disappointment for the reader, and victory for the writer and fellow paddlers.

For the most part, the run was a piece of cake. The South Fork lived up to its reputation as a tough river, made even more so by the high water. Endless rollercoaster rides through crashing waves and holes flew beneath our raft in a huge liquid blur. We only had one swimmer (me) come out of the raft when a wall of water grabbed me by the life jacket and ripped me free of the SOTAR at Devil Slide. But, I was quickly rescued and pulled back aboard by the crew during a short lull in the rapids. We also chose to line the raft around the most difficult part of a rapid called Fall Creek. This mammoth rapid contained a compression wave at the base of a cliff that could easily flip a 20-foot raft. We lined past the wave, but still had to make a death-defying ferry past a huge rock flanked by a whirlpool hole. Furious paddle strokes, fueled by pure fear and adrenaline, delivered us into the safe haven below Fall Creek. The South Fork's reputation as being supposedly too difficult to raft succumbed to our state-of-the-art equipment and techniques.

There are no difficult rapids after Fall Creek, and as we ate lunch on the rocks at the end of the rapid, I reflected how rafting had evolved in recent years.

Back in 1981, I led what at the time was one of rafting's most advanced expeditions... the first raft descent of California's Upper Kings. We had two Avons—the best rafts at the time—one oar raft and one paddle raft. The going was extremely slow. On the second day we made less than two miles. We had to run one raft at a time with members of the other raft stationed on the downstream bank with throw ropes to pull the raft into tiny eddies. The biggest problem was that in each rapid the raft filled with water and became too heavy to maneuver well. The bathtub design had to go.

By Spring of 1983 I had White Water Manufacturing, of Grant's Pass, Oregon, build a self-bailer prototype. We tested the new craft on various Class V rivers and found that it performed superbly.

The self-bailing raft was light and nimble, with all of the qualities we were seeking. While the old-style paddle boats required teams to paddle and bail at the same time, the new self-bailing raft took care of that. Now, paddle boats made more sense than oar-boats on exploratories. We installed foot cups so that paddlers could lean out and paddle strongly without falling out of the boat. And, we learned to shift our weight, dig in, and brace, giving the raft power, stability and finesse. Portages were much easier with the reduced weight-to-person ratio.

Our 14-foot SOTAR had been our magic carpet on the South Fork Salmon, delivering safely through more than 38 miles of pulse-raising rapids. When we reached the Main Salmon, it was like a lake compared to the South Fork. The 22 miles from the South Fork confluence to the take-out at Vinegar Creek only took a few hours on the bloated waters of the Main Salmon.

During that first week in June, 1985, it would have been hard to envision that a half-dozen years later the South Fork would be rafted regularly, and that proposals for permit systems would ever be made.

Rafting has come a long way since our first descents of the Upper Kings and South Fork Salmon!

THE UPPER YOUGHIOGHENY RIVER
"Fear and Loathing in Friendsville, Maryland"
By Kevin O'Brien

"Raft Guide—A.K.A. 'captain', 'boatmen', etc. The man or woman responsible for yelling at the customers in rapids and entertaining them the rest of the time. Needless to say, most raft guides are semi-psychotic most of the time. When not rigging rafts, packing or unpacking lunch, guiding or sleeping, raft guides engage 'merc-talk', plot guide strikes, and plan trips to the Grand, Costa Rica, or Nepal."

William Nealy, Whitewater Home Companion, Volume II

Whitewater rafting on the rivers of Appalachia has become big business over the last decade. The clientele are, for the most part, a likeable bunch; New York City cops, auto workers from Detroit, car salesmen from Cleveland, mothers from New Jersey.

Leaving behind their nine-to-five world, caution to the wind, they flock to the Lower Yough, the Cheat, the New, and numerous other Class III-IV runs of the Mid-Atlantic region, heady with the pursuit of adventure.

On moderate rivers whitewater rafting is a relatively safe, harmless activity, suitable to the masses. Outfitters are quick to point this out in their brochures: "Bring Grandma! Bring the kids! Fun for the whole family!", and so on.

Pitching to the entire spectrum of well-moneyed, summer-vacationers inevitably leads to the roping in that uniquely American phenomenon; denizen of the motorhome, fugitive of Wally World, vacant-eyed, slack-jawed, bovine...

The Tour-On.

The Upper Yough, a steep Class V section of whitewater in western Maryland, is no place for Tour-Ons. Commercial outfitters have run trips on it since the early eighties and, for the most part, are selective of their clients. It is a demanding run for both guide and passenger, not to be taken lightly.

"Previous whitewater experience required. Guests must be in

good physical condition...."

Words right out of the company's brochure popped into mind as I stared from the raft at my approaching clients. Obviously they hadn't read it.

"Calvin? Are you Calvin?", the heavy, red-faced man was bellowing at me.

"I'm Kevin," I replied.

"Where the hell's Calvin?", he repeated, quizzically looking down the row of rafts at the other guides. I could see them beginning to smirk.

"There is no *Calvin*. That's *me*!", I answered, unsure of what I'd just said.

Staring blankly at me for a moment, he pointed to the woman tip-toeing down the bank.

"Calvin, this 'eres my wife, Phyllis."

Phyllis, a large, pink-skinned woman, hair piled high in a spectacular bee-hive, paused in her descent, tilting her silver-rimmed, bejeweled sunglasses to peer at me over the top, smiling.

"Howdy!", was all she said.

"Glad to meet you, son", hollered Hank as he thundered aboard, extending a hand the size of a ham.

Howdy? Son? I'd heard those words before. An alarm, deep in my brain, began to sound.

My God! I thought. That was it! They're *Texans*! The alarm in my head rang shrilly.

It's no secret that Texans and whitewater are a lethal combination. Primarily desert-dwellers, moving water is alien to them, severely limiting their ability to balance on even the widest cross-tube. Their inherent braggadocio and yahoo-ism prevents them from comprehending even the most basic paddle strokes and commands. Their cowboy boots, which they are reluctant to part with, tear holes in rafts.

I'd had Texans in my raft on other rivers. It was never a pretty sight.

Consigned to my fate, I helped Phyllis aboard, got the two situated with paddles and life jackets, and shoved off into the current.

Guiding on the Upper Yough makes for a high-energy

diversion from my usual work as a free-lance writer and photographer. Given the nature of my career, it also serves as a way of making quick cash, helping to appease the wolves, seemingly forever at my door. I'd signed on with one of the larger outfitters that morning, replacing one of their regular, full-time guides who, when last seen, was drunk out of his nut, fire-dancing with customers at about 4:00 A.M.

Floating through the wide, flat section above Gap Falls, the first major rapid of the day, Phyllis began what seemed to her rendition of a chicken. Hands tucked tightly into her armpits, she began flapping her elbows rhythmically, forward and back. Hank, sitting across from her, stared at the shoreline, oblivious.

"Uh, Ma'am. *What the hell are you doing?*" I finally asked.

"A-robics," she puffed, in between flaps.

"23-foof-24-foof...." She was counting now.

Hank, with us once again, looked approvingly at his wife, explaining over his shoulder. "She's been doing this for a month, gittin' ready for this trip."

Phyllis puffed on, reddenning by the second.

As we entered the small wave train signalling the approach to Gap Falls, I emplored Phyllis to get with the program.

"Uh, Ma'am... you better grab your paddle," I suggested.

"78-foof-79-foof...." Phyllis kept puffing.

"Uh, *Ma'am!*"

"Just to 100," she gasped, barely missing a beat.

"86-foof-87-foof...."

Hank, picking up the cue as I began paddling hard, dug in his paddle, wailing his Texas battle cry.

"Let's git it!" he hollered, catching sight of the approaching hole.

Punching the corner of the hydraulic pivots the raft hard into the eddy on river right. Hank, unprepared for the sudden deceleration, sprawls forward onto the side-tube. Phyllis, her arms frozen in mid-flap, is hurled to the bottom of the boat. Hovering in the calm eddy, I wave to the other rafts on our trip, congregated just downstream. Satisfied all is well, they disappear around the corner. It was the last we'd see of them for awhile.

Turning back to the crew, I see Phyllis righting herself onto her tube, straightening her chrome-rimmed sunglasses. Her conical coiffure now listing 45 degrees to starboard.

"Damn!" Hank cried. "Wudn't 'at a pisser?!"

I wasn't about to argue. Hank's the kind of man that knows a pisser when he sees one.

It seemed obvious from our Gap Falls performance that a rehash of paddling techniques was in order. Weaving our way through the Class III below I went over the commands once more.

Phyllis, listening intently as I described different strokes, practiced them in mid-air. Attempting a hard back-stroke, she clipped Hank behind the right ear.

"Goddammit, Phyllis. Put that dang thing down!", he shouted.

"You need to practice these strokes," I intervened.

"We know all 'bout oars. We got a canoe back home," Hank assured me.

Undaunted, I continued my hopeless soliloquy as we approached the next drop.

At Bastard Falls the river begins its descent in earnest, dropping over 150 feet per mile. The rapids—Charlie's Choice, Triple Drop, and National Falls—follow one another in quick succession with little room for recovery between them. It's no place for swimmers.

"Now, on the count of three, I need you to give me a really hard forward stroke so we boof into the eddy, OK?" I was going over the method of running Bastard Falls.

From our tiny eddy on river left we could hear the rapid thundering below.

"Any questions?" I asked, preparing to push off.

"What's a *boof?*" inquired Phyllis.

"Never mind. Just paddle hard on three," I replied.

By now I was certain that any attempt to interpret river terminology, no matter how basic, was futile.

We peeled out of the micro-eddy and headed for the drop. Nearing the top, I began my cadence.

"One." Both paddlers dug in.

"Two." Another hearty stroke.

"Thr..."

Eye-balling the oncoming hole, Hank burst into action,

discarding his paddle and lunging to the floor of the raft. Phyllis, her mighty third stroke completely missing the water, shouted.

"Get up Haaaaa....!"

Our momentum gone, the nose of the raft augers into the stiff hole at the bottom of the pourover. Hitting the floor, I catch a fleeting glimpse of Phyllis as she sails overhead, landing in the foam somewhere beyond.

I clamber over Hank, struggling to unclip my throwbag.

"There she is!" cries Hank, spotting the tip of her breaking the surface. "Phyyyyyliiiis!"

A lucky toss and the rope hits her right in the numbers. Hand over hand I reel her in. Hank helps me hoist her over the side.

Spread eagle on the floor of the raft, Phyllis lay gasping. Moments later, having caught her wind, she turned to Hank, violently demanding, "Why the hell'd you stop paddling, Slack Ass!"

The ensuing argument continued all the way down the left side of Charlie's Choice, where we emerged, mercifully unscathed.

Eddying out above Triple Drop, both passengers now stonily silent, I describe the next series of stair step ledges, holes and the wave train, all funnelling into the huge hydraulic at the bottom, National Falls. I wrap up my summary of the rapid with the warning.

"...and you *don't* want to swim here!"

Rounding the large rock at the top of the channel, we line up for the series of holes. Sensing the seriousness of the oncoming rapid, both passengers are stroking to beat the band.

Slam! We burst through the first hole with plenty of momentum.

Wham! We plough through the second, which slows us only slightly.

Hank, sensing our prowess at having punched the first two holes, decides to throw in a backstroke.

Woomph! We slam into the hole sideways, tilting the boat up on its side, completely vertical.

Hank, formerly on the downstream side, now finds himself launched into the air. Deftly latching onto the boat's grabline in mid-flight, he continues tumbling into the foam, pulling the raft, and us, over on top of him.

"Balls!" I mutter, just as the lights go out.

Black fades to green...fades to white...and bubbles.

Breaking the surface, I look upstream and see the raft is still caught in the hole. I make out Hank's burred head bobbing on the wave train downstream. To my right, Phyllis rockets from the whitewater, eyes wide. By now a familiar sight.

As the three of us approach National Falls I can see Hank is set up for the left line. I decide to give him a wide berth and aim for the right side of the hole.

Tumbling over both edges of the huge hydro almost in unison, we emerge below, bobbing side by side, lucky to have cleared the recirculating backwash. Looking upstream, we watch Phyllis, backstroking furiously, as she's sucked into the maw of the hole.

"Oh Baby. Oh Baby. *Oh Bayyyybee!*" Hank whimpers as he watches his wife disappear into the abyss.

Up... down. Up... down. Three cycles later Phyllis finally emerges in the green water below the backwash.

The rest of the trip, watching the show from below, rallies around and helps us gather up our stray gear.

Back in the raft, Hank stares upstream, the previous quarter-mile of whitewater still visible, winding down the valley.

"Ya know," he begins philosophically, "I think we may be in a little over our heads."

Phyllis was staring blankly into space. Her hair—deflated—hangs limply to one side. Her sunglasses, both earings, one false eyelash, and three fingernails are gone, floating in the darkness at the bottom of National Falls.

Defeated, I paddle them over to the river-right shore, pointing out the trail to the take-out. I try to console them. Tommy's Hole, Zinger, F@#k-up Falls, all the rapids below, will still be there, I tell them, should they decide to come do battle another day. Tired and relieved they begin the long hike down to Friendsville.

Paddling back across the river, I grab the beefiest customer I can find among the other rafts. Paddling R-2, we'll finish out the run.

Back in Friendsville, I search in vain for Hank and Phyllis. Johny Raygun, the guide who's slot I filled that day, waves to me from the liquor store. He catches up with me, reeking of singed hair and stale beer.

"Those folks who walked out said sorry they missed you," he tells me, handing over a fistfull of money. "They left you a twenty buck tip!"

I count the money. "There's only $15.50 here," I reply, looking at him accusingly.

"Oh yeah," he grins. "I bought a six pack. Want one?"

Sipping my beer I notice, out beyond town on route 68, a huge Winnebago briefly silhouetted against the orange evening sky. Cresting the distant hill, it vanishes from sight, bound for Texas.

SHUTTLES

"When I first experienced whitewater, ...I knew that as much as I wanted to do anything, I wanted to run rivers. The sound of rapids ahead, the tug of water..., the filaments of current curling around rocks, the heaping up of the waves, all produced a mind set that would lead me to the inevitable contest. Somewhere a river waited for me, and that river would put me to the test and be the losing of my innocence. "

Elliot DuBois, An Innocent On The Middle Fork: A
Whitewater Adventure in Idaho's Wilderness

First, some guy from Phoenicia invented the wheel. Later, Henry Ford mass marketed the idea—four wheels at a time. Then, while climbing up the take-out trail after a recent run, I realized I'd left my car keys in Jerry's van... eighteen miles upstream. *Back to square one!*

Of all of the less savory aspects of whitewater rafting, the shuttle ranks high on my worst offenders list. Shuttling is nothing like travelling, which I enjoy immensely, especially when travelling along rivers. Travelling gives me time to reflect upon past trips, to scout new rapids, and to revel in the anticipation of a new run. It's the *shuttle* that I've never been a fan of. I mean, it wasn't until my late teens until I managed to overcome inevitable bouts with car sickness. And it wasn't until just recently that my shrink cured me of the phobia that *I'd* be the one who gets to the take-out and says, "Oh no! I forgot the keys!!!"

Still, like many of you, I've come to accept the shuttle for what it is. In the grand scheme of things, the shuttle is a necessary evil—like dank, pungent heaps of polypropylene, the deafening whir of LVM's, cold booties, and leaky handpumps. But accepting shuttles as a part of rafting doesn't mean I have to *like* them!

To start, my shuttle complaints arise out of the fact that the second someone becomes a shuttle *driver*, he or she undergoes an instantaneous transformation. The brain goes out the window, the rules of the road become irrelevent, and the singular thought of seeing and running rivers seeps into every reflex necessary for highway survival.

During my tenure as a shuttle observer — both as a passenger and as a driver — I've managed to break shuttle drivers down into seven categories: Swivelheads, Rubberneckers, Leadfoots, Enforcers, Bobberheads, Wannabees, and Orienteers. Since you may have never noticed the subtle, but important, distinctions between these types, I'm including a detailed analysis of each for you.

SWIVELHEADS. *Early Warning Signs:* The same person that awes campfire circles with tales of mythical river adventures. *Favorite Saying:* "Last year, me and Bob did the first descent of the Upper Left Fork of the Right Fork River. It was AWESOME!" *Physical Characteristics:* Had neck vertebra surgically replaced with ball bearings so he can face passengers, and has thigh indentations from driving with knees. *Driving Technique:* Hands are only used for telling stories; needs three lanes for safety during the most grandiose tales.

RUBBERNECKERS. *Early Warning Signs:* Lots of topographic maps on the kitchen table. *Favorite Saying:* "Hey! What was that river we just crossed?!" *Physical Characteristics:* Two-foot long neck from craning to see over guardrails and embankments. *Driving Technique:* Can consistently maintain a 3-inch distance between guardrails and the passenger door while bombing down a highway at 55 miles per hour.

LEADFOOTS. *Early Warning Signs:* Drives a Porsche 928, Camaro, or souped up GTO. *Favorite Sayings:* "Doesn't this van go *any* faster?", "Get off the damn road!" *Physical Characteristics:* Right foot has no arch and makes a significantly deeper footprint than the left foot; has a killer handshake from slamming stick shifts through the gears. *Driving Technique:* Leans forward, clenches teeth, and slams the pedal to the metal.

ENFORCERS. *Early Warning Signs:* Marine Corp enlistees, security officers, and old grumpy men. *Favorite Saying:* "You can take a piss when we stop to get gas!" *Physical Characteristics:* Short guys with overly-muscled chests, old guys with permanent frowns. *Driving Technique:* Cruise control set five miles per hour below the speed limit.

BOBBERHEADS. *Early Warning Signs:* Takes a nap at every lunch stop; last one out of tent in morning. *Favorite Sayings:*

"Huh?", "I'm fine to drive, really." *Physical Characteristics:* Eyes at half mast, combed hair last Tuesday. *Driving Technique:* Long periods of perfect driving followed by sudden veers toward a cliff, guardrail or river. .

WANNABEES. *Early Warning Signs:* Couldn't get a guiding job, so volunteered to drive shuttles for a big outfitter. *Favorite Saying:* "(Insert famous person) said he'll take me down the (insert famous river) next Summer." *Physical Characteristics:* Cut off shorts, department store sneakers, and thick glasses. *Driving Technique:* Just like they taught you in driver's education.

ORIENTEERS. *Early Warning Signs:* Car compass mounted on dashboard or windshield. *Favorite Saying:* "I think I know a shortcut", or "Maybe it was that *other* road." *Physical Characteristics:* Permanent cowlick from scratching head, and a permanent look of confusion. *Driving Technique:* Don't know— nobody has been able to find him.

Beyond the obvious problems of handling and spotting troublesome shuttle drivers, there are the woes associated with shuttle vehicles. Now I don't expect a single car dealer to substantiate what I'm about to say, but I know damn well that every shuttle vehicle I've ever owned has a factory installed urgency sensor.

This annoying little devise monitors undetectable electronic signals from every other part of the vehicle... from fuel pumps to fan belts. It also monitors external information such as weather, miles from the nearest gas station, and guiding or dinner-date commitments. As the cumulative levels of urgency input rise— things such as heavy rain, wilderness desolation, or stringent time deadlines — the urgency sensor kicks in. Then, just as two or more of these factors congeal... WHAM! A signal goes out to the tire or radiator hose to blow. Happens every time!

But I like to learn from adversity. Nowadays you'll see me heading up the river in whoever's car has a trailer, roof rack, and the least amount of gear piled on *my* dry clothes. I even encourage my friends to buy big suburbans, cherokees, and winnebagos to keep me comfortable. In exchange, I'll pitch in a little gas money, tips on new runs, and some friendly advice on how not to wind up like some swivelhead, leadfoot, or orienteer.

TAKELMA GORGE

"With difficulty we manage our boats. They spin about from side to side, and we know not where we are going, and find it impossible to keep them headed down the stream. At first, this causes us great alarm, but we soon find there is but little danger...; and it is the merry mood of the river to dance through this deep, dark gorge; and right gaily do we join the sport."

John Wesley Powell

I was beginning to think that the "Fraternal Order of the River Protectorate" stood guard over the put-in for the run down Takelma Gorge. Yeah, big mafioso guys with submachine guns and names like "Bruno" or "Luigi" hanging around Natural Bridge. They'd let you run the river, but you had to take a vow of secrecy to do it. Tell anybody about the Gorge, and Bruno would cut off your thumbs.

That was the only explanation I could come up with for the utter lack of information on this section of Oregon's Rogue River. I knew that this isolated section of river, nestled deep in the hills near Crater Lake National Park, had been run before. Probably lots of times. So why all the tight lips?

Even my best river informant shut me down when I called to ask about Takelma Gorge. "Hey, Bob, it's me... Jeff."

"Oh, hey there Jeff. What's up?"

"Well, I want to check out this here Takelma Gorge. Dan said you've run it. What's in there?"

"It's a pretty good run... a couple of portages... one rapid has.... Hey, Jeff, is that sound coming from your phone?"

"What sound?"

"That clicking."

"What clicking?"

"I think they're listening. I mean, you just can't be too careful, you know."

"What?"

"Sorry, man, I like my thumbs... gotta go."

It had become obvious that any attempt to discover the gorge's secrets was going to have to come from atop a raft. I called around to the usual group of friends and managed to fill a paddle-boat. Bill Bowey, our forever intrepid kayaker, was to be the "canyon probe." Anytime he gave us the thumbs down, we hopped out and scouted or portaged. A thumbs up either meant it was runnable, or that Bill was about to use us for some entertainment.

We met at the parking lot for the Natural Bridge Interpretive Site. The place bore no resemblance to your typical river put-in. This was the stomping ground of tourists, where white socks, black shoes, and big straw hats were de rigueur. Our shiny blue SOTAR stood out in this meeting place for weekend warriors and Winnebago owners like a fox in a chicken coupe, quickly attracting the attention of curious onlookers.

Walking down the paved trail to the river, I mused over a small metal sign a few yards short of the cliffs: "Stay on the trail, dangerous currents below."

"Alright," I thought. "They left the welcome mat out for us!"

But in this instance, the sign wasn't kidding. Just upstream of our intended put-in site, the Rogue River coursed through a river runner's worst nightmare... an underground tunnel. This is a land of incredible volcanic activity. Much of it recent. In this case, molten lava flowed across the course of the Upper Rogue, diverting the river through everchanging channels. During one such diversion, the river found its way into a lava tube. Here, surface lava cooled faster than the molten lava flowing beneath it. As the source of the lava petered out, the liquid rock flowed out from beneath its solidified roof. The result was a subterranean tube over 100 yards long.

Following the paved trail to the upstream end of the Natural Bridge Interpretive Site, paddlers can watch the entire Rogue River disappear into a four-foot-wide hole. For a kayaker coming down the upper river, the hazard wouldn't be obvious until it was too late. However, we were only here to exchange a light round of "...what if's" and "man, could you imagine..."

We headed back downstream to the raft, only to find the crowd of onlookers swelling in ranks. This, I'm sure, was not a normal sight for these folks. I mean, here they were, heading up to Crater Lake National Park, when they decide to catch one more scenic attraction. Next thing they know, they're face-to-face with a hoard of neoprene-clad, foul smelling river rats who are debating whether it's better to rappel or just leap the thirty feet from a cliff down to the river below.

Unphased by the commotion, we decided that lowering the boat— and ourselves—by rope was probably the safest option. One by one, the river lemmings made their way down to the raft. Meanwhile, thirty feet above us, scores of bewildered and excited faces anxiously awaited the opportunity to watch what would surely be our immediate demise.

"Left turn... good... right turn... good." Our pretrip test seemed alright. We looked to Bill for the thumbs up, but he was already gone. Half way down the first rapid, we saw the stern of his kayak pitch upwards, followed by his bow, then by his stern again. "Well, boys, looks like it's read and run time. Forward paddle."

In all the excitement, no one had bothered to scout for a clean line through the first hundred yards of Class III+ boulder gardens. So, we picked what looked like the cleanest slot, only to be immediately confronted by a very large, very hard, and very immovable boulder. Since it wasn't about to step aside, we had to. Quickly.

"DRAW LEFT!" Bill had already made the safety of an eddy at the base of the first series of drops. I caught his smirk out of the corner of my eye. "NO! RIGHT TURN!!" Our pre-trip test should have been about 45 seconds longer. Bouncing off rocks like a marble in a tin can, I couldn't help but think "that ought to give those blood thirsty tourists a kick."

Despite our shaky start, the team quickly pulled together. We were able to nimbly dance our raft through tight slots and around randomly strewn boulders as the Rogue vacuumed us toward the heart of the first gorge.

"Whoa!" If ever one unidentified word could capture a feeling, it was now. Staring downstream, the Rogue disappeared into a canyon. No, make that an abyss. And out from the abyss, the Rogue spit and fumed like an angry serpent. Walking downstream, we stared through the misty cloud of serpent's breath at our first major obstacle. An eighteen-foot waterfall. Quite unrunnable.

"How do you want to portage that?" asked Dave Prange, a

veteran of prior hairball descents.

We quickly devised a plan that involved pushing the boat, unmanned, over the falls. Dave would keep a line on the boat in case it decided to get stuck in the falls, and I would dive into the boat as it passed beneath my feet downstream.

As always, the best laid plans—make that *all* of our plans—can go astray. The raft made its glorious descent over the waterfall, and accelerated into the narrow canyon where I stood. Everyone was doing just what they were supposed to, and it looked like it was up to me to snatch defeat from the jaws of our minor victory.

I jumped into the raft, landing squarely in the upstream compartment. Before I had figured out what I had done, the current dragged the tube under and flipped the boat. Now, trapped under the boat, I was hoping that it was someone else's turn to finish off our plan. Brad ran down to me and helped right the raft. I then jumped in and finished off the water level portage.

Fortunately, my escapades had been concealed from the rest of the troops by the cliffs around the falls. Accordingly, I vehemently denied any accusations that made it sound like I screwed up. Needless to say, I don't think they bought my story.

To the casual observer, it probably looked like we had no idea what we were doing. El contrare! By getting all the screw ups—half a dozen rock collisions and one flip—out of the way early, we had befriended the law of averages. With this knowledge came the confidence to proceed into the more difficult rapids below.

Paddling from one gorge into another, we weren't sure which gorge our predecessors had dubbed "Takelma Gorge". Each time the basalt cliffs closed in over our heads, the river narrowed and plunged toward rocks and steep chutes. Some chutes were so narrow that we had to simply aim straight, come to a bone jarring stop, then lift a tube and continue through. Some drops couldn't be run at all, so we'd have to toss the raft over some big boulders, or carry a few yards down the bank to keep going. But our technique seemed to work, and we were making good time bouncing and paddling our way down the Upper Rogue.

Finally, the canyon walls peeled back. Sun glistened on the slick waters, and silence permeated the hills. We slid peacefully toward the take-out, revelling in the peaceful setting surrounding us.

Climbing the grassy banks at the take-out, I noticed an outdoorsy couple peering our way from there canoe-topped VW bus. We carried the raft over to a small flat a few yards from our pickup truck and popped the valves. Over the whoosh of air, I heard a strange voice. Turning, I saw the couple standing over me.

"What's the river like up in there?" they asked.

"It's a pretty good run... a couple of portages... one rapid has...."

About then, I caught a strange flash of light from the corner of my eye. It looked like it was coming from a small wooded area. I turned my head to see Bruno standing behind a tree, a shiny pair of tin snips in his hand.

"That's it?" the couple asked... "Good run... a couple of portages?"

"Sorry," I said, "I like my thumbs."

MIDDLE FORK OF THE KINGS RIVER

By Mike Doyle

"They seem like daredevils, this group that rides the raggedy edge of risk. And they are problematic individuals, these fellows. Some of them drink a little too much or laugh too loud. They are in entirely too good a mood."

Tim Cahill, A Wolverine Is Eating My Leg

To bail or not to bail.... No, this isn't another article about the advantages of a self-bailing raft over a "bucket boat," or vice versa. This story is about a critical question which arises during many ill-fated journeys: at what point do we call it quits?

We've all heard stories of mountaineering expeditions turning back due to reasons such as illness, bad weather or injury. The decision sometimes results from an incident in which no other alternative exists. Most of the time, though, the decision is subject to a group decision which isn't always cut and dry. Egos become involved as well as rationale like "we may never be this close again."

The options of turning back in whitewater boating aren't always as simple as in mountain climbing. Mountain climbing is a struggle against gravity until the goal is reached. To turn back is an easier option since it's usually downhill. Whitewater boating is the opposite. Gravity is your friend until the point that you decide to turn back, either out of the canyon or back upstream. Only on rare occasions during first descents can one choose to abandon the expedition and exit the river by heading downstream.

Whitewater exploration in California had peaked during the early 1980's. Many groups of kayakers and rafters were bagging first descents at a frenzied pace. Two groups of kayakers were in a head-to-head competition in trying to run the remaining unrun California rivers. The first group, consisting of Chuck Stanley, Lars Holbek and a handful of other expert kayakers were exploring most of the Sierra Nevada rivers at a quick rate. In one week-long

119

period in 1980, they bagged three previously unrun rivers back to back to back.

The other group of kayakers, led by Reg Lake, Royal Robbins and Doug Tompkins, had set their sights on the grandest of the Sierra Nevada rivers. They were called the "Triple Crown Boys" and by 1984 they had descended from the headwaters of the three largest rivers in the Sierra Nevada range. The San Joaquin, Kern and Kings rivers were all navigated by this group, and tales of the five to eight-day journeys from 12,000 foot put-ins became legendary among California's boating communities. These expeditions were so extreme that most of them have never been attempted since.

Not far behind the kayakers were the rafting first-descenders. These groups thrived on the belief that "if it can by kayaked, it can also be rafted!" Most of the time, the humbling conclusions resulting from these expeditions was that "if it can be portaged with kayaks, it can also be portaged with rafts."

By 1990 the fervor of first descents in California had passed. Perhaps part of the reason for this was that the "glamour" aspect of first descents had worn off. To many, this looked like way too much work! The other reason was that California had plunged itself into a four-year-long drought, and the end of it was still nowhere in sight.

By 1990, all of the major rivers in California had been kayaked, and all but one had been rafted. The one that remained unrafted was truly the most intriguing, for it was this one which had only been kayaked once. The "Triple Crowners" who had run it called it the most spectacular of all their first descents, and it also was by far the most difficult and dangerous. This river was the Middle Fork Kings.

The Middle Kings watershed originates in one of the finest wilderness areas in the United States... the northern portion of Kings Canyon National Park. 14,000 feet peaks highlight the area. The forboding upper reaches of the Middle Kings have names which send chills down the spine of boaters: Disappointment Peak, Disappearing Creek, and The Enchanted Gorge. A distant view of the spectacular lower portion of the Middle Kings can be had from the Kings Canyon Highway at Confluence viewpoint. It is truly one of the most spectacular river vistas in North America.

By May of 1990, after seeing the lower canyon for eight years on the way to many Upper Kings trips, the time seemed right to attempt the Middle Kings. Of course the California drought had rendered many rivers unrunnable, and the ones that we had been rafting just didn't have the normal "punch" to them. The low water had bolstered our boating confidence levels since most of the rivers didn't live up to their fierce reputations unless they're pumping around 2,500 cfs.

I talked to Reg Lake at the San Francisco Outdoor Adventure Fair that spring and he informed me that the lower gorge of the Middle Kings had no sections which were impassable. There was always a way to portage at river level. Knowing that important fact seemed to set the final plans into motion.

By May of 1990, Dave Hammond and I were training on the West Walker River in a twelve-foot SOTAR in preparation for the first raft descent of the Middle Kings. Dave is my partner in Beyond Limits Adventures, a commercial rafting company in Riverbank, California. That Spring we had also trained for the expedition on the seldom-run Upper Middle Fork Stanislaus, a Class V run just north of Yosemite National Park.

Our rafting technique consisted of two paddlers side-by-side in the middle section of the 12-foot raft. This "R-2" configuration allowed us to quickly catch eddies, jump waterfalls, and punch hydraulics with a comfortable degree of stability. Usually, when portaging was necessary, one person could schlep the boat over the rocks or line it through the rapid while the other paddler carried gear downstream. After our first descent on the South Fork Merced and its 20 or so portages, we became very proficient at schlep-and-line portaging techniques.

On May 26, Dave and I found ourselves at the Kings River base camp packing gear for our assault on the Middle Fork the next morning. We had semi-seriously talked about doing this run in the office, but now we were face-to-face with the reality of our conquest. Our general feeling toward this expedition was far from one of jubilation, it was more like "let's get this trip over with!"

By 6 a.m. the next morning we were in Dave's van heading up to Wishon Reservoir. After a few wrong turns we were lost. We turned back to find the main dirt road. We had to meet our horsepacker by 8 a.m. to allow him enough time to get us to the put-in, and himself back by nightfall. We were just about ready to give up when we figured out the right road and sped on.

We arrived at the trailhead by 8:45 a.m. and the packer was waiting for us. "It's getting late," he said, "so pack up and let's get on the trail." The rushed feeling I had as we were heading into the unknown in the middle of the biggest downpour of the year made me think again that maybe we should bail out now. "We're in the middle of a four-year drought," I thought, "and it has to start raining *now*?!!"

Deciding to go on with our plan, we hastily threw our gear together and loaded the pack horses with our 14-foot raft and equipment. Goodbyes were said to my wife, Bonnie, and Dave's girlfriend, Carol. As we headed out, I waved to my 10-month old daughter, Beth, and again felt like this wasn't such a hot idea. Had we really thought this plan through? No. Should we turn back now? Nah, four days later it'll be over, so let's just do it!

It was now snowing, and we were at 8,000' elevation. The scenery should have been great but it was so stormy and misty we couldn't see much of anything except the horses in front of us. The snow was coming down hard. We startled a black bear that was hanging out in a meadow. We'd been on the trail for three hours and our guide announced that he'd never been to Tehipite Valley, our destination put-in, but he kind of knew where the trail was. "Par for the course," I thought to myself.

The snow now covered the trail and the horsepacker had to bushwack certain sections. At 2:30 p.m. we arrived at what our packer thought was the canyon rim above Tehipite Valley. "Good luck," he said as he quickly dumped our gear, tied up his horses and disappeared back up the trail. It was pouring rain by now and our gear was soaked. "We've made it this far, so let's pack up and get to the river. It's all down hill from here," said Dave.

The fog was very thick and you couldn't see more than 50 feet ahead. Just as we were leaving, we were surprised by a group of four hikers coming up the trail. They couldn't believe their eyes seeing the two of us with our raft and equipment.

"What are you guys doing here and how did you get all that

equipment this far?" Dave told them about the horses and they asked what we planned to do. As Dave described our plan, I could see a distinct look of disbelief in their faces. Their next statement should have been enough for us to turn around and head back.

"You're more than two miles from the canyon rim, and once you get there you've got five miles down the steepest maintained trail in California to get to the river!" We felt defeated already and again thought about turning back. "If you guys do what you say you're going to do, then you're the baddest m-f'ers I've ever seen." The one guy said, "That river down there is suicidal and it's probably rising as we speak." That wasn't exactly what we wanted to hear at that point.

Not wanting to think about our choices too much, we loaded up and said goodbye. The next two miles were brutal, dragging and hauling the raft mostly uphill, a hundred different ways. About 6 p.m. that evening we arrived at a place that felt like we were standing on the edge of the earth. From a rock outcropping we couldn't see much, but we could tell that 5,000 feet directly below was Tehipite Valley. From here on it would all be downhill.

The rain kept pouring, making the trail slippery enough to easily drag the raft behind us. Dave started cutting off the switchbacks and dropping straight downhill to make better time. We would let the boat slide in front of us on a line and then slide after it 50 to 200 feet at a time on our backs. Unfortunately the last shortcut led us away from the trail and down a gully. About 500 feet later we were stranded in the dark, in the rain, on the face of a waterfall. We decided to set up camp for the night under a manzanita bush.

The next morning I awoke in my drysuit to a moderate drizzle. It had rained all night long and the inflated raft didn't work too well as a shelter. The grommets from the self-bailing floor allowed a constant and annoying trickle of water to drop onto me all night. We quickly packed up, pushed the boat over the falls and kept going. The gully we were in was becoming a creek, which, according to the maps, would eventually lead us to the river.

My altimeter showed we were still 1,500 feet above the river but it seemed as though the other side of the canyon wasn't that far away. I had the ugly feeling that this gorge was going to empty into Tehipite Valley in the same way Yosemite creek empties into Yosemite Valley, in a 1,500 foot waterfall. Since we couldn't leave the gorge with the raft because the terrain was too rough, we kept going down. We found that we could just toss the inflated raft over the countless waterfalls and climb down behind it.

We were now 800 feet above the river and we heard a roar that sounded like 25 rocket engines going off. My head snapped to and fro as my eyes scanned the hills for the landslide. I quickly looked for cover, only to find there was none. Luckily, and much to our relief, the slide was happening on another side canyon.

We came to the top of a seemingly bottomless waterfall. Dave crept out to the edge, with me holding his life jacket as he looked over. He saw the bottom 100 feet below. "No worries... it goes," he said, and we pushed the raft out as far as we could. I waited for it to hit. No sound. Dave crept out and saw that the raft was lodged on a four-foot wide ledge halfway down the falls. The gorge's steep, crumbly granite walls forbade access to our raft. It again seemed as though our expedition was over.

But no, Dave decided otherwise and rigged a seat harness for a descent over the edge. It didn't seem like a smart thing to do, but again it was our best option. After an amazing display of spiderman-like leaps, with 75 feet of line attached to him, Dave made it to the raft. I had to belay Dave by hand since there were no tie-offs for the rope anywhere. Dave tugged the line three times and I let it free. The roar of the falls drowned any verbal communication between us so I made my way up the canyon wall and traversed out of the gorge down to the valley.

Two hours later I found Dave and the raft at the valley floor. After talking about the amazing ropework which got him to this point, we pushed over the last few hundred yards of gravel on the valley floor to the Middle Kings. "All right! We're here. We've survived the toughest part of the trip," I thought to myself. I was wrong.

We dropped our equipment and paused by the riverside to look up at the valley walls. As the mist from the storm cleared, spectacular vistas of Tehipite Dome appeared. This impressive rock formation looked like a huge granite thumb towering 4,500 feet above the valley floor. We saw waterfalls, swollen with rain water, thundering hundreds of feet down to the river. This valley, sculpted by glaciers ten thousand years ago, was truly enchanting.

We packed the raft, got on the river and took off. The river was flowing about 2,000 cfs, three times what we had hoped for. The first mile dropped 120 feet but it was easy Class IV. We came to the end of the valley where the river sliced through a 3,000 foot high granite wall. All I could see was mist arising from below, so we pulled out and went down to take a look. From our rocky perch we caught our first glimpse of the hell that we were about to experience for the next three days.

To sum up the next three days, I'll say that rafting was the furthest thing from our minds. We were in a survival mode, the raft and its equipment were nothing more than 300 pounds of high-tech burdens that unfortunately had to be drug behind us. The Middle Kings wasn't meant to be rafted, or even walked next to. It was a death trap. One slip and you were gone, swept away down raging torrents, over 20-foot falls, and under house-sized rocks. And it never let up. If anything, it kept getting uglier. There wasn't even a remote chance that any of the next five miles was runnable. It wasn't even worth thinking about. All we could hope for was to try to get ourselves downstream and out of this mess alive.

By day four, we had gone eight miles on the river and had entered grade 5, level Z on the survival scale. The river averaged 260 feet per mile with some miles approaching 400 feet of drop. At 2,000 cfs this created a river that was not only impossible to run, it was death defying to portage.

The portages were endless. Most involved climbing down the river bed with our dry bags while scouting for portage routes, then hiking back up and getting the raft. The rapids, for the most part, were too violent to line. Instead, we'd spend hours portaging the raft along long, unrunnable cataracts, then the canyon would wall up and we'd have to paddle to the other side of the river. Each ferry required adrenaline-charged paddling as the raft drifted ten feet upstream of more death drops. There were no eddies to catch so we'd have to jam the boat on shallow rocks, jump out quickly, and grab the raft before it was swept over the falls.

The really bad part of this portaging was the fact that our

bodies became so beaten and tired. Dave had been wearing his drysuit for the past three days when we arrived at a beach for a night's camp. The process of taking the drysuit off at night became very painful due to a bad rash that Dave had developed over his entire body. I told Dave his butt looked like an orangutan's. I think he laughed.

We spent our days in the canyon portaging from 5 a.m. until 8 p.m.. Then we'd eat, try to sleep, wake up and repeat the process. We fought off the frustration we felt as each section became more difficult to portage and as huge boulders broke loose from under our feet. We constantly tried to figure how far we had come, but every landmark and side creek that we came upon would add doubt to where we actually were. During the steepest sections we would go about two miles for every 10 hours of portaging. We couldn't give up, for the alternative would be even harder. No matter how bad it got, to go on was the only option.

On day six we heard a helicopter fly over. I hoped it wasn't looking for us since the worst was now behind us. I figured we had only five miles to go until our take-out. We were already two days behind schedule and I was sure that everyone back home was freaking out.

By now the river was becoming runnable. Class V+ rapids that I would normally consider unrunnable revealed runnable routes. A typical rapid would be a half-mile long slalom, with 20 crux moves in it. One rapid took an hour to scout and as I came back I had memorized all the moves. We ran it perfectly, but if we'd missed any position by more than a foot or more we'd have been history. We were running the best whitewater we had ever seen.

The last two miles went by like a breeze, not even a scout. Stuff we'd probably have portaged two weeks before, now seemed like a cakewalk. The end was in sight. It had been six days since we had left the van at Wishon Reservoir. We got to the beach and found a gift from one of our guides, Pat Schimke, who had hiked in and waited for us for a day and a half. Two submarine sandwiches and a twelve pack of beer. We had made it. We hugged each other and cracked open a brew.

Even though our journey wasn't finished, the rest was easy.

We hiked up the two mile Yucca point trail to the highway and hitched a ride to the Kings Canyon Lodge. A couple from Switzerland picked us up and asked where we'd been. I told them we'd been rafting and they said that it sounded like fun. Dave and I looked at each other and smiled. Since it was a short ride to the lodge, I chose not to elaborate!

My only mission now was to call Bonnie and tell her we were OK. We got to the lodge, I placed the call and told Bonnie we had made it. Everyone was glad to hear from us, to say the least!

After I hung up, reality set in and my body seemed to suddenly shut down. The survival mode was over, and now the pain of the past six days was hitting hard. Dave was already checking into a room at the lodge. It was all we could do to open the door and collapse on our beds.

Would I do this trip again? Definitely not. This is the kind of experience you have once in a lifetime, if you're smart. Yet, in a way, I'm glad we did it. We were faced with the "bail-out" point at least a dozen times, yet we kept going. We kept going mostly because we didn't have a choice. The feeling of completion, of victory—you could say, was especially sweet!

Another group of rafters planned to repeat our trip the next month with two rafts and 12 paddlers. They wanted to put in 15 miles upstream from Tehipite Valley and run the entire Middle Fork Kings. I made sure I called them the next week and gave my recommendation. "DON'T DO IT!"

They didn't.

ROBE CANYON

"One thinks that running a big rapid is an experience comparable to that which a mouse has when flushed down a toilet! Now consider a generous assortment of exposed rocks randomly sprinkled down the rapid, add a border of logs and brush, include at times water so cold that it drains a swimmer's energy in seconds, and the full dimensions of the whitewater challenge become clearer."

Roderick Nash, The Big Drops

Throw the rope!! *Throw it! Don't drop it!!"* Jerry had a legitimate concern. His raft was surfing Don's Hole like an angry bronc'. Sure, I was only half a throwbag's toss from his raft and could have hit him easily, but I had my own problems.

Just seconds earlier I had to backpaddle for all I was worth at the top of the same ledge-hole to avoid sending my kayak right into Jerry's lap. Instead of jumping the hole, I was piledriven right down to bedrock and went completely under the raft. Having substituted my elbow for a shock absorber, my throwing arm was paying the price. I could hardly swing it back to toss the rope. Jerry was on his own this time!

After a few very tense minutes, we tugged Jerry and his raft out of Don's Hole, intact. Though we were all safe and sound, this unexpected bit of excitement made for a nerve-wracking introduction to Washington State's toughest raft run—Class V-V+ Robe Canyon on the South Fork Stillaguamish River.

Robe Canyon is the place that bumper sticker creators had in mind when they coined the phrase *Shit Happens*. If it hasn't happened to you in a while, just try rafting this section of the Stillaguamish River. You're bound to increase your odds. In my few runs here, I've seen more broken paddles, popped oars, bent frames, and bruised egos than on any other river in the West. But that's the type of irresistible challenge that puts the cheese in the trap, and brings the Northwest's top rafters to the put-in.

From its headwaters in Washington's majestic North Cascades, the South Fork Stillaguamish—or *The Stilly* as it is known locally—tumbles through mile after mile of meandering Class II+ rapids as it swings past post-boom era mining towns like Monte Cristo and Silverton. At one time, railroad lines traversed the canyon, providing what was supposed to be efficient access to the rich mining areas in the Cascade valleys. But unstable cliffs, constant floods, and deep seasonal snowstorms kept full rail maintenance crews steadily employed as the local barons ordered the lines to be kept open. When the silver and other lodes finally petered out, the railroad lines fell into disrepair, leaving little more than interesting hiking trails along the river today.

Contemporary explorers come to the Stillaguamish valley for different reasons. Some come to ascend the granite heights of Pilchuck Mountain, Big Four Mountain, or Monte Cristo Peak. Others come in search of the wildlife and wildflowers dancing about the surrounding Cascade ridges. And still others come loaded with kayaks and rafts to ply the Class II+ rapids of the upper river, or the Class III to IV rapids between Riverbar and Verlot.

Only the most skilled—or misinformed—of boaters use the access points near Verlot for a put-in. Though the river's Class I+ rapids look incredibly inviting at this point, five-and-a-half miles of easy floating brings rafters face-to-face with a stark gauntlet of granite cliffs, steep drops, and wall-to-wall whitewater. Here, just outside of Robe Valley, is where Robe Canyon begins.

In the next three miles, the Stilly drops from 100 to 180 feet per mile as it makes its way through a tight, cliffbound channel. This has been the private domain of expert kayakers for much of the past decade. Few rafters have dared to toss their hats into this ring. And the reasons are obvious.

Rafters in Robe Canyon are mere third parties to an epic wrestling match between water and rock, swatted about the surface like pesky flies. In places, the rapids are comparable to any of the toughest drops in the west: big boulder-studded drops and powerful ledges often drop away ten to fifteen feet at a time. In fact, Robe Canyon can feel like 42 of the West's toughest rapids jammed into a mere few miles of river.

With so much whitewater packed into such a short distance, each major drop chisels away at your energy level, and begins to

A rare raft descent through Robe Canyon on Washington's South Fork Stillaguamish River.

defuse the very machinery that makes up the Class V psyche. Even the user-friendly Class V's become supreme challenges later on in the trip. And, unless you've got an endless supply of river stamina, you're bound to find yourself panting in an eddy saying "Hey, buddy... can you spare an adrenaline gland?" For most rafters, it's the fear of a flip or a swim that keeps the energy level meter high off the scale, and it can take days to come back down from such a feverish level of aquatic intoxication.

As rafters come to better know this beast, their encounters have gradually filled in a portrait of its character. It is an invariably stealthy opponent, with a voracious appetite for raft material, oars and paddles. In fact, it rarely loses a bout outright, and hoards severed pieces of gear like so many well-earned trophies. Success has come to be measured more in terms of outright survival than by clean runs, and failure can mean the loss of a raft, or worse.

These are not the things first-timers in Robe Canyon like to think about. But, then again, Robe Canyon is not the type of place for any form of thought. Seriously! Just stick your brain in a petri dish before undertaking this run. This is a river where instinct and ability to react make or break a trip. All of this is important for the first-timer on the run since the only way to avoid becoming "Robe Meat" is to successfully fend off about 2,000 granite molars along your descent to Granite Falls.

Back below "Don's Hole," Jerry readjusted his oars and continued his descent. We marvelled from the safety of our kayak-sized eddies as a wonderful variety of expletives, distorted facial contortions, and spectacular jousting maneuvers emanated from the central compartment of his oar boat. In terms of quality, Jerry was having a great run, displaying an array of necessary skills possessed by few oarsmen. And as the rapids began to unwind, and the river slowly returned to its former state of composure, it was obvious that this was going to be a successful run.

When we reached the canyon take-out, the beast took its final swipe. Here, rafters must catch a small eddy at the base of a 50 foot high cliff and carry straight up and out to leave the river. Meanwhile, the nearby roar of unrunnable Granite Falls echoes upstream through the canyon, providing the final bit of inspiration to complete the grueling task.

By the time your booties hit flat ground again, the whole Robe Canyon adventure seems too good to be true. Still, I've yet to hear any rafter stare back down at the river, reflect upon the day's events, and say... "Hey, Jeff, let's do that again tomorrow."

BIG SANDY RIVER
"Six Frames Per Second"
By Kevin O'Brien

*"People who do dangerous sports... will tell you that they
are really quite terrified when they first do it. But quite rapidly,
the experience changes fear into ecstacy, often all at once, and
you get hooked. A total adverse reaction becomes an addiction. "*

Park Dietz, Psychiatrist, as quoted
in American Whitewater

Scrambling onto the rock ledge gains me an unobstructed
view upstream of the entire rapid. I hang one camera
around my neck, lay the other at my feet within easy reach.
The raft is just visible, the two paddlers dwarfed by the house-
sized boulder at the entrance to the rapid...

"They're coming...."

Bracing my shoulder against a rock wall I raise the camera and
focus. Meter the rocks. Meter the water. Average it and set the
aperture. Looking up I see they are in the big eddy now, in the
heart of the rapid...

"Have to hurry..."

Check the settings. Power? Motordrive? Shutterspeed? I fire
a frame, making sure the film winds.

"Forget the second camera. No time...."

Peering through the lens, re-focusing, I see they're out of the
eddy, paddling hard toward the lip of the falls....

The thrill of facing a challenge, tempered by the fear of the
unknown; key elements in the first descent of any steep, dangerous
whitewater rapid. Elements difficult to capture on film.

The visual elements, however, could be captured. Therein lie
my personal challenge, as a photographer, preparing to shoot the
first attempt to raft Big Splat, a legendary Class V+ rapid on the
Big Sandy River in West Virginia.

I'd come to the Big Sandy that morning expecting a fine day
of shooting on one of the state's more photogenic steep whitewater
rivers. A recent thunderstorm had washed all traces of haze from

the air, leaving behind warm spring sunshine and a cloudless cobalt sky. Budding foliage—layers of green, luminous in the morning sun, etched by black shadows—lined the walls of the narrow valley. Cutting through the sandstone bed at the valley's base flowed the river; sparkling white rapids alternating with aquamarine pools, flowing clear in the wake of the storm, two days gone.

Near the put-in at Rockville I'd met up with Dave Martin and Dave Meyers, two veteran whitewater guides scraping out a living that Spring guiding rafts on the steep creeks for one of the local outfitters. Like most guides of their caliber, they spent even their days off paddling whitewater.

Today would be a "shake-down cruise"; Dave Martin, anxious to try out his new self-bailing DIB four-man, topped off the final crosstube, his leg pounding piston-like onto the tired footpump, wheezing in the wet sand.

The other Dave, having unloaded the last of their gear from his clapped-out Subaru wagon, slammed the hatch shut, checked the lock and set about hiding the key. He had to be careful, it was his home for the season.

They'd be paddling the small four-man raft "R-2" fashion. Sitting side-by-side in the center compartment across from each other afforded them plenty of space and made for a light, maneuverable ride.

The gauge on the bridge read 6'3"—a reasonable level rendering most of the drops below solid Class IV. Helping them tie in the last of their gear—pump, throw bag, water, 'biners—I went over possible shooting spots where we could rendezvous downstream.

"How 'bout Splat?" asked Dave Meyers, grinning at me as he popped his head through the neck hole of his faded nylon paddling jacket.

His suggestion that they might attempt the most difficult, and as yet unrafted, section of the river took me by surprise, and was the catalyst for several minutes of animated debate.

In the end, no definite decision was reached, but we agreed to rally downstream above the drop and have a look.

The Big Sandy, from Rockville to its confluence with the

Dave Martin and Dave Meyers making the first raft descent of Class V+ "Big Splat" on West Virginia's Big Sandy River. (Photo by Kevin O'Brien)

Cheat River at Jenkinsburg, drops an average of 85 feet per mile. Along the way it flows over shallow, sculpted slides, through tight channels and abrupt ledges, forming waterfalls.

Friendly, forgiving Class IV. A definitive pool-drop run.

But about 4.5 miles into the run, the valley narrows and the river channels down. Huge boulders sit balanced on tiny, improbable pedestals. Flowing around and under the base of the largest of these boulders the river funnels into sharp ledges, undercut at oblique angles. Pooling briefly in a sloping eddy at midpoint, the rapid terminates in a fifteen-foot vertical falls, thundering onto a final slanted, undercut slab of rock.

Viewed from the sandstone ledges flanking both sides of the rapid, or from the waterline below, the scene is primordial. Obscure angles of rock and turbulent whitewater combine to form an indelible impression of chaos.

This is Big Splat.

For years Big Splat had reigned as an indominable symbol of unrunnable whitewater. The impossible rapid. True Class VI.

Paddlers portaging around the rapid often paused to stare down into its maw. In their mind's eye they ran each ledge and hole, piecing together a feasible line of descent. Satisfied that, at the right level, under the right conditions, it *could* be run, they inevitably hoisted their boats onto their shoulders and continued hiking downstream.

The early 1980's began a renascent period for whitewater boating in the tri-state corner of West Virginia, Pennsylvania, and Maryland. Squirt-boating had burst onto the scene and a new generation of bold, innovative paddlers were pushing the radical, low-volume kayaks to the limit.

Jess Whitmore of Friendsville, Maryland—boat designer, squirt guru, whitewater visionary—spearheaded the movement, when in the Spring of 1983, at the height of his powers, he made the first descent of Big Splat. In his wake followed the inevitable series of latter descents, often involving more balls than brains, reducing the rapid to a Class V+ testpiece.

During this same period, raft descents of steep, 100+ feet per mile rivers had come into vogue. The Upper Yough, Top Yough, and others were being offered on a commercial basis by several outfitters. Perpetually destitute local hardboaters could now make a living pushing rubber down the steeps, consummating a circuitous Class V lifestyle. Honing their skills to a fine edge, these guides pushed rafting to the extreme. In their eyes the former Class VI bastions now offered an entirely new set of challenges...

First raft descents.

I focus on the green, translucent tongue of the falls, centering it in the frame, making it the focal point of the shot. As they approach the edge I see them take one last, violent stroke, propelling the nose of the raft out over the lip.

"Shoot now!"

I press the shutter and the motordrive begins blasting away at six frames per second. I see their flight over the falls in a series of flashing, staccato images:

— The raft tips vertically and both men lean back to counter the angle.

— The raft remains vertical as it dives into the deep crease between the base of the falls and the slanted rock.

— Raft and crew vanish from sight, swallowed in the foam pile.

— In a violent blast of spray, the raft rockets sideways out of the boil, still upright, the crew intact!

Dropping the camera I watch as Dave Meyers tumbles off the upstream tube. Clear of the boil, he swims safely after the raft. A minor flaw in an otherwise impeccable run.

The raft drifts far downstream before Dave hoists himself aboard. When they finally eddy out, we howl back and forth, exchanging a "thumbs up."

The camera's framecounter registers twelve shots. I try to signal them again, but they're already heading downstream, buzzing on adrenaline. I pack up my gear and hustle to catch them at the take-out.

Behind us Big Splat flows on, eternal, indifferent to our petty victories.

THE TAOS BOX
"RAFTING ROULETTE"
By Timothy Hillmer

*"The gorge was dark; seven hundred feet below, the Rio
Grande trickle was a shiny, lead-silver color, like a delicate vein
in a black stone. I got dizzy looking down. And afraid. The fall
was so great. And for some reason that silver ribbon trickling
through the blackness viewed from warm seven o'clock sunshine
made me shudder. "*

John Nichols, If Mountains Die

U pon scouting N.C.O. Falls of the Rio Grande for the first
time, I paused for a moment to wonder about the
unknown origin of its name. Located deep in the remote
gorge of the Upper Taos Box of New Mexico, N.C.O. had been
christened after a strange, three-lettered inscription was found
engraved on a rock near shore. My imagination ran wild.
Nefarious Calligraphers of Obscenity? Nymphomaniac Creatures
from Ozone? Neurotic Cannibals of Oklahoma? Beware of Class
V+ rapids with mysterious names.

I soon lost all interest in deciphering this riddle. At the time I
was more concerned with a hellacious, 10-foot vertical drop at the
entrance to the rapid, which descended into a gnashing, boat-
crusher of a hole. As I stared into the frothing power of the
reversal, I thought back to the first Class V+ rapid I'd ever run,
Lewis' Leap on the Cherry Creek section of California's Upper
Tuolumne. I had run it at a more courageous time in my career,
six years earlier. Time has a way of mellowing machismo.

But N.C.O. Falls beckoned. With Lewis' Leap still sifting
through my mind, I returned to the raft. I stared upward at
overcast skies and felt the beginning of a steady drizzle on my
wetsuit. Minutes later, I was plummeting over the violent entrance
drop with our crew from the Boulder Outdoor Center, only to find
the tube I had precariously entrusted my weight to was suddenly
being sucked under by the hydraulic. In a flash the entire boat
stood on end and dumped me into the foam as a sacrifice to the
river gods.

137

Like being pulverized in a washing machine filled with black ink, I had been unknowingly yanked into the darkness under the raft, where I probed the rubber floor like a blind man trying to find an escape hatch. Squirming like a trapped rat, I kicked and pushed at the boat in vain attempts to get it off, then felt the rapid suck me away and under. I didn't relax, put my feet downstream, or let the lifejacket support me, thus ignoring the classic advice of all river guides. I flopped on my stomach and paddled the basic "save-my-skin" stroke for all I was worth. Just downstream lurked menacing Hell Hole, a killer undercut waterfall. I pushed away from rocks and slithered over ledges, each time sucking air into my lungs before vanishing into the next wave. I was scared and the thought of Hell Hole shadowed my every stroke. Suddenly I saw the lemon flash of Larry LaBocchiaro's yellow kayak. I grabbed the stern and received a quick tow to shore.

There in the shallows of the Rio Grande, spitting out water and coughing like a black lung victim, I felt no adrenaline rushing through my body, no cheerleader morale pushing me back up. My left knee had been banged all to hell. It was raining and overcast, and the canyon walls of the Rio Grande Gorge towered 700 feet in the air like fortress palisades. Hell Hole waited downstream.

Somehow my bold run through Lewis' Leap six years earlier, with all of its Class V bravado, seemed light years away. Humbled and beaten by the river, I recalled something once said by a veteran boatman before descending the Upper Kings River in a paddle raft for the first time. He was asked if he was scared of what lay below. His confident response was, "You've got to want to be here and you have to be ready to die." The words of a hero or the words of a fool?

At the bottom of the Rio Grande I discovered I was not yet ready to die for the river. Not even close. I felt no betrayal or cowardice, only a growing awareness that the river was teaching me a lesson. With only two of the Upper Box's major rapids behind us (Class IV + Upper Powerline Falls and N.C.O.), we had only begun this attempt at a first raft descent.

My only comfort as I climbed back into the paddle boat to resume my bow position was the welcome I received from the crew, all seasoned river guides. Momentarily I wondered whether

The Upper Taos Box, New Mexico. (Photo by Eric Bader, Boulder Outdoor Center)

this was the reason I had come here, to share a challenge with comrades who sought the same quest. There was not a soul in the raft I did not trust my life to. Pete and Glen Dunmire, a brother duo who had climbed all of Colorado's 14,000-foot peaks the previous summer using mountain bikes as their sole transportation. Alicia Thompson, the lone woman on the trip, who had already participated in numerous Class V first descents in Colorado, even though she had been guiding a mere two years. Dirk Hovorka, a wisecracking geologist and rock climber whose strong paddling and timely sense of humor kept our crew confident and loose. Our captain was Eric Bader, owner of Boulder Outdoor Center and a kayaking veteran who had run the Upper Box five times. Four expert kayakers joined us as safety boats: Mike Bader, Larry LaBocchiaro, Jim Cardamone, and Kevin Padden. Already Larry had proven how valuable kayakers can be when rafting intense Class V. Thank God for legless daredevils in little plastic boats.

The rapids of the Upper Box that followed were a relentless blitzkrieg of whitewater. Our self-bailing, 14-foot raft was a true savior, pounding through waves like a Viking battering ram.

Hell Hole was terrifying to behold, a tremendous ledge drop with a monument-sized undercut rock dead center, guaranteed to pin a swimmer for eternity. We discovered a perilous sneak chute on river left and were able to negotiate it without incident, slithering by the hole and keeping a respectful distance from the deathtrap.

Next came Long Rapids, a twin set of Class V's separated by a slim eddy on river left. It devoured us with the table manners of a chain saw. Our raft swamped in the first section and came crashing down toward the lone eddy with freight-train speed. Pete Dunmire latched onto a throw-bag hurled our way, only to be ripped from the boat in his attempt to hold on. We thundered down into the second section, still full of the river and out of control. We slammed into a mid-stream boulder, hurtled over a seven-foot pourover ledge, then plowed bow on into a black anvil of rock at the rapid's base. Everyone dove to the high side and the boat careened off like a bumper car, then slid backward into the calm pool below.

Survival is a sweet revelation. We soon discovered that Pete had been able to get to shore immediately, thus avoiding a perilous swim. Before setting off again, we christened Long Rapids with a new title: Vertical Deceleration — V.D. for short.

The quarter-mile calm which followed provided an unusual stillness at the heart of this Class V gorge. The dusty red canyon walls soared overhead like giant sheets of cracked adobe. A dark stripe of basalt trimmed the entire rim of the canyon for as far as the eye could see. Small meadows and beaches lined the shore. I considered it a gracious reward after our harrowing morning — a river and canyon as priceless as the fabled palaces of El Dorado. A place Coronado and his men called "the land of the Grand Quivira" — land of many riches. A desert jewel.

The overcast afternoon brought with it the most harrowing rapid yet: Boulder Fan. A screaming series of Class V chutes and ledges, it demanded a complete river-left-to-right move in the center of the rapid. And waiting at the bottom was a deadly corkscrew drop which poured into an undercut shelf. This was no place for swimmers. Our run was surgically precise and on target, carving through the upper boulder garden like a slalom racer, and avoiding the killer drop at the bottom. Glen hooted with joy next to me, his black beard drenched from the face-slam of a wave. Class V nirvana.

We continued on through a series of Class IV+ rapids and pulled out for the day above the next big drop: Big Arsenic. We stacked our boats and gear on shore, then hiked three miles up a Park Service trail to the rim of the canyon where our van waited. We spent the night in Taos at the home of a local kayaker, Ben Goodin, who entertained us over Mexican food and beer with colorful descriptions of the two remaining rapids: Big Arsenic and Little Arsenic, the toughest on the river. In the morning we would hike down and tackle them.

But that night, with Ben's words still fresh in my mind, I re-read a section of my river journal where I had once printed a favorite passage from Norman MacLean's powerful memoir of Montana, "A River Runs Through It": *The river was cut by the world's great flood and runs over rocks from the basement of time. On some of the rocks are timeless raindrops. Under the rocks are the words and some of the words are theirs. I am haunted by waters.*

So I slept that night, haunted by a different demon, knowing that tomorrow there would be choices made and consequences faced at Big and Little Arsenic. Let it be.

"Kid, there are two kinds of boatmen: those that have been hammered by the river, and those that are gonna." (Grand Canyon River Guide.)

Perhaps I am of a superstitious sort, but I believe in bad vibes. Some rapids give them off like radiation. If that were the case, then Big Arsenic was a nuclear nightmare. Falling a total distance of 30 feet over a series of rock ledges and boulders, it was a jagged staircase of a waterfall. After hiking down from the rim that morning, we scouted it with extra care. The river had dropped from the previous day's flow of 1,700 cfs, to a still-high 1,650 cfs. As we studied Big Arsenic, we discovered a sneak route down the river-left side of the falls, a clean chute which avoided the jumbled hydraulic of the main drop. Downstream, however, maybe 25 yards away, lurked an ominous pourover hole capable of stopping and flipping a 14-foot boat. The rapid continued beyond, feeding into a maze of sharp rock and swirling current.

I did not like what I saw and did not feel in the right frame of mind to run it. Yes, it was runnable. Yes, at a lower water level I would have run it. The gambler within me was itching. Rafting roulette. But at this high level and with slim chances of missing the stopper hole, I did not like the possibility of swimming. Perhaps my plunge at N.C.O. the previous day had affected my decision. As the others suited up in their river gear, I hiked downstream to set up safety with my throwbag. For the first time in my rafting career I left my paddle crew and walked around a rapid alone. It was the hardest decision I had ever made on a river. But something was missing. I no longer felt the desire to risk being lucky. I felt badly for abandoning my team, but on a river like the Upper Box, the choices are our own. So are the consequences.

Their paddle run was superb. With Mike Bader taking my place in the raft. They exploded down the chute and pulled the boat right with a series of piston-like draw strokes. It was over in seconds, and they floated by the dangerous hole with ease. One unforgettable move right. It was that simple.

As I rejoined the raft in the eddy downstream, I was greeted by ecstatic whoops of joy. A part of me felt elation for their achievement, while another felt sadness, wishing I could have been with them. But I knew their adrenaline-charged euphoria from my own past experiences. This was the first time I was witnessing it all as an outsider looking in. And yet I knew I'd done the right thing for myself. Their celebrating seemed distant and foreign now, like a prize one fights hard for, then easily gives away years later. It endures in memory.

We wasted little time in moving ahead through a rollercoaster string of Class IV standing waves. Around a bend, the river suddenly dropped away and we narrowly caught an eddy on river left, beaching our boat on a rock, then pulling it back upstream. With the afternoon sun blazing down on the black, ebony-like rock of the shore, we trekked through the clustered tangles of poison ivy to scout Little Arsenic. I climbed a large slab of rock and perched on its crow's nest of a pinnacle. What I saw was stunning.

Keeperland. Green water was nowhere in sight, only churning

white. Like 10,000 giant teakettles boiling and surging over, it was a breathtaking vista of guillotine sharp ledges, of enormous boulders rising like Druid tombstones from the riverbottom. And this steep, Class VI strangler was almost undescribably technical, a quarter-mile of white thunder. If a boat were to flip at the top, or if someone were to fall out, the roaring current would carry them down into a maze of bone-crushing drops. Curtains.

Again, I carefully inched my way along the rapid, spending nearly 45 minutes walking the major section. I saw life-threatening obstacles everywhere: a monstrous pourover rock at the very top, an unavoidable drop-off over a steep shelf about half-way down. At the bottom lay the nastiest dragon of all, a river-wide corkscrew falls, boulder studded, undercut in two places, and recirculating like a Maytag gone berserk. This was extreme rafting. As close to the edge as it can get.

If I could not paddle this rapid with everything I had, fearless and unafraid of falling out, then I would not do it. All or nothing. Get psyched or surrender. Pete Dunmire studied the rapid apprehensively, unsure of his own decision, then decided to run it. Larry LaBocchiaro, after a kayak run in which he'd overturned and rolled up just in time to plummet over the bottom drop, took my place in the raft. I felt pressure to rejoin the paddle crew, to hike back up and in some way renew myself after walking Big Arsenic. But that was not the point. I had nothing to prove to anyone.

I have seen gutsy, "right stuff" rafting in other parts of the country at various times in my career. Yet nothing could surpass what I witnessed at Little Arsenic that afternoon. There was nothing macho or cocky about their run. With the finesse of a water strider fighting madly to stay above the fury, I saw twelve arms arch out into the current, their blue paddles flashing like turquoise against the foam. I saw them use the river the way a skater uses ice, their angles geometrically precise and always in control as they cut to the right of a deadly pourover, powered through a ledge reversal, then steadily continued to the river left and charged into the violent hole at the bottom. With shouts of support ringing from the shore, I watched as they sliced through, then continued down into the less hazardous section of Little Arsenic, their raft disappearing momentarily in the trough of a wave, then reappearing with the rising crest as if at sea in a storm.

With the afternoon sun descending, I rejoined the crew and we quickly paddled through two more Class IV rapids and down to the confluence of the Red River with the Rio Grande. In the remaining eight miles of gentle waves and mild current, I thought about how my perceptions of Class V rafting had gone from the macho extreme of Lewis' Leap so long ago to a more cautious, safety-conscious vision. Amidst the celebrating and hoopla surrounding our first descent, I felt left out and distant, yet somehow wiser, as if I had moved into a new awareness of why I run rivers.

Looking around at the spectacular canyon, I thought not of the dramatic rapids, but of the special nature of our endeavor into this wilderness. For some of our crew it had been the thrill of experiencing Class VI for the first time, of testing the current and themselves. For others it had been a renewal of the special magic all rivers carry, that Merlin-like spell which is both bewitching and hypnotic. But for myself it had been a chance to become immersed once again within this world and watch my own perception grow stronger. And each time I learn anew of the frailty of human strength against the current, of the power of accepting one's limitations and the peace which follows.

Hail to the Rio Grande del Norte, truly the grandest river of the North. Hail to the teacher of waters.

(Special thanks to *Paddler,* which first published this story.)

THE THOMPSON RIVER

"There exists in rapids oscillations beyond prediction, and your misfortune may be to hit that build-up at exactly the wrong time. "

Doug Reiner, as quoted in Roderick
Nash's The Big Drops

I was standing on a cliff, high above British Columbia's Thompson River, trying to impart a more experienced and realistic perspective on the distant river below to my fellow team of skeptical rafters. My five man crew—all seasoned veterans of steep western rivers—were having a difficult time making the mental transition from technical whitewater to big, powerful rivers. Big rivers, and truly big water, were very foreign to these guys. No rocks. No chutes. No waterfalls. *Wimpwater.*

"That's it? That's the Jaws of Death?!"

"It's bigger than it looks. Honest."

"Well, I hope so. Is it washed out? I mean, there's nothing there!"

"Well, wait until you see it from a raft!"

Today, the Thompson was anything but wimpwater. It was only late Spring, a time of year when the Thompson hasn't yet subsided to levels considered "appropriate" for our little self-bailing 14-foot raft. More than 60,000 cfs was barrelling across the river bottom like a horizontal avalanche. It made for big water by my standards. Heck, big water by *anybody's* standards!

Still, my buddies were unimpressed. Thoroughly under-whelmed. The little flickering line of white snapping across the surface of the distant Thompson River didn't look like much from where we stood. So, it was going to take a first hand whooping to teach these guys some respect.

This was not my first trip to the Thompson. I had found myself on the Thompson many years earlier. After a season of guiding throughout Washington State I packed up my car and headed north into Canada, looking for something different to run. I picked up a brochure from a local outfitter in Yale, British Columbia and gave him a call. As it turned out, a trip was leaving the next day for an overnight run down the lower Thompson. The highlight of the trip was to be a dash through Hell's Gate on the mighty Fraser River.

Lacking both a boat and boating partners, I decided to lay the money down and be a passenger for a change. It was a perfect introduction to Canadian Whitewater.

The next morning I met our guide, and soon found myself straddling the tubes of a 28-foot J-Rig. The Thompson was easy going on these huge barges. All I had to do was turn every so often to keep the tan even, and occasionally pump the guides for stories about their rivers and boats. The J-rig—a huge motorized pontoon raft resembling a green 28-foot long package of hot dogs—was perfectly suited for late Spring conditions on the Thompson. Its incredible flotation, and sheer size, can overcome almost any hydrological obstacle that old man river could toss in its path.

The importance of size and flotation became real obvious on the second day of the trip, when our guide decided to give us a tour of the infamous eddy below Hell's Gate. At Hell's Gate, tourists regularly descend an aerial tramway down to the riverside to watch 275,000 cfs of water shoot through a gorge only 110 feet wide. At the tail end of Hell's Gate, a healthy portion of that flow does a U-turn and heads back upstream. The result is spectacular. Sitting in the middle of the eddy, our raft was gradually sucked down beneath the swirling surface of the eddy. What once floated 48 inches above the water, sunk to 36 inches above the water, then 24. About the time I started to get *real interested* in our fate, the guide cranked up the engine and powered the raft into the calm waters below.

The stories from that trip filled the car as my latest group of river voyageurs and myself drove the final few miles to the Nicoamen put-in for the Lower Thompson.

Paddling out into the current, I started feeling like a school teacher taking a van full of unruly prepubescent kids to the zoo. "Do we have to go? This isn't any fun. Got any gum? You suck."

But that gradually changed. Coming up to the first big rapid, The Frog, I noticed that the huge rock formation that usually dominated the middle of the river was gone—buried deep within the Thompson. And in its place, giant whirlpools and swirling eddies danced back and forth unpredicatably. It was hard to believe that this was the same place that offers delightful, glassy surf waves later on in the season. The crew became quieter each time the raft would ride up on a boil, pause for a moment, maybe sink a little, then continue downstream. The river was toying with us, and everyone started to realize it.

By the time we got to Jaws, the mental metamorphosis was complete. Nothing had given us any trouble at all, but the overwhelming power of such a huge amount of water had made its impression. Our respect for water had almost hit a crescendo when there, just beyond the next few eddies—Jaws!

Entering the first waves was like pulling the bar down over your lap when you get on a rollercoaster. Your heart begins pounding, you tremble with excitement, and your mind says something like "You think this is fun? You ain't seen nothin' yet!"

The waves were huge. We'd glide up a big glassy eight-footer and disappear into a trough. Then we'd glide up a big, glassy nine-footer, and disappear into a trough. Then we saw it—Jaws!

Before we even hit the curler, I felt like my entire body had been smacked in the funny bone. My body convulsed with fits of laughter as the sweet irony of revenge rang throughout my conscience. "We're gonna fli-ip, we're gonna fli-ip. Told ya, told ya!"

Jaws was huge. A ten-foot-high curling wave, breaking just as we were reaching the vertical plane. Dave Prange and Jim Clements—two powerful paddlers—hung out over the bow, one foot on the thwart, and dug their paddles deep into the heart of the wave. Meanwhile, I lay giggling in the stern, at ease with the futility of our plight, and prepared for a big flip.

THWOMP!! Jaws came crashing down. Sixty-four liquid elephants right in our laps. The explosion of water littered the river with foam, paddles, and bodies. And somewhere beneath the overturned raft was me, clinging to a thwart and still laughing my ass off. "Told ya, told ya!" All I wanted was for the storm to end so everyone could say "yeah, you were right." But the current kept pulling at us. And as long as it did that, I felt very happy glued to my thwart, peacefully sucking air from my cave-like pocket.

Finally, the storm did end. But even then, it took almost a half-mile of river to reflip the raft, gather the crew, and paddle over to an eddy. By the time our brains were back in gear, we were paddling hard for the shore at the Fraser River confluence.

Last week, the same guys found themselves standing around a campfire, listening to stories of rivers, and tossing in their own two cents from time to time.

"Ever done the Thompson?" someone asked.

"Nah, I drove along it one Spring. Didn't look like much," someone replied.

The veterans looked at each other and smiled. "It's bigger than it looks. Honest."

WITHDRAWALS

"As we drift down the river, Rich plying the oars at a leisurely pace, (Jenny) asks us if we don't get bored sometimes with this effortless mode of travel. Sure we do, but none of us will admit it."

Edward Abbey, Beyond the Wall

I was sitting on the couch minding my own business when my roommate cranked on the faucet in the kitchen sink. "Legs up, feet downstream!" I thought. My legs snapped forward. Shit, this is bad news. Six weeks without a river trip and I'm already having major withdrawals. Another shaky day of cold turkey right here in my living room. Water. I need fast, moving water.

I guess that I should have seen it coming. Last night I spent an hour admiring my paddle. A whole hour! I mean, it's probably the same old rock banger you've got, but it was just standing there. Propped up in the corner like a scolded child. It's been a good friend to me over the years... gotten me down some pretty tough rivers. Now the poor thing just stands there. Neglected. Sheesh, I was getting really choked up over the whole thing. It was embarrassing.

I headed to the bathroom and stuck my head in the sink. A far cry from the real thing, but it satisfied my whitewater craving for a bit.

The same thing happened to me late last Fall... only worse. After two months of riverless weekends, I showed up at work with my river sandals on. Man, was my boss pissed off! But I can't figure out what the big deal was. I mean, they matched my suit and tie and all. Maybe they still smelled like my gear bag.

The same day as the sandals incident, I made a one-and-a-half hour detour on my way home from work... exactly the same time it takes me to get to my favorite river. As I crossed the bridge at the usual take-out, I slammed on the brakes, parked it right there by the yellow line, and headed for the bank. By the time I figured out where I was, there was a three mile traffic jam and some guy with a badge asking me my name. "Forward paddle," I mumbled.

Wrong response.

Anyway, I'm back in therapy again. One-on-one stuff. But, I don't really think those doctors are trained in this kind of thing. I mean, it's not a sexual dysfunction, or some sort of Freudian abnormality. At least I don't think it is.

The good thing is that this therapist is cute. Real cute! And young too. The kind of gal that'd make you forget about things like river running. I'm even thinking about asking her out, but you've got to make the right impression, you know. Dress right, and all.

Yeah. I wonder what I'll wear to the session.

I know. I'll wear my wet suit!!

THE NEW RIVER
By James Snyder

"There is something ominous about a swift river, and something thrilling about a river of any kind. The nearest upstream bend is a gate out of mystery, the nearest downstream bend a door to further mystery."

Wallace Stegner

Night runs are one of the best forms of entertainment in the world. As far as I know, the tradition began with a couple of screwed up shuttles, and continued with some missed take-outs, but was popularized by raft guides on Pennsylvania's Lower Youghiogheny River back in the mid-sixties. Even today, raft guides constitute the majority of night riders in the sport—probably because they know the rivers well, have easy access to equipment, and are close to whitewater.

Night runs are almost always on familiar stretches of river, at familiar levels, with familiar friends. But the trips almost always have a strange quality to them. Perhaps it's due to the weird spirits that dance across the river only at night. Or, it could be due to the way night riders *feel* their way through the rapids rather than relying on the perceptual deceptions relayed by their eyes. And maybe it's due to some primal fear of being swept away by the dark... swallowed by the night.

At any rate, night rafting is exhileratingly spooky, and that's why people keep doing it. Jadedness falls from your spirit like a penny from a holey pocket, without a chance or reason to pick it up.

Several factors make night runs wonderfully different from day runs. First, since I like to make night runs with no moon and a heavy fog, there's a certain degree of difficulty in spotting rocks. Under ideal conditions you may have about fifteen feet maximum visibility. If the rock is of the huge New River variety, you might even get lucky and be able to see twenty feet. But, even at normal river speeds, this means you've got about two or three seconds of reaction time before you get intimate with the local geology. If you waffle a bit (which way do we go?), you're bound to cut your reaction time while pumping up your excitement level.

Next, there are usually few visual clues to mark your downstream progress. The trip takes on the effect of sitting in a motionless boat while the world spins under you, bringing on endless adventure. Rocks loom like silent black monsters, and holes lurch up out of the inky blackness, approaching within inches of your boat as you struggle to avoid impending doom. And with each missed rock, new monsters dance beyond the next shadow, dancing with the music of the river, just waiting to tango with your boat.

Waves are what really make the night trip worthwhile. Smooth, green waves are invisible in the dark, slipping unseen beneath your raft even while riding their paths. They sneak beneath you like imaginary elevators, releasing you from gravity for a moment, and just as quickly returning you as if nothing happened. It's like hitting one of the magical road bumps highway engineers install as antidotes to boredom. These little hiccups in earth's gravity always get rave reviews.

White breaking waves are much harder to deal with. They appear as ghosts on the river horizon, dancing left and right, suspended in the air. The closer you get, the faster the apparition approaches. In the final moments, you are sucked into the liquidy cloud as if by unseen magnets, consumed by friendly little bubbles, and released. The sensation is so intoxicating you get to the point where flipping and swimming would just add to the adventure, only to be held back by the final ounces of sobriety guarding your well-being.

While swimming can be an almost comical daytime pursuit, it is fraught with danger by night. A person's dark little head is hard to distinguish from a black field of water, especially with a thick, black sky as a backdrop. Swimmers tend to disappear quickly into the night. Once departed, they are very much on their own—their only contact with their crew, and the security of reality, is through sound. Gurgles, whimpers, and uncontrollable animal sounds provide tracking signals for the remaining crew, who usually respond with calls from the raft like, "Where are you?! Swim over here! We can't see anything!"

Sound is to the night what sight is to the day. It is the mind's sensory guide. The only clue you have to finding your way down a darkened liquid corridor. Different rapid features make different sounds, providing audible signposts as you approach. If one side of an approaching rapid roars with carniverous amplitude, it's a sure sign to head the other way!

Sound is also the biggest safety tool in the night runner's gear bag. It connects you with your crewmates, with other rafts, and with anyone beyond the shoreline. The comfort of another paddler's response qualms night anxieties, and provides reassurance that all is well.

Occasionally, a call to another raft evokes no response. Then, silence can be overwhelmingly disconcerting. What do you do? Race downstream in pursuit of the boat? Or do you wait? On one trip, we were faced with exactly that situation. Concerns quickly turned to fear, fear to terror, and terror to anarchy. Every paddler had a different idea on what to do. Our raft spun so many times that we became disoriented. We finally decided to paddle hard downstream, and began working hard toward that goal. After a few minutes of frustrating forward strokes, we discovered that we were stuck in one of the New River's massive eddies, and that we'd been paddling upstream all the time.

On one fine night, I borrowed a raft from a friend—mainly because the company I worked for didn't endorse night runs—and took off on a New River descent.

I'd spent many years guiding on the New River, and knew its features like the back of my hand. By day, it was a comfortable place to be. For me, it was a free-flowing easy chair, devoid of the perils I'd felt there earlier in my boating career. But by night, it was a blackened collage of sound and fury. An invitation to new adventures.

We were having a fine time on the early part of the trip. The flatwater was as slick and thick as rolling mercury, fueling such high moods that we felt mad as hatters. We entertained ourselves by making noises, occasionally spooking the fishermen who walked the banks late at night to avoid the daytime crowds.

Somewhere above Surprise, the first major rapid, I deduced that the level was about three feet—pretty high for a night run. At that level, Surprise is an eight foot breaking wave with lots of pizzazz. We quickly decided to opt for a far left line, choosing to maintain our merry mood while slipping past the danger. In fact, we opted for the far left line at Upper Railroad also—another big rapid with a big flip hole lurking somewhere on the right side—and slid through unharmed.

Next up was Lower Railroad. Coming into this rapid, I felt my skin begin to crackle. There were no cues anywhere along the approach as to the only clean route available, and the river surrounded us with its confusing roar as we searched for the entry line. Fortunately, we wished our tails off just enough to ace the rapid and emerge unscathed.

At some point, deep in the darkest section of the gorge, I felt the mood slip from blissful mirth to genuine endeavor. We were more than satisfied with our accomplishments thus far because we had met some big challenges and bore well under the pressure. We started thinking about the end of the trip, and how it wouldn't be too much farther until it was all over—only a couple more major rapids with comparatively little hazard.

One of the last good rapids between us and the take-out was Undercut. At Undercut, you must enter on river right, but more than half of that water drives directly into a large undercut rock—hence the name.

"Entire ten man rafts can pin under there without leaving a clue as to their presence," I explained to my crew. "Another problem is how the water that seems to approach from one hundred feet to its left actually feeds right into it. I think we should stay way left to make sure we're safe." I then steered the raft toward the center of the river.

We couldn't see either the shore or the undercut rock through the darkness, but I had been guiding for many years and could sense when the raft had slipped off to the left side of the central currents. This time, "slipping off" would prove to be an understatement.

As usual, the thunder of the rapid enveloped us with uncertain speed as we approached the rapid. We were on the edge of our tubes, waiting for something to happen, while the roar just got louder and louder. The ensuing action was a relief, curing our feelings of apprehension by diverting our attention to self-

154

preservation.

"It's all in the anticipation," I've heard the old guides say while pointing out the similarities between sex and whitewater. I should note, however, that I've encountered some credible arguments to the contrary. In fact, the next few moments fueled the argument that the *event* can be much more overwhelming than the *anticipation*.

We fell sideways over a five-foot drop into a pounding hole, where one of the crew members was jettisoned from the raft. He had flown over three people's heads on his way out of the boat, and had plunged into the foam at the very limits of our visibility. Meanwhile, our raft stuck in the foamy hole, forcing us to lean hard against the current and stroke with unprecedented fervor. Even with our greatest efforts, we could do no more than hold our own against the river, moving neither upstream nor downstream. Our lonely mutineer was setting himself feet downstrean as he started to slip out of sight into the darkness. "Swim! Swim!" a chorus of concerned voices bellowed. "I'm OK" was his blissful reply.

I was the only one who realized that we had about twenty seconds to retrieve him before he would be in Bloody Nose—a treacherous and aptly named rapid. Bloody Nose is a shallow sixty-foot slide into a fierce hole that put rafts through angular gyrations only Gumby could appreciate. The bow turns up and to the left, ninety degrees each, simultaneously. It's a neck of the woods where a low center of gravity is not too bad of an idea.

"Swim!" we yelled to him, but he kept floating feet first, calmly reassuring us that he was "OK." "SWI-I-I-I-M!" He finally turned on his stomach as our freed raft floated toward him to pick him up.

Now, on the very brink of the approach to Bloody Nose, there is a border rock on the river left shore. Our raft was being hurled toward that rock with incredible speed, with our favorite swimmer assuming a perfect position to become the meat in a hypalon sandwich. Fortunately, fate smiled down upon him, giving the hungry rock only a taste of the soles of his sneakers as he used it to push his way back toward the raft amidst our hurried tugs at the shoulders of his life jacket.

Surprise Rapid, New River, West Virginia. (Photo by Kathy Rech, North American River Runners)

In the midst of our rescue efforts, I had quit worrying about the swimmer, and begun yelling "Highside! Highside!" It was a sub-conscious response to our own violent collision with that same rock. So powerful was the impact that the thwarts buckled and the outer tubes crushed together. Although we were all thrown to the floor, we instantly sprung back to our paddling positions and bounced right back into action. In seconds, we had the raft straightened, and smashed through the final hole in an adrenaline-charged crescendo.

Slipping into the newfound calm, the silence was profound. Peaceful and forgiving. "Wow," someone mumbled. "Very true," I thought, thankful that we had only a few rapids to go.

Our trip was essentially over. In fact, the final rapid—Fayette Station—is an optional run. It is actually better taking out upstream of this rapid since it provides an easier path to the vehicles. But, somehow, our trip seemed to be ending too soon. And, upon discussing the matter, I discovered that the feeling was mutual. The river had beaten us thus far, and we now had a score to settle.

We passed the gauge, and proceeded into the rink to battle the final dragon.

Passing the gauge, we noticed that the level was three-and-three-quarters feet. A handsome level. A proud level. It embellished our already wild run. Now, all we needed to do was ice the cake. With a hearty "let's go for it," we dug our paddles into the current and continued downstream.

Fayette Station, at this level, is little more than fun waves. There are really no significant hazards, except maybe one—a huge hole half way down the right side of the rapid. But I wasn't even considering getting near that hole that night. In fact, I hadn't considered the hole at all. After all, the only way you could possibly drop into the hole was to fall off the wave train, and slip to the right. And the only way to do that was to get disoriented.

Well, disorientation is never more than a short spin away on night runs, especially on smooth, green waves... invisible in the dark, slipping unseen beneath your raft, imaginary elevators, the speed bumps of the night. We slipped across a wave, and levitated above one of the speed bumps. It drove us off our home run route into a dead-end course with thunder city, where we didn't even have a second to voice our regrets.

In an instant, we accelerated into a trough, and collided with the wall of water backing the hole. Every paddler who had been sitting on the right side of the raft exploded over the heads of the left side paddlers. Meanwhile, the raft stuck, trying to flip to the left, where I was sitting. I called upon an unusual kayak technique, called "splitting a hole," to stay in the boat. I braced my paddle against the wall of water crashing into the raft from upstream, feathering the blade at just the right angle. This generated some extra gravity, which I used to press myself deeper into the well of the edgeless raft.

It was working well. But as the person to the right was flying over my head, I felt a determined hand grab the right shoulder of my lifejacket. And then, an even more determined second hand grabbed my lifejacket's left shoulder. Of course, none of this activity slowed his descent. He plunged into the falls, still firmly attached to my person, and posing a serious threat to my well-being. The water violently ripped him under the boat, but did nothing to weaken his iron grip.

There we posed, raft on edge, me bracing against the falls, and "Aquaman" steadily building a "you too" kind of attitude.

I was not to be easily persuaded out of the safety of the raft. It was dark and wet beyond the tubes, and I had no desire to leave my precarious perch. I'm sure that Aquaman was also fighting persuasions... the vicious persuasions of the downcurrent pounding on his head, and the disheartening persuasions from his weakening grip. He was at war with the will of the river, using me as a grip on reality, and too scared to succumb to the river itself. It was a natural thing to do. After all, he *was* in a man-eating hole, in the middle of the night, with no one downstream should his grip fail him.

Finally, a brutal lack of air signalled the end of the match. The twilight warrior released my lifejacket and relented to the mercy of the river gods. After a brief purgatory beneath the raft, he was released. Allowed to return to the everyday world—reborn.

We pulled the raft and crew together before the take-out, unscathed. We all achieved a new zest for life. A slightly changed outlook on night rafting. And a curious new admiration for the joys of sunshine.

The rest of the excursion was a blur of returning equipment, sharing farewells, and eating some breakfast. There was no time for even a nap before I resumed my guiding duties for the next day.

As fun as all of this sounds, I didn't mention a word of it to anyone for quite a while. It took some time to sift through the events, digest the experience, and decide if fate had been kind to us or not.

In the end, the trip itself had become insignificant. It had been a step through a door through which few would venture. It was a risky step, bringing us face to face with untold joys and our deepest fears. I searched deeper, until the significance of our adventure was revealed.

The river showed us to be somehow alone—together.

CAL SALMON

"...We rounded a bend and came to a rapid known as Grant's Bluff or Freight Train.... It is not the type of drop you want to swim. Nasty reversals and big rocks, and what seems to be river-wide holes, can cause even the best boaters to wish they were back at Otter Bar Lodge soaking in a hot tub, drinking a glass of fine wine and having some smooth, aged cheese on a whole wheat cracker."

Brian Clark, River Runner Magazine

Have you ever watched a special on Sea World. You know, the trained animal shows, where a seal barks and someone throws him a fish. Well, that was me. The seal. But no one was throwing me a fish, and I wasn't really barking.

I probably sounded like I was barking. But it was just my water-burdened throat fighting with my lungs for a gasp of air. On my second bark I got sucked back down for another thrashing in some rivergod's washing machine.

It's weird what your mind does while your body goes ass over teakettle through a river's liquid darkness. "Bummer," I thought "my mom's gonna ask someone what the last thing I said was, and they're gonna have to tell her *'ARK!'* You know, Mrs. Bennett. Like a seal... *'ARK!'*"

The parade of cars should've told me something. Here on the Cal Salmon, cars usually make their way upstream in the morning, downstream in the afternoon. Pretty typical stuff. But today was different. Not only were there more cars on the road than I'd ever seen before, they were all heading in the opposite direction. Downstream. And it wasn't even noon yet.

By the time we reached the put-in at Nordheimer Flat, only a few boaters were left to be found. "What's up?" I asked one of the guides.

"Oh, not much. You gonna run it today?"

"Yeah."

"A bit high for me. Good luck."

I didn't get it. A little bit of brown water and everyone skittered downriver like geese heading south. It just didn't figure.

Well, actually it *did* figure. But *I* didn't get it. I'd run the Cal Salmon two years earlier at about 4,300 cfs. Pretty high water by Cal Salmon standards. In fact, many of the commercial outfitters start cancelling trips around 4,200 cfs. But now the river was running over 7,500 cfs, and, in the midst of this torrential downpour, it was still coming up!

Since the put-in was at a wide, shallow gravel bar, the extra 3,200 cfs didn't look any different than I'd remembered. Not different enough to stop us from getting on the water anyway. We filled our two 14-foot self-bailers with strong paddle crews and headed downriver.

It only took about three minutes to figure out why everyone had packed up their rafts and gone home. The river was big. I mean, *REALLY BIG!!* The Cal Salmon had gone stark raving bonkers. Our raft felt like it was tied to a locomotive that was dragging us downstream at about twenty miles an hour.

"OK..." I shouted "This is gonna be Airplane Turn. Paddle hard!"

All of the familiar landmarks were there. The bends in the canyon. The boulders along the banks. But the rapids were gone. The big boulders that formed the Airplane Turn were about six feet underwater. I hadn't even noticed the Maze or Lewis Creek Falls. But in their place, a long series of tailwaves bounced our raft around like a beachball at a pool party. It was time for a plan.

"OK everybody. This is way bigger than anything I've seen in here. Plus, we haven't seen anything yet. So, let's get conservative. Avoid the holes. Power up those waves. Be ready to high side...."

It was a lame plan! But it was the only thing that was going to work. Now, as if to convince myself that we were going to be alright, I started singing aloud: *"...the weather started getting rough\the tiny ship was tossed\if not for the courage of the fearless crew\the Minnow would be lost\the Minnow would be lost..."*

We whisked through the canyon with lightening speed. Big rapids came and went in a blur of foam and fury. One of the biggest rapids—Cascade—showed up all too fast. Although we had our butts puckered up on those raft tubes like nervous starfish on rocks, I didn't know if the extra bit of suction could beat the wall of water that had to be waiting at the base of the rapid.

At Cascade, the river divides itself between two chutes. The left side provides a boulder maze, requiring a fast left-to-right move at the bottom to avoid being pancaked in either a hole or on a VW size boulder. The right side is a steep chute. Almost a waterfall. One of those deals where you line up, hang on, and see what happens. But that was at *regular* water levels. There was nothing *regular* about the water level we were seeing today.

Rather than chance a blind run, we stopped on the left bank to scout out the rapid. Much to our relief, the river had filled in the worst parts of the drop, making safe passage possible along either route. We headed back to our boats and ferried to the far right bank. Making the final adjustments, we reached the top of the chute along the right wall and hunkered down a bit in the raft. In a flash of white and water, it was all over. We floated free of Cascade and continued on our race track descent toward the take-out.

Next up was Achilles Heel, a long, steep rapid that tended to slam rafts onto a high, banked curve along the right wall, then straight down over a five or six-foot drop into a nasty hole. Again, at medium flows, rafts could make the pull in order to avoid the hole, or simply hit the hole with momentum. But at higher levels, the hole developed a healthier appetite for synthetic materials. In fact, one raft spent about five exasperating minutes recirculating in the hole when we made the run at 4,300 cfs. Finally, the rafters jumped out of the raft and swam down to an eddy, letting the river bounce the raft around for another few minutes before letting it go.

We were going to creep through the boulders near the top of the rapid, then paddle like hell to avoid the hole. But, somewhere high above us, someone heard our plan and said "yeah, sure, watch this."

Our raft shot across the rapid like a loose cork from a warm bottle of champagne. We were on an inflatable rocket sled. I didn't even have a chance to say "we're screwed" before we were perched upon a pillow, high on the right bank, staring straight down into the guts of Achilles Heel.

"FORWARD PADDLE!!!" I guess I should've been honest with my crew. What I really meant was "you guys forward paddle,

I'm just gonna sit back here and hold on for all I'm worth."

But everyone knew exactly what I meant, and they weren't about to let me be the only one arm wrestling a safety strap. I mean, this was a perfect opportunity to match grip strength against the best the Cal Salmon had to offer.

We slid a few inches higher on the pillow, then violently changed direction. Sitting in the back of the raft, I felt as if the entire San Francisco 49ers defensive line had landed on me. I couldn't see a thing, but could feel a wall of water wrapping itself around my shoulders and dragging me backwards into the hole. We had slammed the hole with some momentum, but had stalled momentarily. I hung on just long enough to watch the water clear away and my crew paddling into a friendly eddy.

We were almost home. One set of rapids to go. By now, we had figured that we were pretty invincible. We started feeling kind of sorry for all those rafters who had left the river and gone home. This was turning out to be a heck of a good time.

Mile six. Here we were. The grandaddies of all Cal Salmon rapids. Last Chance and Freight Train. Also known as Big Joe or Grant's Bluff depending on who you talk to. This was the original home of whitewater carnage. In fact, Gayle Wilson's two videos, Whitewater Bloopers I and II, provide hours of entertainment at the expense of countless paddlers who have been thrashed here.

Last Chance gets its name from a big eddy at the bottom right side of the rapid. The idea is to swing around some boulders, start pulling to the right, and avoid a big hole at the base of the rapid. Done correctly, you'll find yourself in a peaceful eddy with a second chance to scout out an even worse Class V rapid downstream... Freight Train. Screw up and you're likely to flip in the hole. Then, that eddy is your *last chance* to swim to the bank before swimming Freight Train.

I had seen this rapid plenty of times before. I knew its reputation, and had seen the calamities. I had probably been a victim to a calamity there once or twice myself. But today was going to be different. The rocks on the right bank were totally submerged. We could bounce along the right bank, and take what looked like a highway around the right side of the hole.

What we hadn't accounted for was the fact that our success

The right chute of "Cascade" on California's Salmon River toys with these low water rafting enthusiasts

upstream had pissed off a river god back at Achilles Heel. And there's nothing worse than cheating a river god out of a good flip and swim session. Now it was his chance to show us who was boss.

We took the most enthusiastic paddlers from the two rafts and loaded them into one boat. At the base of Last Chance two people waited with throw bags in case anything went awry. We talked over our paddle itinerary and headed for the current.

Coming around the top of the rapid, it was immediately apparent that something was really wrong. We were way out in the middle of the river. Nowhere near the right bank, as we had planned. The current was much more than we had expected, and we were on a collision course with the big hole.

Rather than succumb to the whims of the river gods, we struggled for the right bank. Big mistake. We hit the hole squarely on our side. I jumped on the downstream tube, took one deep breath, and kissed the daylight goodbye.

It's amazing how little a life jacket does for you on a flooded river. My feet could have been pointed straight at the surface for all I knew. Still, it feels kind of good to swim like hell. Like you're gonna save yourself or something. Even if you don't know up from down.

I popped to the surface and was amazed to find the raft right in my face... with my buddy Doc still hanging onto it. I started to reach for the flip line before I realized where we were. First one rock slammed my leg, then another. We were at the top of Freight Train. I remember saying to myself "this is gonna suck!" then getting a deathgrip on a handle and crossing all my toes for good luck.

There is nothing in the English language that can describe the violence of a Class V swim. Even holding onto that raft, it was all I could do to prevent being dragged down like a two-ton anchor. Waves buffeted us from all sides. "Have we made it past the big hole?" I silently questioned. I looked skywards toward my angry river god and listened. Combined with the thunder of the whitewater, his answer resounded like a massive whale belch... *NOPE!!!*

The pressure was awesome. Try as I may, my grip was sheered from the raft. Leaving the thunder of the surface storm, I entered the dark world of river demons. Rather than fight it, I rolled up into a tight ball, like those cannonball dives that kids do. If I didn't struggle, I could save my oxygen in case I was down long.

Time is a very relative concept, something that your mind tends to screw with when you can't see your watch. Especially when you're in life-threatening situations. As I rolled through the dark bowels of the Cal Salmon, my time and reality had become painfully slow. I wanted to hit the fast forward switch. I wanted to read the end of the book first.

WHO-O-O-OSH! I was jettisoned toward the surface, blasting out of the pillow just before slamming into the walls marking the exit from Freight Train. "ARK!" I snapped a lung full of air and looked to the right. At first I thought it was an illusion. A sick, demented mirage tossed there by my river god. But no, it was real... the raft was within an arm's length of me. I flung my arm toward a handle and breathed a huge sigh of relief.

"ARK!" Well maybe I breathed too soon.

Like a baby doll being held out a car window, I hung onto the side of the raft, swinging behind it to the safety of the pool below. Soon, Doc and I had the raft flipped back over, and paddled it down to the eddy at the Butler Creek take-out.

We decided to head back upstream together to see how the rest of our team was doing. In a few minutes we were standing amidst some rafters staring down at Last Chance and Freight Train from the towering cliffs known as Grant's Bluff.

"Just get off the river?" someone asked.

"Yeah," I said.

"You should've seen this flip a couple of minutes ago! *AWESOME!*"

Before I could respond, my mind flashed back. I was instantly transported back to the bottom of Freight Train. I couldn't breathe. Staring at the rafter in front of me, I struggled, struggled some more, and finally answered...

"A-A-A-ARK!"

REVENTAZON RIVER

"Ha ha! We are here! I don't know exactly where, but somewhere on top of a rapid...."

George F. *Flavell*, The Log of the Panthon

Somewhere between a mysterious fruit tree and the west bank of Costa Rica's Reventazon River, the epitome of logic rolled from Dave Prange's lips with a prophetic ease: "If it tastes good, it probably won't kill you."

I couldn't remember reading that saying in my old boy scout manuals, but I was too hungry to really give a rip.

We'd been paddling for hours in continuous Class IV and V rapids without a bite to eat, and it looked like dinner was little more than a wistful dream at this point. In my hands were small, edible-looking orbs harvested from a nearby tree moments earlier by one of our team members. I sank my teeth deep into the curious, sweet smelling fruits, devouring four of them in about 45 seconds. The fresh supply of carbs and sugar quickly permeated my tired body, nourishing new found paddling strength. But as vigor returned to my muscles, a dark, damp feeling began crawling up my spine and penetrating the little terror factories in my mind.

"How far is it to Siquirres?" I asked.

"Twenty-five miles," blurted Dave.

Steve thought "twelve miles."

Doc tossed in a confident "beats me."

So much for consistency. It was obvious that no one knew.

Here we were, 20 feet from spiders, lizards, monkeys, snakes, and who knows what else, pondering the possibility of a night in the jungle. "I'd rather be buried up to my neck in a schoolyard with my head painted like a soccer ball," I thought to myself. "How the heck did we get into *this* mess?"

Actually, our Reventazon River adventure had begun on a pleasant note. Earlier that morning, four boats had left the eddy behind our riverside camp, upstream of the village of Angostura. I was in a paddle raft, joined by members of Team SOTAR and Team Oregon, both of which were here to compete in the 1991

Costa Rica Rally against some of the best rafters in the world. Two paddle-cats travelled alongside, one manned by Doc Loomis and Dave Mullins, and the other by two of Russia's best known rafters, Misha Kolchevnikov and his friend Shoritz. Finally, Steve Scherrer, owner of Alder Creek Kayak Supply in Sandy, Oregon, joined us, expertly darting his Prijon Invader kayak among the rafts like a nervous minnow being chased by submarine predators.

At the start of the trip we found ourselves bobbing through easy Class III rapids, past huge jungle vegetation, and finally past the small town of Angostura. For many of us, this was our first introduction to jungle boating. And, the experience was breathtaking. The scenery was remarkable—straight out of a National Geographic magazine. But, as the trip progressed and we drifted deeper into the heart of the Peralta section, the more I started thinking "travel to beautiful tropical countries, experience world class rivers, and get your paddling ego stomped."

The river had picked up in intensity shortly after passing the bridge at Angostura. The first major horizon line sent us running for the left bank to scout a rapid called Jungle Run. This hole-ridden beast drops about ten or fifteen feet in about 50 yards. Not very steep by river running standards, but add to that the fact that much of that drop was swallowed by two channel-wide ledges, and that nearly 4,000 cfs filled the channel. The combination of gradient and flow provided a set of hydraulics capable of flipping large rafts end for end.

Since this was truly a wilderness adventure, we decided to slip through a left-side cheat route, thereby avoiding the carnivorous Class V+ holes that gave Jungle Run its mean reputation. Still, as soon as we rejoined the main channel, the river sucked us back into its tireless cavalcade of bank to bank wave trains.

The Reventazon slammed along its corduroy bed with more whitewater—*bigwater* kind of whitewater—than any of us had seen before. We had paddled big, pushy rivers before, but nothing this continuous. It was truly amazing to watch the effects of so much water descending upward of 85 feet per mile... so long as we stayed upright. And occasionally, staying upright became a legitimate concern. Long series of four to eight-foot-high waves would lull us into a false sense of security. These liquid carnival rides were breathtaking and exciting, giving us views far downriver from their crests, and leaving us blinded by walls of water in their troughs. But every once in a while innocent looking waves would hide sharp ledges and keeper holes until the very last second. The sudden sight of these monsters sent us leaning forward over the bow, paddling as hard as we could to maintain some momentum, and pulling as much clean water as we could to break through the reversals.

Although any one of us was a prime candidate for a whooping, Misha and his paddling partner, Shoritz, inadvertantly volunteered to be first. We were beginning to feel pretty confident about the huge holes and waves. Then, at what seemed to be a straight-forward Class IV bend, a hidden rock reached up and snagged the frame of Misha's homebuilt cataraft. The two paddlers found themselves instantly kneeling in waist deep water, fighting back the current as the cataraft held tight.

Misha's solid aluminum thigh brace snapped nearly in two, sending him into the river, where he was picked up by some other members of the team. Shoritz, however, was staying with the cat to help pull the boat off the rock. It took about ten minutes of line throwing, and some heavy tugging, before the cat floated free of the rock and into the eddy where the rest of us stood.

The river's first swipe had potentially devastating effects. Misha's thigh was badly bruised, and the broken cataraft frame left a dangerously jagged edge right where Misha's thigh would have to go. If he leaned the wrong way, or was hit with a strong wave, the broken steel would cut his leg. Getting back on the cataraft would be risky, but hiking out of this location was an even riskier alternative.

We spent a few minutes pounding the sharp edges with rocks, until the narrowed tubing slipped into a small pocket on the intact portion of the frame. A couple of straps from the other rafts held the tubing together, allowing Misha and Shoritz to remount their cat and paddle downstream.

Once back on the river, everyone paddled with a new found sense of self-preservation. Eyes flashed back and forth across the horizon like sonar, looking for keeper holes and other subsurface hazards. But soon, we were back into the fun mode, bounding over the crests of the big waves, and gritting our teeth through endless lines of big curlers.

Soon after the Turrialba River poured in from the left bank, the river spread out into a wider, ledge-filled channel. Although we were still moving downriver with incredible speed, we were able to spot hazards sooner, and plan our moves earlier. When big ledges spanned the entire river, the easier drifting times gave way to some very tense moments wrestling the raft out of big holes.

Deep in the heart of the Grand Canyon, there lurks a rapid known by every river runner—Lava Falls. This gigantic rapid later gave birth to its name progeny—Lava South—which inhabits Chile's Bio-Bio River. Now, here on the Reventazon, we were face to face with Central America's own version of Lava Falls—*Lava Central*.

Beyond the bow of our raft the river bed narrowed considerably while tilting precariously downward. Many people have dubbed Lava Central "El Horrendo," and for good reason. In 75 yards the river bottom drops more than 25 feet. The effect on the river surface is breathtaking. Irrationally placed curlers, migrating haystacks, and exploding waves block any line of safe passage. We pointed ourselves toward the first curler, locked our feet deep into the footcups, and worked into a fast paddle pace.

Soon, the raft arched high into the air. From the back of the raft, the bow paddlers appeared to be standing on the front thwarts, their torsos stretched over the bow while their paddles swept the air in an attempt to find anything that would lend resistance. In the next second, I would be high above them, staring over their heads at the next wave as our raft descended deep into the bowels of the Reventazon. Although this gigantic liquid see-saw ride seemed to last an eternity, I'm sure that we descended the entire 75 yards in less than a few seconds.

The excitement of Lava Central/El Horrendo left me winded and weary in the back of the raft. My guiding voice was all but gone now, and my attention span was growing shorter with each passing mile. Fortunately, the Reventazon offered a moment of appeasement, allowing us to catch our breath and lower our pulse rates before moving on.

Next came La Ceja, a rapid similar in size to Lava Central. By now I had moved to the front of the raft with Dave Prange and had turned the helm over to Doc Loomis.

Half-way through La Ceja a portion of the river made a gravity-defying tip skyward, hung there like a giant liquid billboard, and released its incredible weight five feet upstream. Dave, readying himself for the pending collision, raised his paddle like a giant tomahawk and stabbed it deep into the wave's face. The river retorted by hurling a wall of water at our chests.

The raft decelerated violently, sending Dave across my lap and nearly over the bow. Only the sharp metallic hinges of his knee brace held him aboard, the thin skin of my left shin acting as an anchor cleat.

"Aieeeaah!" I screamed as my eyes probed the foam for the source of my pain. "G-r-r-r-r." The moment I realized that it was Dave's brace that was the root of my agony, my body snapped straight. At the same time, my arms shot outward, giving Dave an adrenaline-charged push... right over the bow and into the river!

Still in the midst of an incredible sea of storm-driven waves, I revelled in the momentary respite from the dagger-like pain, then paused to wonder how Dave was doing with his swim.

Dave had hardly hit the water before he was stroking his way right back into his seat—something I'd do if pushed into a Class V rapid! He popped over the bow like a spooked seal and began paddling again, having hardly missed a stroke. Not until we were all the way through La Ceja did we truly realize what had just happened. We chuckled, shared apologies and paddled on.

Coming to the end of the Peralta section, the river whipped up to a final fury, descending through the staircase rapid known as The Land of a Thousand Holes. Between our raft and the Peralta footbridge, the river lied in wait, daring us to find a route through the endless series of huge offset ledges and disconcerting boulder gardens.

We had only come nine miles, but the river had chipped away much of our enthusiasm. A sneak route appeared along the right bank, and provided an inviting opportunity to avoid the nasty holes. We slinked through the narrow passages proffered by the boulders, and ferried across to the eddies beneath the footbridge.

Normally, paddlers would exit the river here, and make their way back to the town of Turrialba. However, our information had been obtained in the midst of a late-night Rally party from an Australian paddle team that had done the river a day earlier. We had heard that the take-out was at a *cement bridge* not at a steel footbridge. While most of us sat in the eddy scratching our chins and wondering where we were, Steve Scherrer walked up to some locals to discuss geography.

As a result of language barriers and miscommunications, we erroneously concluded the take-out was 11 kilometers downstream. So, we climbed back aboard our craft and headed downriver.

It took us only half-an-hour to figure out that we'd been mistaken. We'd missed the Peralta take-out, and were now on the Pasqua section of the Reventazon. With no guidebook in hand, no locals on the banks, and nothing in our memory banks regarding the distance to the next town, we paddled on.

About an hour later we started getting concerned. We pulled into an eddy beneath an old homestead, only to find it abandoned. While we stood there tired and bewildered, Misha disappeared into the jungle, emerging moments later with fists full of the mystery fruit. The rest of us, half-starved and wondering whether the Pacific Ocean was the next major landmark, retraced Misha's footsteps and began devouring the fruit. Dave's words about tasty fruit not killing anybody convinced me to imbibe in the gluttonous feast. Fortunately, these delicious morsels later turned out to be guava, but we were nervous about our intestinal futures in the mean time.

It was a 16-mile paddle down the Pasqua section to the next take-out. Though easier than the Peralta section, the river still dropped 55 feet per mile through long sections of Class IV+ whitewater. Big rapids like Gran Pillow (named after Pillow Rock on West Virginia's Gauley River) and Muerte Verde (which translated means "Green Death") passed beneath the rafts' floors and disappeared into the already cluttered minds of the paddlers. The singular goal of getting out of the jungle by nightfall, and back to camp to continue training for the competition, affected our every thought.

Finally, the new highway bridge at Siquirres rose above the river like the first sight of land for a shipwrecked sailor. Whoops of joy echoed into the jungle as we slumped over our final few strokes into the eddy.

It would only be two hours of anxious waiting for our botched shuttle, and a long, kidney-jarring ride back to camp before we could share our stories with our friends.

Looking back, the Peralta run is not all that bad. It's big, it's wild, and it's jungle. Next time, the peace of mind I'll have knowing where the take-out is will make a big difference.

If I ever tell anyone else to do the run, I'll tell them to *bring a guidebook*!

SNAKE RIVER
"CAN I KEEP YOUR OARS?"

"Tuber—A.K.A. 'hole bait', 'dead meat.' A tuber is a root-like vegetable or someone who runs rivers in innertubes, usually without benefit of helmet, life jacket, or common sense. Despite the charming egalitarian aspect of the 'sport,' innertubing is proof that natural selection is still hard at work."

William Nealy, **Whitewater Home Companion: Southeastern Rivers, Volume II**

Every once in a while, one of my river buddies does something so monumentally stupid, so utterly ridiculous, so void of sensibility, that I have to ask myself... *why didn't I do that first?!*

That was precisely the question running through my head as I watched Mike Blumm blow up his innertube.

It wasn't the mere act of inflation itself that had me so bedazzled, it was the fact that Mike was about to toss his bloated artificial donut into the raging torrents of Wild Sheep Rapid—the longest Class V rapid in the Hell's Canyon section of Idaho's Snake River.

After a few more minutes of watching Mike forcing recycled canyon air into his tube, I thought I had the scene figured out. This was a put on. A practical joke. I was sure of it. But I wanted to play along. So, I began walking down the hill, closer to the situation, moving in for a better look.

I strained to wipe away my skeptical smile as I stepped the final few feet to Mike's side. I put my hand on Mike's shoulder, and began to talk. "Thing's OK at home, Mike? You get fired and not tell us? Wife been seeing another guy? Not enough raisins in your raisin bran?" Mike just kept about his business, staring intently at the river.

"Shit," I thought, "this is for real. *He's really gonna do it!*"

It was clear to any casual observer that this little stunt was attributable to a temporary lull in sanity. Canyon fever. But, after a couple of minutes of discussion, Mike was able to convince me that this adventure had been carefully planned.

"Carefully planned?!" I exclaimed. "What the heck kind of planning goes into tubing a Class V rapid?!" Boy did I have a lot to learn.

First of all, explained Mike, there is the careful selection of the innertube. Now, don't ask me what that means. I never quite got the theory down on innertube selection. All it probably means is that the tube holds air. Next, you have to plan not to forget your helmet or life jacket. No biggie there for any person of average intelligence. Finally, and most importantly, there's the "tell-all-your-friends-you're-gonna-do-it-so-you-can't-back-down" part of the plan. This final part of the plan provides some trip insurance in case you think about chickening out at the last minute. Having overseen all of these fine planning details, Mike was ready.

I watched Mike hike down to the river to survey the rapid one last time, and began to pity the poor ole guy who first spots Mike's body floating past Heller's Bar. But, as one never to let an opportunity slip through my hands, I offered my final words of encouragement: "Hey, can I keep your oars if you don't make it?"

Mike ignored my pessimistic bon voyage, poked his derrier through the tube's hole, stepped to the river's edge, and unceremoniously backflopped into an eddy. He then began to backstroke furiously out into the current until, about a thousand backstrokes later, he found his desired entry line for the rapid. I think. Well, either he found his line, or his arms gave out.

Mike's knees and helmet began to bob as he accelerated down the slick tongue toward the first line of waves. Soon the river swept him into a confusing display of foam and current. I felt overwhelmed by the grace of his descent, and admired the audacity of his futile endeavor.

Faster and faster, the river swept him toward the first mega hole. And, as his tube paused, poised above the lip of a huge, gaping hole, I reached a moment of realization... a realization that I was about to become the owner of Mike's oars.

But, it was not to be. For the next few seconds, Mike managed to utilize his innertube to its fullest capabilities... displaying true tubing finesse whether above, below, or in hot pursuit of, his innertube. And somehow, he survived.

We were finishing up our lunch about the time Mike completed his hike back upriver to join us.

"How was it?" we asked.

"Fun," he said. "A little bigger than I thought it'd be."

As we loaded up the rafts for our own runs through Wild Sheep, Mike seemed extraordinarily calm. It was as if a month of stress and anxiety had been lifted from his shoulders.

We set up camp early that day. Above the roar of the next big rapid—Granite Falls—and beneath overhanging cliffs adorned by ancient Indian petroglyphs, we basked in the late afternoon sun, and traded old river tales over cool gulps of beer.

As the conversation turned back to Mike's exploits, we noticed that he was absent from the circle. Gone. Someone mentioned having last seen him walking toward Granite Falls. Scouting perhaps? I mean, Granite *is* the biggest, wildest rapid in Hell's Canyon.

Mike stumbled back into camp, exuding that same maniacal glare of intent he'd shown at Wild Sheep. "I'm going to take that innertube through Granite," he said. "Right through the big hole!"

"All right," I thought. "A second chance. Maybe *this* time, I'll get some new oars!"

THE PACIFIC OCEAN
"REALLY BIG WATER"

"Nobody ever did anything foolish except from some strong principle. "

Melbourne

We were at the end of our rope. My best whitewater videos had been played to death, now looking like they'd been shot during a North Dakota snowstorm. The low water runs of late Spring had become no water runs by late Summer. Worst of all, my neoprene was dry! For the first time in six months! And it even smelled OK! This had to end.

My friend Doc called me out of desparation.

"Hey Doc, what's up?"

"I've got an idea!"

"What?"

"Wanna do some big water?"

"What? The Thompson? The Snake? Did a dam break somewhere? I don't have any vacation time left."

"No, man. Close by stuff. The Pacific."

"The *what*?!"

"The ocean! The Pacific Ocean!"

It had to happen... 897 flips had finally gotten to Doc's brain. The cold water had locked up the mental gears. He was being totally irrational. Irrational *and serious.*

"The Pacific?"

"Yeah! Eight foot waves! I'll bring my raft!"

Well, if anyone is foolish enough to sacrifice their raft for some new hair-brained odyssey, I want to be there. And this truly qualified as hair-brained. A gazillion acre-feet of water pummel your front tube within 80 feet of your beach towel. I couldn't wait!

With Moolack Beach, Oregon, providing the backdrop, Doc and Dave Prange pointed their shiny yellow SOTAR toward Japan, stirred the surf with their paddles, and headed confidently to sea.

Well, that lasted about 96.5 seconds before Poseidon started slapping their raft around like an errant beachball. The cartwheels, handstands and somersaults that intermittently disrupted their paddle strokes would have made any circus troupe green with envy!

This was *big* water all right. With *big* quantities of *big* flips!

It took only 15 minutes before Doc and Dave marched onto the sand, pulled their shoulders back, and declared their first ocean rafting trip a great success. (Note: Ocean success bears no relationship whatsoever to river success!)

Since that first trip, Doc and Dave logged additional adventures at other famous Northwest beaches. Even had an excited — albeit nearsighted — seal try to mate with their raft one day.

So there you have it. It's a tough precedent to follow. But next time you're really bored, grab your nose plugs, shark repellent and zinc oxide. Get your raft and give these guys a call.

The Pacific Ocean is always running!

Surfer dudes at The Pacific Ocean. (Photo by Doc Loomis)

CATARACT CANYON

"We always thought we needed a certain amount of thrills to make life sufficiently interesting for us. In a few hours' time in the central portion of Cataract Canyon we experienced nearly enough thrills to last us a lifetime."

Ellsworth and Emery Kolb

Get in a raft with a river guide and you're liable to hear enough tall tales to write a novel. Some of them true. For me, it always helps to keep a healthy supply of enduring stories in my repartee to fill in quiet moments, flat stretches, and to avoid questions like, "how deep's this river?"

While the best river stories usually stem from first hand experiences, a good secondhand tale can't be overlooked. Such is the case with the following story.

During my early days as a raft guide, I had the good fortune of befriending an ex-Colorado River guide. All his boating skills were acquired while getting his raft stomped by the big rapids of Cataract Canyon, which, during high water, is one of the most treacherous sections of the Colorado River. Though the end result was a fine set of well-honed big water skills, his initiation to the business of running rivers was downright embarrassing.

The swamper is the low man on the guiding totem pole. Swampers load and unload rafts, set up porta-potties, and fill the position of an all around *gofer'*. In Cataract Canyon, swampers hang out by the guides, watching their every move, sometimes waiting years for the moment when they can take the helm.

Arnie had just bluffed his way into his first river job, swamping for a big outfitter of marginal repute. His verbal resume had consisted of trips from the Rogue down to the Stanislaus, with a few rivers in between.

Arnie spent the beginning of his first season swamping during high water trips through Cataract. During the peak of runoff, raft companies sent motorized pontoon boats or triple-rigs through the big drops. This allowed for a greater margin of safety, but imparted nothing upon the swamper. After a couple of these trips, Arnie split for the Colorado Rockies for a few weeks of backpacking.

Upon his return to Utah, he was surprised to find things had changed. A guide strike was on and the company was understaffed. The top two-thirds of the totem pole had been hacked off. Arnie was now a head boatsman.

A trip was heading out the next day, and Arnie's services were badly needed. "You want to guide it?" asked the owner. "The river's still high. It's a real scream in there. But these folks really want an oarboat trip, you up to it?"

Arnie hadn't expected that question quite so fast. His expertise was dishwater, not whitewater. But Arnie was quick on his toes. This was an opportunity that had to be grabbed. "Uhm, well, uhm..." If he was going to do this trip, he'd have to say yes before his throat totally sealed off. "...err, yeah."

Arnie was now locked in. No turning back. He dragged his knotted stomach over to a friend's house and bummed some beer.

"Hey, Arnie, I heard you're gonna row it tomorrow."

"Yep."

"One trip just got back. A real nightmare. They lined up wrong at Satan's Gut and flipped, big time. Everyone held onto the raft. And with the oars and ammo cans and all, some folks got pretty banged up. A couple of broken arms or legs or something. Yeah, a real nightmare."

Arnie's mind was spinning. *Flips...oars...broken arms.* He was starting to wish he had been on the level about his experience. Or lack thereof. But it was too late. By the time morning arrived, he found himself on a bus heading toward the put-in.

The first couple of days of most Cataract Canyon trips take in miles of peaceful water, easy rapids, and glorious canyon scenery. While the passengers partook in these casual observations, Arnie honed his rowing skills. He pulled on the left oar, then on the right. Anyone who knew anything would have wondered what the heck Arnie was doing working up a sweat in Class II water. But he was pulling it off. He told stories from his first Cataract trips as if he'd done it for years. Everyone was convinced of Arnie's skills... except Arnie.

After a couple of days on the river, they had reached the lip of the inevitable. The grandaddies of Cataract Canyon rapids—Mile Long and The Big Drop. Arnie's heart was wrestling his stomach for a position in his throat. A creeping fear began to take over the thought centers in his brain. "What the hell am I doing here?" he thought. Meanwhile, his mouth moved with the disguise of confidence which he had perfected over the course of the last two days of guiding.

Flying through Mile Long, Arnie's oars danced along the surface like wounded crickets, catching the current and the tops of waves, and flailing in the troughs. But he was doing alright. Hanging tough and keeping the raft straight.

Before long it was all over. Arnie and his crew had survived Mile Long, slurping down their victory like so many shots of confidence. But more rapids—worse rapids—waited downstream.

Arnie's biggest moment came way too soon. Quivering with excitement and terror, he went into a short guide's speech he'd heard the old timers say before: "OK, down there is Satan's Seat and Satan's Gut. The Big Drop. It's what we're here for. Remember everything about what I said when we started this trip. Don't panic, hold on tight, and *DON'T FALL OUT.*"

Following final preparations, Arnie tugged heavily on the oars, straining hard to get the boat out into the main current. Soon, truck-sized walls of water began dancing like angry spirits on the river's surface. Arnie's mind was becoming overloaded. "*A real nightmare...lined up wrong...flipped...held onto the raft...broken arms...broken arms...broken arms.*" His friend's words rang loudly above the roar of the rapids. Then it happened.

"SNAP!" An oar let go with a sickening pop. "KAPLOOSH!" The first set of waves exploded over the boat, nearly capsizing the raft. Paralyzed with fear, Arnie could do nothing. Huge diagonal waves reached skyward, forming ever narrowing corridors of doom, funneling the raft and crew toward extinction.

"JUMP!"

The crew looked startled.

"C'MON! JUMP!!!"

Arnie had gone berserk. No one could have guessed what was running through his mind. The perceived inevitability of a flip in Satan's Gut had warped Arnie's sense of judgment. He felt that it would be better to simply swim the Gut than to hold onto a tumbling raft full of arm-breaking oars and ammo cans.

"JU-U-U-UMP!"

No one budged an inch. For many of the passengers, this was their first taste of wilderness adventure. This was supposed to be fun. Exciting. Not a Hollywood version of "Arnie Goes Psycho." They hunkered lower and lower into the raft, holding onto ropes and frames with white knuckled vengeance.

"JUMP!"

Arnie went overboard. No kidding! Right out there in the middle of Mother Nature's personal drowning pool. Out there under the vultures and Utah's blazing sun.

It took a few seconds before Arnie found the surface again. He came up within an ear shot of the raft. Seeing his crew glued in place, he shouted his final words of misguided encouragement before concerns for his own well being became paramount.

"JUMP!" Blub, blub, blub, blub...

Now the raft, totally unguided, floated perilously toward Cataract Canyon's biggest, ugliest holes. Nearby, Arnie bobbed through the churning brown waters like a cork in a sea storm. Both raft and Arnie had the worst of possible lines. A big hole drew near. The roar of the water was sickening.

In a moment it was all over. Somehow, the raft had slipped through unscathed. The crew was safe. A perfect run. But Arnie was nowhere to be found.

"There he is!!" Shouted someone from the raft.

Arnie had taken an awful swim. He had entered the hole straight on, dead center. He was no match for its powerful grasp. He was sent deep into the bowels of the Colorado once, tumbled and released, and sucked back down for another ride. By the time he had reached the calm pools below, he had expended all the energy he had in his fight for survival.

"Arnie, hang in there. Just a second." One of the least adventurous passengers—a true city slicker—had unstrapped a spare oar and set out on rescuing Arnie.

By that time, other boats had converged for the rescue, but Arnie's crew reached him first. They hauled him over the gunwales and laid him on the pile of gear, letting the sun revive him.

By the time he came around, there was little left to Arnie's Cataract Canyon trip. The peaceful calm of Lake Powell waited downstream. There would be no opportunity for vindication. No chance to replenish his ego. Just hour after hour of the longest days of Arnie's life.

His story has reached near legendary proportions in some circles. Quite an unwelcome infamy. Fortunately, his real name is seldom revealed.....

MIDDLE FORK OF THE STANISLAUS

*"To walk by a river or flow with it down rapids and through
quiet stretches, to swim in it, to feel on your skin the power of
its currents, is to have a direct experience of the flow of time
and history and the cycles of the earth that bring the rain and
snow, the winds and the waters that flow down the mountains to
the valleys to the ocean again. This is the mystique of the
Stanislaus. "*

Harold Gilliam, as quoted in Tim Palmer's
Stanislaus: Struggle to Save a River

Bagging first descents is high stakes stuff for boaters at the
leading edge of California's whitewater fast lane.
Reputations are made or fade on the first drop of a paddle,
and plans of pending first descents are as well guarded as the
Queen's jewels. To make matters worse, just about anything that
could've been run, already had. Kayakers like Lars Holbek, Chuck
Stanley, Maynard Munger and Bryce Whitmore were carving up
every spare mile of free flowing water before I even knew what
whitewater was all about!

Fortunately, *firsts* come in all shapes and sizes. If a river has
already been run in a kayak, there's still room for a *first* raft
descent. If it has already been rafted, do a *first* in a canoe. And,
if it's been canoed? Heck, get Bob Carlson to sell you a river
board and have at it!

Every once in a while, a *first* flows past the noses of
preoccupied boaters for years before someone jumps up and takes
notice. Such was the case with the Middle Fork of the Stanislaus.

The Stanislaus used to be a common river name in any
California boater's vocabulary. The delightful rapids of the Main
Fork, between Camp Nine and Parrot's Ferry, were the baptismal
waters of a whole generation of boaters. However, the Army Corp
of Engineers, armed with bulldozers and blueprints for a massive
dam, quickly put an end to this section of river. The once wild
Stanislaus now lays dormant, entombed beneath the stagnant waters
of New Melones Reservoir.

During the Spring of 1979, with the main section of the

Stanislaus slowly backing up, two groups of kayakers, led by Chuck Stanley and Lars Holbek, set out up the logging roads above Camp Nine. On June 12, the two groups made a successful bid at a first descent of the eight mile Class V section of the Middle Fork of the Stanislaus, tracing the valley beneath Mt. Knight, and ending at Camp Nine.

It wasn't until 1986 that anyone started giving any serious consideration to rafting the Middle Fork. Part of the reason was its inaccessibility; the Middle Fork requires some tough driving on deeply rutted dirt roads, followed by a two mile hike through lovely Sierra forests, narrow trails, and thick stands of poison oak. Then there was the problem of finding adequate water. The Middle Fork only flows when Sand Bar Flat Dam spills an adequate amount of water, usually some time around the peak of run off.

In mid-June of 1986, a team of rafters led by Beth Rypins were hanging out at Sourgrass Ravine on the North Fork of the Stanislaus, after having first driven to the Middle Fork for a scout. A small group of boaters, consisting of Mike Doyle, Steve Ellsburg, and myself, struck up a conversation with Beth, the gist of which proved to be the deathknell of her team's hope for a first descent.

Mike and Steve listened attentively as Beth filled in the remaining information gaps on this unrafted section of river. Walking back to our end of the campground I noticed a certain eagerness in Mike's steps, a quickening in his words. I could read the signs. But I had to be sure.

"So, Mike, what do you think?"

"Let's run it!"

That was all it took. In a few more days we were rolling across the shoulder of Mt. Knight, connecting logging roads in an effort to find the Middle Fork trailhead, and listening to Dan Buckley read aloud from "A Guide To The Best Whitewater In The State Of California." The van began to crackle with excitement as he talked about gradients up to 170 feet, Class V+ rapids, and whitewater that "borders on excellent."

The reality of our situation hit as soon as the van door flew open. The small pine needle-covered clearing at the trailhead erupted into a rainbow of yellow rafts, blue helmets, red lifejackets, and green dry bags. Everything we needed for two days of wilderness rafting laid scattered upon the ground like a tool shed after a tornado. Getting this stuff to the river was going to be a chore!

We divided the equipment up as equitably as possible. Rafts were rolled into long cigars to make them managable during the two mile hike. Sleeping bags and safety gear were packed tightly into dry bags and strapped to our backs. Any unnecessary items—like food—were left in the van.

That's right. I said "like food." In the war against poundage, food was one of the items slashed from our list of necessities. Anyway, Mike had his fishing gear with him, and guaranteed us fresh trout for dinner. The only food items making it to the river were some freeze-dried bags of soup. Not much for eight guys on an overnight expedition!

By the time we reached the river, the group was too fatigued to enjoy the first glimpse of the magnificent canyon scenery. Many were face down in an eddy, slurping up water as fast as they could swallow, or scrubbing off the poison oak encountered during the final descent to the river. But soon, people started regaining their senses, separating out their gear, and blowing up rafts.

The moment I regained my senses, I heard Dan beckon us to join him on a short cliff separating our eddy from the rest of the river. "Uh, guys, you better come have a look at this."

I wasn't about to budge. I'd already hiked as far as I wanted, and three more yards would bust my limit. Unless Dan had found the fountain of youth, el dorado, or a lemonade stand, I wasn't gonna' move.

But I was still curious. I hadn't really seen the river yet, and I had five rolls of film to burn. So, reluctantly, I fell into the short line of boaters, and made my way up to the granite plateau beneath Dan's feet.

Turning my head to the left I immediately encountered a magnificent blast of stunning Sierra scenery. Towering cliffs reached down from the sky, ending in pine-covered talus slopes that slid at precipitous angles toward the water. Those boulders that had reached the river formed a quarter-mile labyrinthe of glistening pools, dancing currents, and head-to-tail Class IV rapids.

I was in the heart of a whitewater Disneyland. So captivating was the scene that I had all but tuned out the flurry of conversations whizzing about my ears. But slowly, words like "awesome" and "gnarly" began to grab my attention, and I turned my head to the right.

We were a scant 50 yards downstream of our rafts, which still bobbed patiently in the eddy. However, half way between us and that eddy, the river plummeted at least 15 feet... all at once. We hadn't even wet our paddles yet, and we were looking at our first portage. We'd become certified experts at carrying rafts, but we preferred carrying to the rapids, not around them.

Amidst the bitching and moaning, the rafts slowly made their way across the plateau, and into a friendlier eddy, past the waterfall. We loaded up, pointed the bow into the current and took off.

Snapping out of the first eddy was like grabbing a passing train. In an instant, boulders started coming at us like a lifesize video game, and with each successful 50 yards, the difficulty level inched higher. The gradient was unbelievable, but quite managable. The slots were plenty wide for a raft, but kept us constantly on our toes.

It seemed like 20 minutes went by before we even had a chance to sit in an eddy and gloat. The momentary calm seemed alien in this fantasy world of continuous whitewater. The crews cackled like kids in a candy store. It was hard to believe that the Middle Fork had gone by for so many years unnoticed by rafters. The river was so perfect that it seemed practically designed for rafts!

For the rest of the first day we picked our way through rapid after rapid, making up the names as we went along... Half Dome, Fresh Squeezed, Beyond Limits. Every so often, Mike's crew would slam through a big rapid, drive into an eddy, and give Mike a chance to cast a fly into the nearest pool. After all, he was our source of dinner, and if he didn't catch any fish, we were going to be awfully hungry. At other times, the rapids got so intense that we simply chose to line our boats, rather than risk an injury so far from the nearest town.

Later the first day we slid into a slow moving pool of water

186

An expert paddle team drops into the huge hole at "Willy's Falls" on the Middle Fork of the Stanislaus River during the first raft descent. (Photo by Mike Doyle)

and put on the brakes at a sandy, riverfront campsite. We had expended plenty of energy that day, and everyone was getting tired. Plus, Mike had been skunked so far. Not a single fish had fallen prey to his hook and line. We needed to give him a final chance at getting us some dinner.

It wasn't to be. Mike didn't get so much as a nibble. Now we were paying for our decision to pack light. The few pouches of freeze-dried dinners that had survived the weight rationing campaign were tossed into a single pot of boiling river water, and divvied out to the paddlers like hobo soup.

While everyone else wrestled spoons into the steaming pot, I reached into my sleeping bag and grabbed my single stowaway granola bar. It was all I could do not to laugh out loud as I snuck off behind a tree to devour my prize.

Coming back into camp, I noticed a marked brightening in the team's spirits. This was quickly followed by the familiar fragrance of our celebratory punch... river hooch juice.

Someone had snuck a flask of 151 rum, together with some punch mix, into their dry bag. What we were missing out on in culinary joy, we would more than make up for with gleeful attitudes. We celebrated our first day's success until the day's full effect slammed down on our eyelids, and sent us stumbling into the trees in search of our sleeping bags.

By morning, it had become obvious that some of the crew never found their bags. And, we were kind of worried whether we would regain our senses. But day two started off much easier than the first.

Instead of the constant barrage of Class IV and V rapids, the river would rock the raft into a Class III trance, hypnotizing us with cool spray from the splash of waves, and the up and down motion of the passing trees. This went on just long enough to shake the cobwebs from our brains. Then, the river began to pounce again, tossing every weapon in the river god's arsenal in an effort to separate raft from crew. Each rapid displayed the full variety of its unique character. Smooth slides, tight boulder slaloms, and frothy waterfalls presented new delights at each turn.

After a few more rapids, we found ourselves at the North Fork confluence, two miles upstream from Camp Nine. The North Fork presented a splendid sidehike into short waterfalls and clear, deep swimming holes.

As we approached the end of the trip, the river exploded one last time. A 200-yard long flurry of boulders and steep drops provided a fitting finale for the Middle Fork.

Soon, we were floating peacefully into the open canyons at Camp Nine. The huge floating logjam at the upper end of New Melones Reservoir displayed a stark reminder to the Stanislaus we had lost years earlier. Talk, however, remained on the accomplishments of the last two days.

In the jubilation surrounding our first raft descent, we realized that the Stanislaus lives and flows, awaiting a new generation of boaters.

SLATE RIVER
By Tim Keggerman

"To think of any river as nothing but water is to ignore the greater part of it."

Hal Borland, Beyond Your Doorstep

I t was the Spring of 1984 and I was standing high atop Mt. Augusta, a 12,000' mountain near Crested Butte, Colorado. Some friends and I were getting in some fine Spring corn skiing. We had stopped for lunch and were looking out over the glacier carve of the Upper Slate River Valley. I thought how nice it would be to ski down, hop into my kayak, and paddle back to Crested Butte by river.

Yeah, at this point in the climb we were all sweating. The splash of water would feel so good. I stood up and walked over to the 500-foot waterfall at the most upper reach of the Slate and soaked my head in the icy spray.

After skiing down some of Colorado's finest Spring snow, we got in the pickup and headed down the valley. With my buddies talking of deep snow and smooth powder turns, my mind was far below the snowline. My eyes remained glued on the small Slate River Canyon to the right of our road. I was thinking, wondering...

A couple of days later a buddy of mine, Dan Hicks, asked me if I had ever run the Slate. "No," I answered, "but I've sure been thinking about it."

We decided right then to head back to the canyon and begin scouting.

After a quick six-mile drive from town, we were at the first potential put-in. The scene was postcard perfect. Mammoth granite ridges towered above the surrounding mountainscape while snow covered fields descended to within 20 yards of the river. Closer to the river, lush carpets of green tundra drifted into thick stands of Douglas Fir and Blue Spruce.

We were one mile downstream from the old mining town of Pittsburgh, flanked by beaver ponds above us and the tight, narrow Slate River Canyon below. The sight and smell of water captivated our senses. Lush green moss glistened with crystal droplets captured from the waterfalls plunging into the river. This was an exotic place just to hike to.

Focusing our attention on the river, we began to notice that all of the visible drops had that Class V look. Steep rapids with churning, grabby holes. We could see very few slow stretches and few eddies. Still, there appeared to be just enough room between the big drops to catch our breath and to scout the next rapid.

We decided that it was still too early to try the Upper Slate. Logs cluttered some of the worst rapids and spanned the river in places. But, with a little more water, these hazards would submerge, taking with them our biggest concerns. As Dan and I hiked back up to the truck, we prayed for some warm snow-melting weather, and a couple of days later we got it!

Before we were to return to the Slate, we checked around with the old timers to find out more about the river. As it turned out, not many paddlers even knew of this hidden canyon, and no one had even *thought* of running it. The Upper Slate! We knew this was going to be fun!

After much anticipation, we found ourselves driving toward Pittsburgh one more time. As we unloaded our boats, the river roared a hearty confirmation of how lucky we were to be there. We were going to have high water on a virgin run. Just enough water to bury the logs, but enough to keep the first descent within the bounds of sane adventures.

It wasn't long before we were staring at the first significant rapid, a beefy, hard surging chunk of water flushing over a six-foot ledge and into a six-foot wide sharp slate crag.

"This drop's too gnarley!" Dan said.

"Yeah!" I said. "Too-nar." The name stuck, and we decided to call the first rapid Too-nar Falls. We also decided that Too-nar Falls was too much for us to run, and the decision was made to portage. But, on our way back to our boats we changed our minds and decided to run it.

Too-nar Falls was an incredible rush! We slid through the rapid intact and sailed toward the next drop on a wave of endorphines ten feet high.

Too-nar turned out to be the first of six big drops that make out one long one-and-a-half mile rapid. We've named the drops Too-nar Falls, Slate River Falls, Virgin Canyon, Jucie Lucy, Dead Man's Curve, and Wicked Wanda. Dan and I ran all of these drops on our first trip, but have retired to some weak-kneed portages around the worst rapid—Wicked Wanda—on subsequent trips. The Upper Slate is a scare ball run to the max, with Wicked Wanda just over our personal max.

As we continued downriver on our first trip, we stopped to scout each of the named rapids for logs and runnable routes. Since we had put on the river late in the day to catch the peak of snowmelt it had already begun to get dark by the time we came to the last rapid.

This rapid looked hideous... a seven-foot wide flume with a three-foot high roostertail dropping nine feet into a boiling cauldron. Four-foot boils backed by undercuts surrounded the rapid on both sides as the rapid clawed its final descent through more four-foot drops and undercuts. The disappearing sun cast an ominous light on the rapid, setting the blackening slate against the white foamy water in a flickering match of light and dark.

Both Dan and I flipped in the first drop. I had quickly rolled up only to find myself at the lip of the roostertail. The roostertail surged and blew me to the right a tad, landing me on a big boil which pulled me down for my second flip. "Shit!" I thought. "This is NO PLACE to be upside down!" I rolled back up just in time to run the last drop bass-ackwards, plunge deep into the bowels of the hole, and emerge upside down one last time. On my final roll I quickly looked back at the drop only to see Dan coming down behind me doing exactly the same routine I had just done.

When we rejoined in the eddy we agreed that had we seen the rapid from any other angle, we would have surely portaged it. It looked too wicked from the river. I saved the *wicked* part, and added *Wanda* because I like to rhyme. Thus, the rapid was christened Wicked Wanda.

As we made our way to the take-out, the last remnants of daylight fizzled out and stars began to light the sky. Carrying our boats up the steep bank to the road should have been a cold ending to our extraordinary trip, but we couldn't feel it. High spirits steamed and danced around our bodies as we clambered into the truck and drove back to town.

We had the time of our lives that evening, celebrating our victory, and revelling in that indescribable feeling of a completed first descent.

Our Slate River adventure has since proven to be a springboard for many other hearty river adventurers. Crested Butte Rafting now runs small commercial rafts down this stretch of river for three to four weeks a year during peak run-off in early Spring. Needless to say, this is a run where previous paddling experience, fearless attitudes, and a thirst for high adventure shine.

SKYKOMISH RIVER

"For a long moment, our raft seemed poised at the entrance to the rapid, and then all was a confusion of exploding waves, shouted commands, and torrents of water hurling over us. We paddled madly—often finding little more than air beneath one end of the raft or another. One second we 'highsided' to one side of the boat as we ran up on a boulder, the next, we shot between converging rocks that I was sure would capsize us. Jerry's voice rose above the din with a 'Forward left!' and soon we were safely tucked into an eddy behind a huge boulder."

Tim McNulty, Washington's Wild
Rivers: The Unfinished Work

Few rapids in the state of Washington generate more stories and tall tales than Boulder Drop on the Skykomish River. It is a beautiful rapid, arranged with the same balance of beauty and rawness that outdoor painters seek to capture on canvas. Glistening sheets of emerald water wind through bright mounds of car-sized granite boulders, intermittently exploding into cottony heaps of foam and confused hydraulics. In the background, the snow-capped peak of Mt. Index sails above the thickly forested banks, fighting for a boater's attention like a neglected cat. And though it is by no means the most difficult rapid in the state (usually it is only a Class IV drop), it is the home of bad karma. A whitewater version of Murphy's Law.

On a typical weekend it is not uncommon to see walkie-talkie wielding rapid traffic coordinators, techno-head rescue teams, knee clacking commercial customers, and jittery guides peering into the heart of the rapid from the North bank. It is an amusing scene if you've been here before, but slightly disconcerting for the first-timer on the "Sky." For all its humor and variety, chaos is inevitably the recipe du jour. Fear and excitement are the main ingredients.

While the river dishes out hearty portions of carnage stew, the gossip columnists of the whitewater world stalk the banks, waiting for the perfect tale of calamity to come their way. All of the best stories seem to filter back to the local taverns and paddle ranches, where boaters report the news before the hapless victims even finish their trips. Of all the yarns I've heard, this one seems to stick out in my memory.

On this particular afternoon, boatloads of commercial customers were careening through Boulder Drop, paddles out of synch, and yahooing for all they were worth. One unfortunate guide had failed to close his throwbag all the way before entering the rapid. Worse yet, only the loose end of the rope was carabinered to the raft. A short way into the first drop the rope began to feed out until, eventually, it snagged on a rock. It wasn't long before the rope snapped tight and the raft came to a sudden halt, sending the guide and his crew into the front of the boat.

Somehow, everyone managed to find a safe seat while the rope held tight. In fact, the crew almost seemed to be enjoying their surfing antics. Then, in a moment of courage and chivalry, their cunning guide dislodged his river knife and set out toward the back

An R-2 (two-man paddle team) moments before their big flip in Boulder Drop, Skykomish River, Washington. (Photo by Doc Loomis)

of the raft to cut it free.

With dagger in hand, the guide took two big steps when... *whoosh!!* The stern sunk, causing the whole boat to flood. As the tidal surge made its way from stern to bow, it dislodged passengers one by one, washing most of them into the drink. Fortunately, the techno-heads and walkie-talkie folks were fast on the scene, and pelted the hapless crew with throw bags and rescue boats before they even knew what hit them.

With the crew and raft finally clambering onto the safety of the riverbank, the news of their misadventure relayed back to Index. From the confines of a local guide shack we tipped a cold one to that guide.

Secretly, I know we were all thinking "*Whew!* glad it wasn't me!"

BURNT RANCH GORGE

*"There's no question the limits of river running have been
extended, the ante's been upped and the definition of a runnable
river sounds different today than it did a decade ago. What, after
all, is a Class VI rapid? Is it something <u>guaranteed</u> to kill you...
or just something that will scare you blind...?"*

David M. Bolling, River Runner Magazine

Everyone was wide-eyed. Bill was gone. I began to think that
these are the types of things that you read about in
newspapers, or on Charlie Walbridge's river accident
statistic sheets. My mood was rapidly deteriorating.

"Where's Bill?"

"Sheez, I don't know, I thought he was in *YOUR* boat!"

"Well, he was... but he didn't swim out of the rapid."

We were in the eddy below Lower Burnt Ranch Falls, a nasty
Class V rapid in the Trinity River's Burnt Ranch Gorge. No, *nasty*
doesn't sum it up... *disgusting* is the word. Here, the river
plummets about 15 feet in fifty yards as big boulders whip the
surface into an indecipherable frenzy. To make matters worse,
clean runs must start in a narrow chute, then make a big left to
right zig zag while lurching from hole to hole.

But somehow, Lower Burnt Ranch Falls has taken on a
reputation as being user-friendly. I mean, I've seen crews
practically set up a mid-rapid poker game while blindly slamming
through the big drops, and emerge unscathed.

But today was different. Our paddlers were coming unglued in
the moves just above the crux, and two out of four boats had
flipped. Fortunately, everyone survived the swim with little more
than a couple of charlie horses and bruised egos. Except for Bill.

Where the hell was Bill?!

A commercial trip down Burnt Ranch Gorge begins unlike any
other trip in the nation. After a brief guide's talk at the Cedar Flat
put-in, passengers are tossed right into the river... literally!
Flipping rafts, swimming rapids, and executing self rescues in
Class I and II rapids are de rigeur on the pre-trip agenda. This is
preventive medicine. As much a form of personal insurance as life

jackets and helmets.

Strange, you say? Hardly! Burnt Ranch Gorge is on the cutting edge of commercial whitewater, and passengers must be prepared for the inevitable bout with calamity.

I had seen this pattern—flip, swim, flip, swim—repeated many times before at Cedar Flat. And today was no exception. Following an hour or so of training, the crews appeared to be in ship shape. So we headed off downriver, ready for another day of great river running.

Gliding towards the first rapid—a shallow Class IV boulder garden known as China Slide—we marvelled at the huge rocky scar etched into the hills on the left bank. Here, in 1890, a half-mile long by thousand foot wide landslide dislodged from the south canyon wall, tore across the river, and backed the Trinity up for twelve miles! We paddled a narrow entry slot through the weathered debris and bounced down the final few feet through channels formed by nearly a century of erosion.

China Slide went by perfectly. Didn't even phase the crew, who had already honed their skills on other Class IV and V California rivers. But we hadn't even patted ourselves on the back when the Trinity tossed down the real welcome mat—Pearly Gates—where the Trinity River plunges eight feet into Box Canyon.

One by one, the rafts paddled out into the main current, ferried across to river left, and turned on a powerhouse of forward strokes. With unbridled whoops of excitement espewing from the passengers, the rafts plummeted down Pearly Gate's twisting ramp, and crashed deep into the churning hole at its base. The crews, soaked and smiling, shredded another big Burnt Ranch Gorge rapid without incident, and drifted safely into the calm waters of Box Canyon. Here, for the first time, vertical cliffs rose directly out of the deep, swirling currents, transforming the Trinity River's deep V-canyon into a true gorge.

Drifting out of Box Canyon, we found ourselves congealing as teams, sharing not only common kinships among river lovers, but our nervous anticipation for Burnt Ranch Gorge's bigger rapids —Upper, Middle, and Lower Burnt Ranch Falls.

Following a couple of Class III drops, the Trinity gave us one more chance to warm up for The Falls. Tight Squeeze, a life-size, aquatic version of bumper pool, clogged the river with car-sized boulders, leaving only narrow chutes and hairpin turns in their wake. Although Tight Squeeze is far from being one of Burnt Ranch's toughest rapids, I had good reason to approach it with caution.

On my first run down Burnt Ranch Gorge, I had miscalculated the current flowing across the entrance drop. In an instant, I found our raft slipping toward a deeply undercut wall. I hadn't even had a chance to shout another command before the raft jammed itself into the wrong chute, tipped up on its side, and planted itself vertically against the wall. Me and the four other crew members found ourselves encased between the raft and the wall, standing knee-high in fast water.

Two of us were able to push the raft far enough away from the wall to allow the remaining crew members to dive away from the raft, and into safer currents. This turned out to be a perfect strategy for the two of us, since the raft, unburdened by the dead weight from extra paddlers, soon popped free of the wall, landed flat, and finished up the run unscathed.

This time, Tight Squeeze would present no problems.

After another mile of increasingly difficult rapids, we slammed through the final 50 yards of ledges and holes above Upper Burnt Ranch Falls, and paddled eagerly into an eddy for a rest. Before we could run the Upper Falls' narrow slot, we relieved our rafts of some air.

Running the steep, narrow slot at Upper Burnt Ranch Falls is the ultimate mind bender. You take off on a power ferry from the eddy, dash across the tail waves of the last drop, and spin downstream to face a six to seven-foot slot. Then you hit a hard forward and wedge the boat into a narrow chasm between two giant house-rocks. While your front paddlers stare down a ten-foot slide to the pool below, the raft squirms and buckles as the current tries to slam-dunk it through the drop.

If you let enough air out of the thwarts, you'll simply spit free like a watermelon seed. Leave too much air in your raft, and you're likely to flip. Fortunately, all of our rafts took the melon seed approach and floated away in the safety of the bottom pool.

Just downstream, Middle Burnt Ranch Falls explodes into a whitewater fanfare that makes the Upper Falls look like a carousel ride. Now things begin to get serious. A four-foot entry drop, backed by a strong hole, must be run perfectly to avoid the worst part of the rapid. This means carving a right to left track across the face of the ledge and ending up in a micro-eddy protected by a wall on one side, and a boulder sieve on the other side. Then, you must slink the raft through a ten-foot wide channel before crashing over the two final seven-foot slides.

A clean run through Upper and Middle Burnt Ranch Falls would usually make most any paddler's day complete. But, due to some sort of perverse twist in Mother Nature's sense of humor, all that a successful run of these falls does is get you to the top of Lower Burnt Ranch Falls, definitely the baddest of the bunch.

We scouted Lower Burnt Ranch Falls long and hard, preparing ourselves mentally for the challenge. Psyched up and ready to go, we boarded our rafts and paddled through a narrow entry slot flanked by two leaning slabs of granite. In an instant, the canyonwalls melted to a gray blur as the rapid accelerated us through its staircase of raft-pounding holes. We held fast, jabbing our paddles deep into whatever current was available. And as fast as the rapid had started, the storm ended. We floated to the safety of a river-left eddy—hidden from view from the rapid—and waited for the next raft to come through.

In the eddy, it felt as if we'd arrived at our own surprise party. Paddles clacked in high-fives above our heads, and stories of fear and success filled the air like reminiscent conversations at a high school reunion.

Then it happened.

The next raft floated by upside down, followed by four bodies swimming frantically toward the eddy. I grabbed a throw line and pulled one swimmer in while the rest of my crew aided the others.

Once everyone was safely ashore, we made a head count: One, two, three, four ... wait, one, two, three, four... *OH NO! Bill! Where's Bill?!"*

"Bi-i-i-i-i-lll!!!"

Our situation below Lower Burnt Ranch Falls turned miserable. Two guides decided to get a closer look at the rapid by

Upper Burnt Ranch Falls is one of the highlights of any descent through Burnt Ranch Gorge, Trinity River, California.

climbing the steep cliff that blocked our view of the Lower Falls. However, after a few anxious moments, they returned with bad news. Bill wasn't anywhere.

Since he had to be *somewhere*, we thought the worst.

Maybe, when his raft flipped in the lower falls, Bill wedged a foot in something beneath the surface. While some of the remaining crew started up the cliff to see if they could find some sign of Bill, the rest of the crew simply took it upon themselves to keep yelling his name. This was part hope, part disbelief.

"Bill! Hey, Bill!"

"What?!"

"Hey did you hear that?!"

"No."

"Listen then,... Bill!'"

"What!"

"It's Bill," I thought. "Bill, where are you?!!"

"Under here..."

One of the rafts was talking! Well, actually, Bill's voice was coming from one of the overturned rafts.

In the midst of the post-flip chaos, no one ever bothered to flip the final raft back over again. Bill had to be under there. "Bill, are you under there?"

"Yeah."

He was really there. A hurricane of emotions overtook us. All at once I was relieved, elated... *pissed off.*

"Bill, come out of there!"

"No."

"What do you mean, no? COME OUT!!"

"NO!"

Bill had freaked. He must have blown a mental fuse during his swim. He wasn't about to leave the safety of his PVC cave.

"C'mon Bill, GET OUT OF THERE!!!"

"NO!!!"

We decided to flip the raft back over again. Then he'd have to come out. We tossed a flip-line over the boat, crawled up on a tube, and started pulling.

"Sheez, this feels heavy. I think he's holding on!"

"Bill, *let go!*"

"No!"

If we were going to get Bill out, we were going to have to pull the raft away from him. Three of us got on the rope and started pulling. Meanwhile, some of the other paddlers started lifting from the other side. The raft was finally coming over.

There was Bill, stuck to that thwart like a barnacle to a dock. But as the golden California sunshine touched his ashen face once again, his terror began to subside. We choked back some tears of joy, gave Bill a hug, and hiked him back to the camp.

As the campfire roared later that night, the tall tales started flying. Bill's story unfolded time and time again, slowly building to legendary status. Even today, the legend lives on... The legend of "Barnacle Bill."

POSTSCRIPT: Contemporary travellers to Burnt Ranch Gorge will not see the same Lower Burnt Ranch Falls that turned paddlers into stuttering, weak-kneed idiots. A massive landslide has created a totally new and different Lower Burnt Ranch Falls which is half the length, twice as steep, and just as fun as the old one. Enjoy!

EPILOGUE

"It is worth remembering that, long after we are gone, these rivers will still run to distant seas, and that our daughters and sons will want to stand on the banks, as we have done, transfixed by the magic of a river's music and lulled by its flow.... They deserve their inheritence. Their children do, as well. "

Paul Vasey, Rivers of America

I have been fortunate, over these past ten years, to witness the joy, the thrill, and the challenge that only whitewater rivers can bestow. While sliding down a smooth tongue, gliding toward the heart of a rapid, I feel a return to the elements, to primal forces far more powerful than the human spirit. On the river, I gain a deeper understanding of my own roots, and begin to understand humanity's reliance upon water for the sustenance of life itself.

And when away from the river, I feel a profound sense of displacement, affecting every aspect of my daily life, as if a part of me had been left at the last take-out.

This sense of interconnectedness has been shared by my predecessors, captured in timeless prose for boaters of all generations. John Muir, the grand architect of environmentalism, once professed, "The rivers flow not past, but through us, thrilling, tingling, vibrating every fiber and cell of the substance of our bodies, making them glide and sing." Henry David Thoreau, writing in his Journals, stated, "The river is my own highway, the only wild and unfenced part of the world hereabouts." And Chief Seattle's inspirational words have appeared with encouraging frequency: "The rivers are our brothers, they quench our thirst. The rivers carry our canoes and feed our children... and you must give to the rivers the kindness you would give any brother."

While contemporary whitewater enthusiasts look upon flowing waters with reverence and respect, others eye rivers as developable resources. A raw product to be harvested, transformed, and sold. The latter group appears in many forms—regional irrigation districts, private utility companies, the Army Corp of Engineers.

They come to the rivers not to float and enjoy the wonders of wilderness, but to dam and divert them, shackling eternal waters behind the transient insults of concrete and steel.

I have strained to eloquently capture my own feelings on this latter type of "river use" but have fallen quite short of my goal. So, instead, I have deferred to the poetry of Margaret Hindes, whose beautiful verse I read in William O. Douglas' "My Wilderness":

Gone, desecrated for a dam —
Pines, stream, and trails
Burned and bare
Down to dust.
Now water fills the hollow,
Water for power,
But the bowl of wilderness
Is broken, forever.

Rivers are the veins of the earth. The lifeblood of the planet. They feed and nourish the land, and rinse away the trivial monuments of man's arrogance, mindless of humanity's misbegotten pride. Rivers are there for all of us to view, to float, and to enjoy. They carry our dreams, and the dreams of future generations.

Whether you ever see any of the rivers in this book, or simply relive our experiences from the comfort of your easy chair, it is you who can help preserve rivers for everyone. Take the first step by getting involved—from joining your local whitewater club to supporting national environmental groups. Then, let the river's own wealth of inspiration kindle your energies and foster your own desires to preserve free flowing water for everyone to enjoy.

I leave you with these words, passed along by Tanaka Shozo: "The care of rivers is not a question of rivers, but of the human heart."

Put some heart into your rivers and they'll last forever.

SECTION TWO:
A GUIDE TO THE RIVERS

INTRODUCTION: This guidebook covers a broad range of whitewater rivers, from commonly paddled expert runs such as the Gauley, Colorado, and Tuolumne, to rare descents on the Middle Fork Kings and the Black Canyon of the Gunnison. Although this guidebook covers all of the rivers and runs in Section One of this book, mere mention of a river in this guidebook doesn't mean that it is runnable, that we recommend that you try it, or that this guidebook will get you down it. Rely on your own knowledge and judgment in selecting rivers that are within your skill level.

BIG SANDY CREEK, West Virginia ■■■■■■■■■■■■■■■

SECTION: Rockville to Cheat River
REGION: Preston County
CLASS: IV-V (One V+)
MILES: 5.5
GRADIENT: two at 30, 3.5 at 80
WATER LEVELS: Needs 5.2 to 5.8 on the Rockville Gauge to be runnable, with a maximum of about 6.5 to 7.0
SEASON: Winter, Spring, occasionally in the Summer
GAUGE: Call (412) 644-2890 to get the level at Rockville
USGS QUADS: Bruceton Mills, Valley Point

DESCRIPTION: The Big Sandy has five very distinct rapids, ranging from big boulder gardens to huge, heart-pounding waterfalls. Numerous Class III-IV rapids intermingle with the biggest drops.

One-and-a-half miles into the trip, a series of rapids leads to 18-foot high Big Sandy Falls (also called Wonder Falls). Next, a quarter mile of rapids leads to Undercut Rock (Class IV). Then there's Zoom Flume, an eight to ten-foot Class IV drop. The next big rapid is Little Splat, an extremely complex Class IV-V rapid. Big Splat, an awesome 25-foot high rapid that ends with a 16 to 18-foot high Class V+ drop that lands on Splat Rock, is the next obstacle. Finally, a long section of Class IV-V rapids leads to an island, where you'll find Class V Island Drop, a big rapid containing two drops. After Second Island (Class III-IV), take a deep breath and celebrate!

LOGISTICS: The put-in is just below the bridge in Rockville, which can be reached by "73/73" crossing over Laurel Run. The take-out can be found on the left bank of the Big Sandy where it runs into the Cheat River. (Best Guidebooks: Wildwater West Virginia, Appalachian Whitewater Vol. II)

CHEAT RIVER, West Virginia ▰▰▰▰▰▰▰▰▰

SECTION: "Cheat Canyon," Albright, WV 26 Bridge to
                 Jenkinsburg Bridge
REGION: Preston County
CLASS: III-V
MILES: 11
GRADIENT: 25
WATER LEVELS: 1.0 to 6.0 on the Albright, WV, 26 Bridge
SEASON: All year possible
GAUGE: National Weather Service in Pittsburgh (412) 644-2890,
             or the Cheat River Campground (304) 329-1299
USGS QUADS: Kingwood, Valley Point

DESCRIPTION: The post-flood Cheat is one great river! It is the largest free-flowing river east of the Mississippi, and displays a boulder-strewn riverbed set in a remote, steep-walled canyon. There are more than 38 rapids rated Class III or better.

The highlights begin with Decision, a long Class III+ rock garden that ends with some exciting ledges. Big Nasty, about three-and-a-half miles into the trip, contains a huge Class IV to V boat-eating ledge-hole that regularly devours large rafts. Two miles later, the river drops through another long rapid known as Even Nastier (Class III-IV).

About two-thirds of the way through the run, the river bends to the right along a high sandstone cliff that rises on the left. This signifies Class IV to V High Falls, a wide reef that drops into a natural ampitheater. Coming out of High Falls, you'll next run into Maze (Class III-IV) then Coliseum (Class IV-V). Upper Coliseum contains a 50-foot wide channel stuffed with a channel-wide hydraulic, then Lower Coliseum (also known as Pete Morgan's) caps off the biggest rapids on the run.

LOGISTICS: The put-in is at the Albright Bridge, the take-out is on river right at the Jenkinsburg Bridge, just above the confluence with Big Sandy Creek. (Best Guidebooks: Wildwater West Virginia, Appalachian Whitewater Vol. II)

CHUYA RIVER, Russia ▬▬▬▬▬▬▬▬▬▬▬▬▬▬▬▬

SECTION: Aktaash to the Katun River or Chemal
REGION: About 200 kilometers south of Garn-altaisk in
Gornoaltaisk, which is in the Siberian part of Russia
CLASS: V-VI in Mushoe Cascade section (upper section), then
Class III-IV(V) in lower section
MILES: About 8 for the upper section, about 15 for the
lower section, plus a few miles on the Katun River
GRADIENT: About 150 to 200 feet per mile on the upper section,
then tapers off dramatically. Gradient of lower run
unknown.
WATER LEVELS: 2,000 cfs ideal
SEASON: After the Spring floods; usually late June, July except
after heavy rains

DESCRIPTION: The Chuya River was made famous in 1989 when the Chuya Rally opened its doors to international competitors, opening a new era of rafting competition and comraderie. The description set out below is rough and merely provides an overview of the Chuya River since it is difficult to describe the river with the same accuracy as others listed in this book

The upper section, commonly known as Mushoe Cascade, contains an unbelievable series of Class V-VI cataracts set in an ominous gorge. Although it is well known by Russian hair boaters, many have died on this section. Don't try it unless you're with veterans of this run.

The upper section ends after about eight miles when the

canyon walls give way to the high plateau country that characterizes the lower section. The lower run is about 15 miles long and is Class III-IV with a couple of Class V's. One Class V, Begemot (Hippopotamus) is right in the race course for the Chuya Rally and contains a powerful stopper at high water. Many paddlers on the lower Chuya River travel onto the Katun River, which is a giant Grand Canyon-like run which can have flows of 15,000 to 200,000 cfs! This run contains huge, fun waves and some large holes that should be avoided.

LOGISTICS: Jib Ellison at Project RAFT started describing the shuttle to me as "First, get on a plane, travel half-way around the world, then get on a bus...." You get the picture. The Chuya River is in the middle of nowhere, deep in the recesses of Siberia. Before you pack your bags, call Project RAFT at (510) 704-8222 for more information.

COLORADO RIVER, Arizona ■■■■■■■■■■■■■■■

SECTION: "The Grand Canyon," Lee's Ferry to Lake Mead
REGION: Coconino and Mohave Counties; Grand Canyon
       National Park
CLASS: II-V
MILES: Up to 230 river miles, 47 lake miles
GRADIENT: 8
WATER LEVELS: 5,000 cfs on up
SEASON: All year
GAUGE: Bureau of Reclamation (801) 539-1311 or the National
      Park Service (602) 638-7843
USGS QUADS: Too many to mention!
PERMITS: Write to the River Permits Office, National Park
      Service, Grand Canyon National Park, PO Box 129,
      Grand Canyon, AZ 86023 or call (602) 638-7843.

DESCRIPTION: The Grand Canyon of the Colorado River is one of America's premier whitewater runs, and probably the best known. In its 230 mile long canyon, the Colorado carves its way through mind-bending canyons, past inviting campsites, and through world-class rapids. Most people make the run in about 10 to 18 days, and it's best enjoyed when there's ample time to hike the side canyons, relax, and enjoy the scenery. 113 to 200 rapids—including the more famous drops like Lava Falls, Crystal, Hermit, Granite, Upset, and others—will excite even brain-dead veterans!

LOGISTICS: The Grand Canyon has a wealth of information available in the form of guidebooks. The put-in is at Lee's Ferry and the take-out is at Pearce Ferry. The trip can also be broken up into smaller segments. The upper trip is from Lee's Ferry to Phantom Ranch, is 87 miles long, and ends with an arduous nine miles hike out of the canyon. Phantom Ranch can also be a starting point for some people who meet up with their rafts, is 138 miles long, and involves the same hike (but at least it's downhill). Additional logistics are best left to specific guidebooks to the area. (Best Guidebooks: The Colorado River in Grand Canyon, Grand Canyon River Guide, Rivers of the Southwest)

COLORADO RIVER, Colorado ■■■■■■■■■■

SECTION: "Gore Canyon," Kremmling to the Pumphouse
REGION: Grand County
CLASS: V
MILES: 11
GRADIENT: 32 avg., 100 max.
WATER LEVELS: 1,000 to 1,500 cfs is optimum; has been run
              as low as 300 cfs, and some hair boaters run
              it up to insane levels of 4,000-5,000 cfs
SEASON: Best late Summer after peak snowmelt; but it can be run
        from April until freeze-up in mid-November when
        water levels are within the recommended levels
GAUGE: Get the USGS gauge for the Colorado near Kremmling
       from the National Weather Service at (303) 691-4393 or
       from the Lakewood USGS Office at (303) 236-5825
USGS MAPS: Kremmling, Mt. Powell, Radium

DESCRIPTION: The Gore Canyon section of the Upper

Colorado is called a great Class V play run by some and a scary Class V river by others. It has been paddled by all sorts of people and even plays home to the Gore Canyon races the last weekend in August of each year. No matter what your opinion, it's a wild and exciting river with some great Class V rapids.

If you put in at the Highway 9 bridge you'll find three miles of painfully slow water that takes about 1-1/4 hours to paddle. The short hike in down the road cuts off this nuisance. The whitewater starts with some fun, playful Class III rapids that pick up just past the Satellite water station on the right. The first real rapid is called Applesauce (Class IV) which is a short, trashy ten-foot slide with a big rock at the bottom. Class III rapids continue to Gore Rapid, less than one mile downstream. Gore Rapid (Class V) is a quarter mile long rapid that starts with some strong moves amidst aerated hydraulics to avoid a boulder sieve, then enters a long series of holes. Continuous Class III and IV rapids continue from the bottom of Gore Rapid to Pyrite Falls 1/4 mile downstream. Pyrite Falls is often considered the last drop in Gore Rapid and is a big Class IV+ drop that contains a shallow shelf on the left (an ankle buster at low water) and a center rock with chutes left and right.

There is a blind drop between Gore Rapid and the next big drop, Tunnel Falls, which should be scouted. Tunnel Falls is a ten-foot high horseshoe shaped ledge with a big hole at its base. There is an interesting run on the left with a 90 degree sliding turn over shallow sliding rocks, a hero chute right into the hole, and a tough ski-jump move on the right. Another half-mile of Class III and IV rapids begin just below Tunnel Falls and continues to a calm pool flanked by a sheer cliff on the left bank just above the next rapid, Toilet Bowl, the most dastardly drop on the trip.

Even though Toilet Bowl looks less austere than the classic rapids upstream, this short weir-like structure can capture and hold both boats and paddlers in its twenty-foot backwash. Anybody caught in its trough is guaranteed a rough swim so paddle like hell and avoid the right side.

The final rapid, Kirschbaum, is a long series of big rocks and big holes that ends with some nasty sieves on the right. It is a great eddy-hopping rapid for veteran paddlers. After Kirschbaum a couple of miles of Class II and III rapids lead to the take-out.

LOGISTICS: The put-in is on a small strip of BLM ground on the northeast side of the Hwy 9 bridge about a half-mile south of the town of Kremmling. Some people use an alternate put-in to avoid the flatwater section, but we're not sure what the current legal status of this put-in is. Check with the locals before trying it. This put-in is found by taking the first left off of Hwy 40 just west of Kremmling adjacent to the highway maintenance facility. Follow this road to a fork and keep going straight (not right) to a locked gate. From there it's a fifteen minute hike down the road to the river. The take-out is reached by going 3/4 mile further south on Hwy 9 from the regular put-in bridge, then turning right on a road marked "State Bridge/Pumphouse Recreation Area." Follow this road about nine miles to the the take-out at the pumphouse. (Best Guidebooks: Colorado Whitewater, The Floater's Guide to Colorado, Western Whitewater)

COLORADO RIVER, Utah ▬▬▬▬▬▬

SECTION: "Cataract Canyon," Moab to Lake Powell
REGION: Grand, Wayne, San Juan, Garfield Counties;
          Canyonlands NP
CLASS: II-IV+
MILES: Up to 112 depending where you put in
GRADIENT: 11; 29 in Mile Long and Big Drop
WATER LEVELS: 4,000 to 60,000 cfs
SEASON: All year
GAUGE: Colorado River at Cataract Canyon, Bureau of
          Reclamation in Salt Lake City: (801) 539-1311
USGS MAPS: Too numerous to mention
PERMITS: Available through Superintendant, Canyonlands
          National Park, Moab, Utah 84532; (801) 259-7164

DESCRIPTION: The Cataract Canyon section of the Colorado below the Green River confluence is home to some legendary big water, rivaling that of the Grand Canyon during peak runoff.

If you put in near Moab, the trip starts with lots of flatwater. The Green River accesses are a little more exciting. Most of the action comes in 16-mile long Cataract Canyon itself, with the worst rapids (Mile Long, Big Drop, Satan's Seat, Satan's Gut, and others) in the final three miles above Lake Powell. Make sure you've got the back of an olympic rower if you don't have a powerboat to drag you 27 miles across Lake Powell to the take-out.

LOGISTICS: The Moab put-in is actually at the Potash Mine 17 miles downriver from Moab off of Scenic Hwy 279. The take-out is at Hite Marina on the south side of Lake Powell near the State Route 95 bridge. (Best Guidebooks: River Runners Guide to Utah and Adjacent Areas, Canyonlands River Guide, Western Whitewater)

GAULEY RIVER, West Virginia ■■■■■■■■■■■■■

SECTION: Both "Upper" and "Lower" runs; Summersville Dam
        to Swiss
REGION: Nicholas and Fayette Counties
CLASS: Upper Section (To Koontz Flume) is Class IV and V,
        Lower Section (Koontz Flume to Swiss) is Class III and
        IV with some V
MILES: Upper is 16; Lower is 8
GRADIENT: 28
WATER LEVELS: 800 to 5,000 (2.4 to 4.5 on Belva Gauge);
        2,500 is considered optimum
SEASON: Best during the 20 days of dam released flows in
        September and October
GAUGE: US Army Corps of Engineers at (304) 529-5127 (for
        flow at Summersville Dam); Summersville Dam
        (304) 872-5809; National Weather Service in Charleston
        for the Belva Gauge (304) 342-7771
USGS MAPS: Summersville Dam, Ansted

DESCRIPTION: The Gauley is *THEE* river of the East. It is where all the hotshots go to strut their stuff, and commercial rafting passengers go to scare themselves silly.

Upper Section: At the standard flow of 2,500 cfs, the 15-mile

Pillow Rock on the Gauley River, West Virginia... where the forces of geology and hydrology battle. (Photo by Kathy Rech, North American River Runners)

upper section, from Summersville Dam to Swiss, is the toughest part of the run. If the Meadow River (about 4.75 miles into the run) is pumping more than a nominal flow into the Gauley, things will get *very* exciting on this run! The river gets going one-half mile downstream of the dam with Class III-IV Initiation and gradually builds until, two miles into the trip, boaters run into Class V Insignificant. Here, the Gauley descends through a series of big, but somewhat avoidable, holes and ledges that tend to munch rafts and kayaks alike. Pillow Rock, at mile four, is one of the river's best known Class V rapids. Here, the river piles through 80 yards of foam and fury as it crashes toward an apartment-sized rock on the left bank where it pillows, falls toward a volkswagen-sized rock, and spits boaters out. Big fun! Around mile five, after the Meadow River confluence, you'll run into Class V Lost Paddle and Class IV Tumblehome. This rapid-combo provides a one-third mile jaunt through huge holes, strange hydraulics, and past nasty undercuts. At mile seven, Iron Ring (Class V-V+) presents one of the river's most fierce obstacles. Attempts to blast a passage for floating logs downstream here in the early 1900's created a mid-stream obstruction that makes route-finding perilous from one's boat. Sweet's Falls (Class V), at mile eight, provides an exciting descent over a ten-foot sliding falls into a big aerated hole. If you've survived this far, you'll make it through the "easy water" to Koontz Flume without any problem.

Lower Section: Again, at the standard release level of 2,500 cfs, the lower run starts with a great rollercoaster ride through big waves and a big hole at Class IV-V Koontz Flume. The other significant rapids include Class IV Lower Mash (big holes and a u-shaped ledge), Class IV Gateway to Heaven (a weaving path past big holes and between two big rocks), Class III-IV The Hole (aptly named and sufficiently descriptive), and Class IV-V Pure Screaming Hell (the final mad zig-zagging dash past even bigger holes and strainers).

LOGISTICS: The Summersville Dam put-in is found by heading south, then west, from the town of Summersville. Non-commercial paddlers can take out at Carnifex Ferry at the mouth of the Meadow River or at Panther Creek Road (a dirt road—Route 22—leads to the half-mile trail to the river). There are other take-outs too, but the last take-out is one mile upriver from the town of Swiss along Route 19/25. Call one of the local outfitters for advice or help with shuttles! (Best Guidebooks: *Appalachian Whitewater Vol. II, Whitewater Home Companion Vol. I, Wildwater West Virginia, Vol. II*)

GUNNISON RIVER, Colorado ▬▬▬▬▬▬▬▬

SECTION: "Black Canyon of the Gunnison," East Portal (3.5 miles downstream from Crystal Dam Outlet) to the North Fork Confluence
REGION: Black Canyon National Monument, Northeast of Montrose in Montrose County
CLASS: V-VI
MILES: 29.5
GRADIENT: 98 avg; 240 max.
WATER LEVELS: Best around 450-600 cfs; do not run higher!
SEASON: Late Summer
GAUGE: Contact Black Canyon of the Gunnison Monument for information at (303) 249-7036 or call (801) 539-1311
USGS MAPS: Grizzly Ridge, Red Rock Canyon, Smith Fork
PERMISSION: Required in advance by Black Canyon of the Gunnison N.M.. Write or call early or you'll get turned away at the river!

DESCRIPTION: From Crystal Dam to the East Portal of the Gunnison water diversion tunnel there is 3.5 miles of Class III and IV rapids. Once boaters pass the East Portal, things get very serious. The river begins to drop 100 to 240 feet per mile through boulder choked Class V rapids in the heart of one of the least accessible gorges in America (unless you're into technical rockclimbing). There are numerous mandatory portages, some of which are very difficult. The second day usually starts with a mile-long portage that can take many hours! Ropes are generally carried to facilitate portaging. Once past Red Rock Canyon (11 miles into the run), the gradient drops off to 24 feet per mile as the river carves its way through delightful rapids before meeting with the

North Fork.

LOGISTICS: To reach the put-in drive east on Hwy 50 out of Montrose about eight miles then turn north following signs to the Black Canyon of the Gunnison National Monument. Before entering the Monument, turn right on a road marked "East Portal" and follow it down to the East Portal put-in. The take-out is at a campground that's at the end of a one-mile long spur road marked with a BLM sign that says "Gunnison River Forks." This road cuts south off C-92 about six miles east of Austin (if you hit railroad tracks crossing C-92 you went a quarter-mile too far). This road is also about five minutes west of Hotchkiss. (Best Guidebooks: Colorado Whitewater, The Floater's Guide to Colorado, River Runners' Guide to Utah and Adjacent Areas)

KINGS RIVER, California ▬▬▬▬▬▬▬▬▬

SECTION: "The Upper Kings," Confluence of Middle and South Forks to Garnet Dike Campground
REGION: Kings Canyon National Park, Sequoia National Forest
CLASS: V+
MILES: 10
GRADIENT: 100
WATER LEVELS: 500 to 2,000 cfs, 1,000 to 1,500 optimum
SEASON: Best after peak snowmelt, usually late June to late July
GAUGE: Kings at Rogers Crossing gives flow at take-out (916) 653-9647
USGS MAPS: Tehipite Dome, Patterson Mountain

DESCRIPTION: This is one of California's premier wilderness trips. The long shuttle and hike-in are overshadowed by the incredible whitewater and majestic scenery. Plan on two days to enjoy the entire ten mile trip, or put in early for a one-day trip.

The whitewater begins a few hundred yards below the put-in with Class III to IV Butthole Surfer and keeps getting tougher. The most difficult section is between miles three and five. This section begins with awe-inspiring Warp Two and Cassady Falls. Warp Two is a ten-foot high slide that sends boaters downriver at warp speed toward Cassady Falls, a horseshoe shaped cauldron wherein the river plunges ten feet into huge boils and foam. The next major rapid, That's Dumb, contains a single steep drop into a massive recirculating hole. Few boats make it through this hole intact.

The rapids mentioned above will seem like a mere warm up when you reach the section between Garlic Creek Falls and Rough Creek Falls. Here the river pinches down between massive cliffs, and both of these creeks cascade down the right wall. When you see the first waterfall, pull over to the left bank to scout. The river drops 160 feet per mile in this section through big boulders and steep drops. Portaging in this section is very difficult because cliffs actually close in on both sides of the river and some huge boulders block the eddies.

The rest of the rapids are pool-drop with massive boulders and ledges, and everything has been run. Portages are usually not too difficult elsewhere along the river. There aren't really any good campsites on this section except at mile 4.7. Bring your Therm-a-Rest and be prepared to deal with what you find.

LOGISTICS: This is one gnarly shuttle! Take Hwy 180 through Sequoia Nat. Pk. to Kings Canyon Nat. Pk. and follow it to a small shoulder/turn-out at Yucca Point 16 miles northeast of Grant Cove Village. The two-mile trail to the river starts here. To find the take-out, follow Trimmer Springs Road from Centerville (18 miles east of Fresno) past Piedra and Pine Flat Reservoir. Eventually, the road turns to awful dirt. Garnet Dike Campground is near the end of the driveable section of road. (Best Guidebooks: California Whitewater; A Guide to the Best Whitewater in the State of California; Western Whitewater)

KINGS RIVER, MIDDLE FORK, California ▬▬▬▬

SECTION: Dusy Branch to Yucca Point Trail
CLASS: V-VI
MILES: 12 to 29
GRADIENT: 222 avg, 260 avg in last 5 miles with stretches
between 300 to 400 feet per mile, and over 500 feet
per mile in the top half of the full run!
WATER LEVELS: 500-1,500
SEASON: Summer
GAUGE: 1/2 of the Kings at Roger's Crossing (916) 653-9647
USGS MAPS: Tehipite Dome, Marion Peak, Mt. Goddard

DESCRIPTION: Totally bitchin'! If you need to know more, read
Mike Doyle's story, then put your boat on your car, turn the pages
of the guidebook, and head toward another river!

LOGISTICS: See the previous Kings story for the take-out,
and consult the topos for a put-in. (Best Guidebook: A Guide to
the Best Whitewater in the State of California)

NEW RIVER, West Virginia ▬▬▬▬▬▬▬

SECTION: Thurmond to Fayette Station
REGION: Fayette County
CLASS: III-V
MILES: 14
GRADIENT: 15
WATER LEVELS: Great run over a broad range of flows. Low
water trips can be made at 2,000 cfs or lower. The river starts
to be considered "high" at 6,000 cfs, and "very high" at 8,000
cfs, although it is run much higher by experts. The New is run
from -1.5 to 12 feet on the Fayette Station gauge; it's best
from -0.5 feet (about 2,000 cfs) to 3.0 feet (about 6,000 cfs)
and really starts rockin' above 4 to 5 feet (about 8,000 cfs)!
SEASON: All year
GAUGE: Call the US Army Corps of Engineers, Huntington, at
304-529-5127. There is an additional paddler's gauge on
the New River at the Fayette Station take-out.
USGS MAPS: Thurmond, Fayetteville

DESCRIPTION: The "New" is synonymous with "Big Water"! Though the river begins with a long, easy stretch, the second half of the run contains lots of heavy water action—big waves and holes. The excitement starts with a jarring hole at Surprise (Class III-IV) about four miles into the trip. Three miles downstream the river drops through Upper Railroad Rapids (a Class III-IV shelf-drop with a big hole) and Lower Railroad (a Class IV cascade through boulders).

The biggest rapids—the Keeney Brothers—start nine miles into the trip. Class III Upper Keeney, Class IV Middle Keeney, and Class IV-V Lower Keeney contain big waves, big holes, and offer big-time thrills! Between 5 and 12 feet, the Keeneys become one giant nerve-wracking ride through mammoth hydraulics and holes. Serious Class V! Ten miles into the trip, paddlers approach the most technical rapid, Class IV-V Sunset, A.K.A. Double Z. After Double Z look out for Greyhound Bus Stopper, an aptly named ledge that can swallow a bus whole. Class IV-V Undercut Rock, A.K.A. Miller's Folley, is at mile 12 and has a nasty undercut rock at the top right and a nasty drop called Bloody Nose on the lower left.

If you decide to take out at the Fayette Station bridge, you'll miss one of the most fun rapids on the trip. Fayette Station is a classic Class IV rapid with big waves and some well-concealed holes. It is a great ending to a great trip.

LOGISTICS: The put-in is behind the parking lot at the Thurmond Store, which is found by taking Rte. 25 from US 19. The take-out is in the cove on the left below the Fayette Station rapids on private property belonging to Wildwater Unlimited. It's a quarter-mile carry to your car. (Best Guidebooks: Appalachian Whitewater Vol. II, Whitewater Home Companion Vol. I, Wildwater West Virginia, Vol. II)

PACIFIC OCEAN, Western United States ▬▬▬▬

SECTION: Washington, Oregon and California coastline
CLASS: I to VI depending on off-shore weather patterns
MILES: Hundreds and hundreds
GRADIENT: 0', but it feels steeper
WATER LEVELS: N/A
SEASON: All year
GAUGE: N/A; however, many National Weather Service stations
    provide information on wave height and wave intervals
PREFERRED CRAFT: Cruise ships, sport fishing vessels and self-
    bailing rafts
USGS MAPS: Too numerous too mention. Better off using an
    AAA map

DESCRIPTION: Despite man's best efforts to tame and harness the earth's water supply, some water is simply to powerful and plentiful to dam or divert. Such is the case with the Pacific Ocean.

Long after your other favorite rivers dry up, this one's still running. Check it out during moderate swells and be prepared for an all-out beach assault together with some strange looks from beach-combers and vacation-goers. Fortunately, there is enough ocean frontage available so that you can pursue the somewhat embarrassing activity of surf-rafting in the privacy of your own cove.

The authors highly recommend that you don't choose a popular surfing location. Chances are you'll really piss off the locals, and probably get your car tires slashed.

LOGISTICS: Head west until you hit water, then drive north or south until you find a nice point break.

PACUARE RIVER, Costa Rica ▬▬▬▬▬

SECTION: "The Upper Pacuare," Bajo Pacuare to San Martin
CLASS: V-VI
MILES: 15
GRADIENT: 76 to 109
WATER LEVELS: 900 to 1,400 optimum
SEASON: All year possible; highest September through December
GAUGE: N/A; But, for more info, contact Rios Tropicales, S.A.
  at P.O. Box 472-1200, Pavas, Costa Rica, phone (506) 33-
  6455; here in the U.S., contact the Nantahala Outdoor Center
  at (704) 488-2175 or Alder Creek Adventures at (503) 668-
  3121 or consult Mayfield's and Gallo's "The Rivers of Costa
  Rica" for additional outfitters who may be able to give up-to-
  date information.

DESCRIPTION: This is one of the world's premier Class V trips.
The Pacuare is a medium-sized river that carves its way through
an extraordinary jungle canyon.

At the recommended level of 1,300 cfs, the run begins with
easy Class II and III rapids in a low valley that get more difficult
as you proceed downriver into the steeper canyons. The big rapids
contain big boulders and sharp ledges backed by strong holes and
swirling hydraulics. A heavy rain early in the day can bring the
water level up *fast* and can create some mind-boggling whitewater.
Scout everything your first time down!

Two standout rapids are Hydraulic Blood (Class V-V+) and
Bobo Falls (unrunnable after the 1991 earthquakes). Both are in
narrow canyons and can be scouted with some difficulty. Scout
Hydraulic Blood from the precipitous left cliff for a zig-zag route
through the big drops, and scout Bobo Falls while carrying your
boat over the boulders along the shelves on the right.

LOGISTICS: The put-in is at a steel bridge at Bajo Pacuare
which is about an hour's drive southeast from Angostura or
Turrialbe. The take-out is at the end of an awful dirt road that
leads down into the canyon from the vicinity of Tres Equis which
is about an hour's drive northeast from Angostura or Turrialbe.
(Best Guidebook: The Rivers of Costa Rica)

PAYETTE RIVER, NORTH FORK, Idaho ▬▬▬▬▬

SECTION: Smith's Ferry to Banks
REGION: Boise County
CLASS: V-V+
MILES: 16
GRADIENT: 106 avg, well over 200 in places
WATER LEVELS: 1,000-1,700 is Class IV-V; 1,700-3,000 is
                 Class V; 3,000+ is V-VI (best for 1st-timers:
                 1,200-1,500)
SEASON: May, July, August, September
GAUGE: Get the Cascade Reservoir outflow from the National
        Weather Service at (208) 334-9867, or call the National
        Weather Service at (208) 334-9867 or the Idaho
        Department of Water Resources at (208) 327-7900
USGS MAPS: McCall, No Business Mtn., Cascade, Smith's Ferry

DESCRIPTION: OK, I've got to admit it. I get nervous even trying to describe the North Fork of the Payette. It's not that any one of the rapids is so scary, it's the fact that they line up nearly back to back for 16 miles.

First timers to the North Fork can divide the run into two parts and begin learning the rapids before committing to the entire run. The lower run (5 miles or so), is only Class IV to IV+ and can be scouted from Hwy 55, which follows the entire run. It contains very obvious rapids like Houndstooth, Juicer, Otter's Run, and Crunch that can and should be scouted from the road. The cool thing about this part of the Payette is that you get the feel for the river without the mega-high danger factors found upstream. Some folks go a little further upstream to the big turn-out near Swinging Bridge Campground to add two tougher rapids, Screaming Left Turn and Jaws, to the lower run.

If you have trouble with any of the rapids on the lower section, go find another river. If they're unintimidating and fun, start driving upstream along Hwy 55, scouting everything along the way. The run from Smith's Ferry starts with Steepness, a plunging rapid that quickly descends through foaming holes and mini-cascades. Near milemarker 93, Nutcracker contains a couple of big holes and one rock that divides the current. At milemarker 88,

The Lower North Fork Payette provides an exciting introduction to the Payette's incredible whitewater.

Bouncer Down The Middle presents a long stairstepped rapid through some sharp ledge-holes that ends at a curve with a river-wide hole.

The most intense whitewater is two miles downstream of Bouncer at Jacob's Ladder and Golf Course. Jacob's Ladder is a long stampede of foam and fury that contains mind-boggling hydraulics and do-or-die moves. The last big drop in Jacob's Ladder dumps boaters into the upper end of Golf Course, a boulder-riddled scramble through a minefield of short ledges. If you survive all of this, get out of your boat at Swinging Bridge and kiss the ground!

LOGISTICS: Hwy 55 heads north from the Boise area right to the take-out at Banks then continues along the river to the put-in at Smith's Ferry. What more could you ask for? (Best Guidebooks: Idaho, the Whitewater State; Idaho Whitewater; Western Whitewater)

REVENTAZON RIVER, Costa Rica ▬▬▬▬▬▬

SECTION: "The Peralta Section" and the "Pasqua Section,"
        Angostura to Siquirres
CLASS: V to Peralta, IV+ past Peralta
MILES: 9.1 miles from Angostura to Peralta, 16
        miles Peralta to Siquirres
GRADIENT: Upper run: 68 to 85; Lower run: 55
WATER LEVELS: 2,000 to 4,000 cfs is best for first-timers
SEASON: All year except during high water. Usually highest
        during the rainy season from September through
        December
GAUGE: Vertical gauge just downstream of the bridge at
        Angostura; 1.15 feet=2,000 cfs, and 1.8 feet=4,000 cfs

DESCRIPTION: The Peralta Run on the Reventazon has been compared to the Gauley, but one notch tougher, and to the Grand Canyon of the Colorado, without the flatwater or eddies. Still, both descriptions seem to fall short of describing this remarkable run.

First-timers should keep their eyes open for a right bend in the river a few miles into the trip with a rock wall on the right. This marks Class V+-VI Jungle Run, an unbelievable rapid that descends steeply through a series of holes, any of which could separate a boater from his boat as well as brains from the boater. Fortunately, there's a sneak route through shallow boulder gardens on the left... use it! Beyond Jungle Run, boaters will be on lightning fast water with big waves and brown, churning hydraulics. Each time you get used to the awesome proportions of the wave trains, a big hole jumps out and pounces on you like a hungry lion. Keep your eyes open!

Downstream of the Turrialbe River confluence, start looking for El Horrendo, A.K.A. Lava Central. Here, the river drops about 25 feet in 75 yards through giant exploding waves. The next rapid, La Ceja, is an easier version of El Horrendo. Next, there's Piedra de Fuego (Rock of Fire), a river-wide ledge backed by a keeper hole. Take the left side sneak route. The final rapid, Land of a Thousand Holes, is within sight of the take-out at a footbridge. Check out the long line of keepers from the right bank, smile, then get back in your boat and stay right to avoid all of them. If you swim here, you'll miss the take-out and probably wave goodbye to your equipment.

The Pasqua section, from Peralta to Siquirres is much like a toned-down version of the Peralta run. There are still many big rapids with towering waves and big holes in the upper half of the run, but it gets easier the closer you get to the take-out. This would be a good warm-up for the more difficult Peralta run.

LOGISTICS: The put-in is at the bridge in Angostura (southeast of Turrialbe) and the take-out is at the highway bridge near Siquirres. For more information contact Rios Tropicales at (506) 33-6455, Nantahala Outdoor Center at (704) 488-2175, or Alder Creek Adventures at (503) 668-3121 (Best Guidebook: The Rivers of Costa Rica)

RIO GRANDE RIVER, New Mexico ━━━━━━━━

SECTION: "The Upper Taos Box," Chiflo Trail to Dunn Bridge
REGION: Taos and Rio Arriba Counties
CLASS: V-VI
MILES: 20
GRADIENT: 120 in the Upper Box, then tapers off dramatically
         for the rest of the trip to the take-out
WATER LEVELS: 500-2,000
SEASON: April-June
GAUGE: Call the BLM at (505) 758-8851 or get the Embudo
       gauge at (505) 243-0702
USGS MAPS: Guadalupe Mountain, Arroyo Hondo
PERMITS: Must be obtained from Wild and Scenic
         Headquarters/BLM at Taos Resource Area, PO Box
         1045, Taos, NM 87571; (505)758-8851

DESCRIPTION: This is the most ferocious section on the Rio Grande, and is usually run lower than 2,000 cfs for safety. The infamous Upper Taos Box is actually an eight mile section between Chiflo Trail and the Little Arsenic Spring Trail. However, the next section upstream, commonly called the Razorblade Run (a Class IV trip), can be added. That adds another seven miles of river. Then, to avoid the hassle of hiking out of the canyon, many paddlers run the final eight miles of whitewater down to Dunn Bridge. The full trip takes two days and is 22 miles long.

The Upper Box run starts with a mile or so of Class II to IV whitewater and long, easy sections, before a powerline crosses high over the canyon. Here, the river crashes into Upper Powerline Rapid and begins gnawing its way through an intimidating series of Class V to VI rapids. The next rapid, Class V+ N.C.O. starts with a six-foot drop, then slams through confusing whitewater on its way through Hell Hole and on toward Undercut Rock. Undercut Rock is usually portaged. Next, there's Long Rapids, about a quarter-mile section of Class IV and V whitewater with only one short break near the middle. Then there's Boulder Fan, a Class V slalom amidst nasty chutes and ledges which is also often portaged at higher flows.

If you survive this, there is the Great Calm to air your brain out. At mile six you'll hit the two toughest rapids on the river, Big Arsenic and Little Arsenic. Big Arsenic's approach is marked by a shallow rapid on a gradual left bend and begins when the river bends sharply left. Portage on the right. Big Arsenic drops 30 feet over rock ledges and boulders. Little Arsenic is described in Tim Hillmer's story as "...a quarter mile of white thunder" and contains a deadly sieve on the left at low water. Scout everything!

LOGISTICS: The put-in is reached by turning left off of Hwy 3 just north of Questa, a small town north of Taos. Follow signs to River Rim Access via Route 376. Once you reach the gorge rim you'll see a trail leading into the gorge. This trail has a sign warning of the cataracts below. Follow the trail to the river at the put-in. The first popular take-out is at the Red River confluence but involves a long, dusty carry out of the gorge. This is near the Cebollo Mesa Campground, which can be found by heading south out of Questa about five to ten minutes, then turning right off Hwy 3 on the east rim. Most paddlers float another 10 miles of easy river and take out at Dunn Bridge which is found by travelling south along Route 3 to Arroyo Hondo, then driving along Arroyo Hondo Creek to the bridge. (Best Guidebooks: Colorado Whitewater, The Floater's Guide to Colorado; Rivers of the Southwest; Western Whitewater)

SECTION: "Takelma Gorge," Natural Bridge to River Bridge CG
REGION: Jackson County
CLASS: V
MILES: 7
GRADIENT: 57; 100 in first mile
WATER LEVELS: 500-1,000 cfs
SEASON: Best late Spring into late Summer (avoid heavy runoff)
GAUGE: Unknown; check with River Forecast Center in Portland
for some information at (503) 249-0666
USGS MAPS: Union Creek, Prospect North, Whetstone Point

DESCRIPTION: The upper Rogue River bears little resemblance to its popular cousin downstream. Here, the river careens in and out of small, intimate gorges that contain many Class III to V rapids, and one big waterfall that must be portaged. Class III+ rapids begin within sight of the put-in and continue around the first corner. Narrow chutes and twisting drops take boaters almost to the lip of the waterfall, which can be portaged along the left bank without too much difficulty.

Takelma Gorge is 4.3 miles below the put-in. You'll first hit Woodruff Bridge three miles below the put-in, then Abbott Creek enters from the right a half-mile downstream. Then, in another 0.7 miles the river enters the gorge. Takelma Gorge itself contains some very tight slots amidst forboding canyon walls and pushy whitewater. Here, the river drops 40 feet in a quarter-mile. At anything above late season flows some of the chutes lead toward some scary pockets against the walls. Fortunately, there is a hiking trail leading upstream from River Bridge Campground that affords first-timers to the area a look into the canyon. In the heart of Takelma Gorge, some giant logs migrated into the main channel and completely blocked any runnable chutes (1991). Fortunately, this is at a wide spot in the canyon, and there is a broad lava bench on river right that provides a safe portage route. However, if the water level were too high, it would be almost impossible to get back in the river below the logs.

LOGISTICS: The put-in is at the bridge along the paved trail at the Natural Bridge Interpretive Site which is a signed tourist attraction located a few minutes west of Union Creek along Hwy 62 (about 60 miles northeast of Medford). The take-out is at River Bridge Campground which is one mile north of Hwy 62 along Forest Road 6210, which cuts off of Hwy 62 five to ten minutes west of Natural Bridge. (Best Guidebook: Soggy Sneakers Guide to Oregon Rivers, Third Edition)

RUSSELL FORK OF THE LEVISA FORK OF THE BIG SANDY RIVER, Virginia/Kentucky ▬▬▬▬▬▬▬▬▬

SECTION: "The Russell Fork," Flanagan Dam to Elkhorn City
REGION: Dickenson County (VA), and Pike County (KY)
CLASS: IV-VI
MILES: 10.3
GRADIENT: 4.6 miles at 180+
WATER LEVELS: Best from 1,100 to 1,500. Much tougher at lower or higher water levels!
SEASON: Four October weekend release dates guaranteed, with sporadic releases in Spring for flood control
GAUGE: Call the Corps of Engineers at (703) 835-1438 or the Flanagan Dam at (703) 865-4413
USGS QUADS: Elkhorn City

DESCRIPTION: The Russell Fork is one gnarly run! Huge, powerful drops, nasty undercut ledges, and an awesome gradient combine to form one of the East's toughest regularly run stretches of water. In October, it is not uncommon to find everything from the country's top kayakers to rafts full of commercial customers crashing and burning their way through Triple Drop, El Horrendo, Climax, and many other tough rapids.

The run starts on the Class II rapids of the Pound River just downstream of the Dam and continues through an easy warm-up section down to the Russell Fork confluence. Once on the Russell Fork, the river grows in intensity as it approaches Entrance Rapid. When a high rock tower appears over the river, it's time to scout Tower Falls, a very pushy staircase rapid. Next comes Fist, one of the few big rapids that comes close to being called *straightforward.* After Fist comes Triple Drop, one of the biggest rapids on the trip. Here, the river descends through three distinct vertical drops—five, eight, and nine feet high—in a very short distance. The next rapid is El Horrendo, a double drop that lands paddlers 25 feet lower than when they entered the rapid. Survivors here get to go on to paddle Climax, a heart-stopping boulder garden with nasty undercuts and inconveniently placed rocks everywhere.

So, how are you doin'? Still alive? Good! The rest of the run to Elkhorn City is much easier and soon tapers off to Class II.

Keep in mind that portage routes are available and should be used if you're over your head. But, the portages are awful!

LOGISTICS: The put-in is just downstream of the Flanagan Dam at the picnic area on the Pound River northwest of Haysi, Virginia. If the flow is coming from the Russell Fork itself, you can put in at the Route 611 bridge at Bartlick a couple of miles downstream. The take-out is at the Route 197 bridge at Elkhorn City. (Best Guidebooks: A Canoeing and Kayaking Guide to the Streams of Kentucky; Virginia Whitewater; Appalachian Whitewater Volume I)

SALMON RIVER, California ▬▬▬▬▬▬▬▬▬

SECTION: "The Cal Salmon," Nordheimer Flat Campground to
         Oak Bottom Campground
REGION: Siskiyou County
CLASS: IV-V
MILES: 12
GRADIENT: 31
WATER LEVELS: 1,000-4,000 optimum, but can be run higher
SEASON: April-June
GAUGE: Salmon at Somes Bar, (916) 627-3291 or (916) 653-9647
USGS MAPS: Forks of the Salmon

DESCRIPTION: This is a delightful pool-drop run through an intimate canyon. Whitewater begins just over a half-mile below the put-in with Bloomer Falls. This used to be a Class VI drop, but is now just a flume with a big boulder in the middle of the current. After a couple of Class IV boulder gardens, the river slams into Class IV+ Airplane Turn 2.5 miles below the put-in. This is a twisting four-foot drop through boulders. About 2.7 miles downstream, the river splits into two channels at Class V Cascade. The right channel is nearly a waterfall, and the left is a fast sluice in heavy hydraulics. Less than a quarter-mile downstream, the river winds through small boulders, veers right and drops over Achilles Heel, a Class IV+ drop that ends with a plunge into a big hole. One mile later is Whirling Dervish (Class IV+), a twisting bobsled ride that takes one dangerously close to a big midstream boulder.

The biggest Class V rapids of the trip, Last Chance and Freight Train, are at mile six below the put-in. Last Chance ends with a big keeper hole that plugs the entire right channel. Then, the river continues through a pool and descends through 100 yards of foaming, snarling whitewater. Last Chance and Freight Train can be scouted on the way to the put-in from a turn-out at a sharp bend in the road.

Just downstream of Freight Train, the river nearly meets the road at the Butler Creek confluence. The run from here down is easier than the upper section but contains many Class III to IV rapids. The highlight of the lower section is Gaping Maw (A.K.A. Marble Rapid). This complex Class IV+ boulder garden is about 2.5 miles below Butler Creek and should be scouted by even experienced boaters. The rest of the run gradually eases off until there are little more than Class II riffles near Oak Bottom.

LOGISTICS: Somes Bar is a small village north of Orleans on Hwy 96. Salmon River Road heads east out of Somes Bar and follows the river to Oak Bottom Campground take-out a few miles up the road. The same road follows the river all the way past Butler Creek, up to Nordheimer Flat Campground put-in, and on to Forks of the Salmon. (Best Guidebooks: California Whitewater; A Guide to the Best Whitewater in the State of California; Western Whitewater)

SALMON RIVER, SOUTH FORK, Idaho ▬▬▬

SECTION: Road End (near the Secesh and East Fork of the South Fork Confluences) to Vinegar Creek (Main Salmon)

CLASS: Under 1.5' on the Krassel Gauge it's III+; Between 1.5 and 4.2' it's III-IV; Above 4.2' it's IV-V

MILES: 57 (36 on South Fork, 21 on the Main)

GRADIENT: 48 on the South Fork

WATER LEVELS: OK, here goes. Everyone measures this run in gauge height. There are three tributaries that each contribute 1/3 to the South Fork, these are the Secesh River, the South Fork Salmon River, and the East Fork of the South Fork of the Salmon River. However, the South Fork has the lowest elevation drainage of the three rivers. So, the gauge is relative at best. The river is considered low at 1 to 3.5 feet, medium at 3.5 to 4.5 feet, high at 4.5 to 6 feet, and very high above 6 feet. Correlations in cfs are impossible, but here are some rough guesstimates: 2'=1,000, 3'=2,000, 4'=4,000, 5'=6,000, and 6'= 8,000 to 9,000. Optimum is 4'

CRAFT: Rafting is usually done only between 3' and 5', 6' is for experts only! Kayakers dig it at all flows.

SEASON: May-July

GAUGE: Krassel Gauge is visual, located upstream of the Secesh and E. Fk. of the S. Fk. confluences on the South Fork below the Krassel Work Center

USGS MAPS: Williams Peak, Parks Pk., Pilot Pk., Chicken Pk., Wolf Fang Peak, Warren, Burgdorf

PERMIT: Required to float out on Main Salmon; contact the Forest Service at the North Fork Ranger District, PO Box 780, North Fork, ID 83466. (208) 879-5204

DESCRIPTION: This is an extraordinary wilderness trip complete with spectacular granite canyons, thick forest scenery, and great whitewater. It can be done in a day at highwater if there are no mishaps, but it's better to spend two days to make the entire trip.

The big rapids begin about mile five to eight (depending on who's guidebook you read) with Devil Creek Rapid. This is a big boulder garden with a large hole on the left that is backed by a big boulder. You'll be able to spot it by the previous rapid, which has a waterfall on the left bank. About two to three miles of great whitewater follows Devil Creek. After a long calm you will find Surprise Rapid. This is a long rock garden at low water that becomes a minefield of awesome holes at high water. Elk Creek rapid, another rapid with giant holes, is identified by a tall cliff on the left with a steep rapid at its base.

The biggest rapid, Fall Creek, is marked by a huge logjam on the right bank and is about 27 miles into the trip. Here, the river descends through a long, steep rapid (1/3 of a mile!) with an endless series of huge waves and keeper holes. Most people scout this one. After turning the corner onto the Main Fork, the Salmon turns flat and serene. The last 22 miles of paddling rarely attain much more than Class II. Note: If you're caught on the Main Fork without a permit, you'll get fined.

LOGISTICS: The put-in is reached from McCall. First follow signs to Ponderosa State Park. At the second blinking light turn right and go 4.5 miles until you come to a dirt road on the right marked "Yellow Pine." Go across the lake then follow Lick Creek Road 34 miles to the South Fork, turn left, and follow it to the end of the road. Note that this route doesn't open until about July 1 in normal years. An alternative route starts at Cascade. Take the Warm Lake Road east from Hwy 55 just north of Cascade and follow it to the South Fork Road. Then, turn left on South Fork Road and follow the South Fork to the road's end. The take-out is 26 miles east of Riggins at Vinegar Creek on the Main Salmon. (Best Guidebooks: Idaho, the Whitewater State; Idaho Whitewater; Western Whitewater)

SKYKOMISH RIVER, Washington ▬▬▬▬▬

SECTION: "The Sky," Index to Goldbar
REGION: Snohomish County
CLASS: III (one at IV-IV+)
MILES: 6.7
GRADIENT: 30
WATER LEVELS: 1,500-5,000 optimum; jumps a half class at
        5,000 to 10,000
SEASON: During winter rainy season, during Spring snowmelt,
        and into late Summer (Best April-July)
GAUGE: Skykomish at Goldbar (206) 526-8530
USGS MAPS: Index, Goldbar

DESCRIPTION: This is one of Washington State's premier
commercial rafting trips, and is a delight for kayakers and rafters.
Stunning mountain scenery, emerald waters, and huge granite
boulders make for a magnificent run. With the exception of one
difficult rapid—Boulder Drop—the river can be done by highly
competent intermediate paddlers. Boulder Drop is Class IV at most
levels, but approaches Class V at some flows. Rapids are
characterized by a steepening of the river bed, or boulder-strewn
ledges. Almost everything can be scouted from the boat.

Boulder Drop is only about a mile or so below the confluence
of the North Fork and South Fork. Here, the river winds
powerfully through mammoth granite boulders, then descends over
a couple of four to five foot ledges and spins toward some big
curlers and tail waves. Scout Boulder Drop from the right bank for
a route through "the needle" center-right, or around the "airplane
turn" at the left end of the rapid. Enjoy!

LOGISTICS: The put-in is either at the bridge in the town of
Index, or below Sunset Falls outside of Index on the South Fork
of the Skykomish. To find Sunset Falls, take Hwy 2 west out of
Index, cross the South Fork, and turn left on Mt. Index Road.
Now, go about a half-mile to a trail that leads down to the river.
The take-out is at a fishing access at the Hwy 2 bridge over the
Skykomish just east of the town of Goldbar. (Best Guidebooks: A
Guide to the Whitewater Rivers of Washington; Washington
Whitewater; Western Whitewater)

SLATE RIVER, Colorado ▬▬▬▬▬▬▬▬▬▬▬

SECTION: "The Upper Slate," Pittsburg to Oh-Be-Joyful Creek
REGION: Gunnison County
CLASS: V-V+
MILES: 4.5
GRADIENT: 72 avg; 150 max
WATER LEVELS: Best 150 to 250 cfs; considered high at 300 cfs
SEASON: About a month during peak snowmelt, usually in June
GAUGE: No gauge is available. However, there is a beaver pond
at the put-in with a beaver dam at the lower end. If you
can paddle over the dam, the river is high enough. Just
be sure that it isn't too high!
USGS MAPS: Oh-Be-Joyful

DESCRIPTION: This is a small, steep pool-drop river with six major rapids interspersed with some pretty constant whitewater action. The major rapids are Too Nar Falls, Slate River Falls, Virgin Canyon, Jucie Lucy, Dead Man's Curve, and Wicked Wanda. The action begins with the six-foot plunge at Too-Nar Falls, and reaches its peak at Wicked Wanda, a seven-foot wide flume that drops nine feet before surging over a series of smaller ledges and past some ominous undercuts.

Although the Upper Slate is primarily the domain of expert kayakers, small self-bailing rafts can make the run too.

LOGISTICS: Take Slate River Road out of Crested Butte toward Paradise Divide. The take-out is at the confluence of the Slate River and Oh-Be-Joyful Creek. You can reach this by taking a short four-wheel drive road south off of Slate River Road less than a mile west of Nicholson Lake. The road is marked by an Oh-Be-Joyful sign and may be impassable for some cars. If your car can't make it, it is a quarter-mile hike up this road. The put-in is about four more miles up Slate River Road just below the old mining town of Pittsburg at an unmarked campground on a beaver pond. For more information, contact Crested Butte Rafting at (303)-349-7423. (Best Guidebook: This one!)

SNAKE RIVER, Idaho/Oregon ▬▬▬▬▬▬▬

SECTION: "Hell's Canyon," Hell's Canyon Dam to Pittsburgh
        Landing or Heller's Bar
REGION: Northern Oregon/Idaho border
CLASS: III+ (IV-IV+)
MILES: 35 to 81
GRADIENT: 8
WATER LEVELS: 8,000 to 30,000
SEASON: All year
GAUGE: River Forecast Center before 2:00 pm at (503) 249-
0666; or call (800) 422-3143
USGS MAPS: Cuprum, He Devil, Kernan Point, Grave Point,
        Kirkwood Cr., Grave Point, Wolf Creek, Cactus
        Mountain, Deadhorse
PERMITS: Obtain through Hell's Canyon National Recreation
        Area, 3620-B Snake River Ave., Lewiston, ID 83501;
        (208) 743-2297

DESCRIPTION: This is a giant river that carves its way
through one of the deepest canyons in North America. The
surrounding cliffs and high-desert scenery are truly remarkable,
and provide plenty of visual excitement for this float trip.

The first big rapid, Wild Sheep (Class IV at low water, IV+
to V at high water), is 6.5 miles from the put-in below Hell's
Canyon Dam. Here, the wide river bursts into a 100-yard long
series of waves and holes that resembles Grand Canyon-type
whitewater at high water (above 30,000 cfs). At lower flows, giant
boulders punctuate the surface, creating a more technical, yet
forgiving, rapid.

Two miles downstream is Granite (also Class IV or IV+,
depending on flows). Here, the river slides down a giant ramp and
crashes into a giant hole before exiting through another 50 yards
of fast and foamy water. With the exception of Waterspout (a
Class III-IV series of waves 13 miles below the put-in) and Rush
Creek (a Class IV wall of water 15 miles from the put-in), the rest
of the river contains long, peaceful pools and easy Class II-III
rapids. The camping is excellent, and many parties take 3 to 5
days to make the run all the way down to Heller's Bar.

LOGISTICS: The put-in is at the base of Hell's Canyon Dam on the Oregon side. To find it, start from Cambridge, a small town north of Weiser, Idaho, on US 95. Take Hwy 71 north to the dam. The take-out at Heller's Bar is reached by going to Clarkston, Washington via Joseph, Oregon, then upstream along the Snake 30 miles to Hellers Bar. There is a take-out at Pittsburgh Landing that cuts off the last 46 miles of flatwater, making this a 35 mile run. Pittsburgh Landing is reached via a horrendous dirt road (Forest Service Rd. 493) that leads over Pittsburgh Saddle from Whitebird and Hwy 93. Contact the National Recreation Area for a list of shuttle drivers. (Best Guidebooks: Idaho, the Whitewater State; Idaho River Tours; Idaho Whitewater; Oregon River Tours; Soggy Sneakers Guide to Oregon Rivers; Western Whitewater)

STANISLAUS RIVER, MIDDLE FORK, California ▰▰▰

SECTION: Mt. Knight Trail to Camp Nine Powerhouse
REGION: Calaveras County
CLASS: V
MILES: 8
GRADIENT: 90 avg; 170 max
WATER LEVELS: 1,200 to 2,000 optimum
SEASON: Short! Flows only when water spills over Sand Bar Flat
        Dam, usually during peak runoff.
GAUGE: Get level from PGE at Sand Bar Flat Dam
USGS MAPS: Crandall Peak, Strawberry, Liberty Hill

DESCRIPTION: This is a rarely run, but incredibly rewarding, section of the Stanislaus River. There is little evidence of human impact in the canyon, and little chance that you'll run into other boaters.

After a two-mile hike to the river, the rapids begin with a Class V drop over a 12-foot ledge followed by a parade of technical Class III+ and IV boulder gardens that goes on for nearly four miles. Picking your way downstream, the river dances back and forth between stunning crystalline pools, long pool-drop rapids, and pulse-raising descents through giant drops.

The action gets hot again about a mile above the North Fork

Jeff Bennett guiding during the first raft descent of the Middle Fork of the Stanislaus. (Mike Doyle photo, Beyond Limits Adventures)

confluence. Here, the river picks back up to Class V with some incredible boulder choked cataracts. Everything can be run, but keep in mind how far you are away from help before trying it. Just above the North Fork confluence is a particularly tough rapid with a large mid-stream boulder and some powerful hydraulics.

Don't pass the North Fork by. A short side-hike up this canyon reward weary travellers with some splendid swimming holes before getting back in their rafts to finish off the final rapids on their way to Camp Nine.

Though we portaged a few times on the first raft descent, the run is now done commercially by Beyond Limits Adventures out of Riverbank.

LOGISTICS: The take-out for this run is the old put-in for the main Stanislaus run. It's found by driving down Camp Nine Road from Vallecito to the Powerhouse. You'll need a Stanislaus National Forest map to find the put-in. Drive up the dirt road that leads up the river-left side of the canyon and continue until you hit the Forebay turn-off. Here, turn right and go 7.5 miles to the unmarked trailhead. (The trailhead starts just left of the letter "m" in "Mt. Knight" on the USFS map.) Then it's a two mile hike downhill to the river. For more information, contact Beyond Limits at (209) 529-7655 or (800) 234-RAFT. (Best Guidebook: A Guide to the Best Whitewater in the State of California)

STILLAGUAMISH RIVER, Washington ▬▬▬▬▬▬▬▬

SECTION: "Robe Canyon," Verlot to Granite Falls
REGION: Snohomish County
CLASS: V-V+ (one VI)
MILES: 12.3
GRADIENT: 56 avg; 100 to 180 feet per mile in the canyon
WATER LEVELS: 800 to 1,600; 1,700 considered very high!
SEASON: Rainy and snowmelt (November through late Spring)
GAUGE: Stillaguamish, South Fork (206) 526-8530
USGS MAPS: Verlot, Granite Falls

DESCRIPTION: The "Robe Canyon" section of the South Fork "Stilly" starts off with 5.5 miles of Class I and II water, then changes moods suddenly and violently. The first rapid is a twisting sluice that winds through sticky holes and sharp ledges. The moment you see the river entering the canyon, get out on the right bank and hike downstream on an old railroad grade to the second tunnel. The next 6.8 miles contain ferocious, unforgiving rapids that will bruise the egos of even the best rafters. Though kayakers regularly paddle this section, it is still for experts only, and only at the recommended flows.

The river in the canyon is constricted on both sides by tight cliffs or steep slopes, and is boulder filled throughout most of its length. Rapids often drop ten to fifteen feet at a time through long series of three to four foot drops backed by powerful cross currents, narrow boulder-flanked chutes, and powerful holes. First timers should scout everything and plan on spending a full day in the canyon. The only mandatory portage, Landslide, is spotted by a huge tan-colored cliff on the right bank and an ominous horizon-line. Don't miss the take-out below the bridge! Unrunnable Granite Falls is just downstream!

LOGISTICS: The take-out is directly beneath the Granite Falls bridge on Mountain Loop Hwy just north and east of the town of Granite Falls. DO NOT go downstream of the take-out, there is an unrunnable cataract there! The put-in is across from the Verlot Public Service Center 9.1 miles northwest from the town of Granite Falls on the Mountain Loop Highway. (Best Guidebook: A Guide to the Whitewater Rivers of Washington)

THOMPSON RIVER, British Columbia, Canada ▬▬▬▬▬

SECTION: Nicoamen River to Lytton
REGION: Ends at Lytton, B.C.
CLASS: Class III+ to IV (IV+ to V at high water)
MILES: 15
GRADIENT: 15
WATER LEVELS: 10,000 to 80,000 cfs
SEASON: All year
GAUGE: Water Survey of Canada (604) 666-6087
TOPO MAPS: Spences Bridge, Prospect Crk., Stein River, Lytton

DESCRIPTION: The Lower Thompson is a big, fun run at water levels of 16,000 to 26,000 cfs. Huge roller coaster waves over long wave trains, and face-blasting plunges through breaking curlers provide plenty of excitement. Kayakers can hang out on the big waves all day, and rafters with intermediate to advanced skills can handle most of the rapids with ease.

The whitewater starts just downstream of the put-in with The Frog. Here, five-foot waves and strange, swirling hydraulics dance about a huge rock formation in the center of the river. At lower flows this is an outstanding surf spot! Next is Cutting Board. At low water, avoid the huge hole on the right. Downstream is Witch's Cauldron, which is followed by the biggest rapid on the run, Jaws, A.K.A. Jaws of Death.

At Jaws the 100-yard wide river pinches down to 50 feet in width, creating a series of six to ten-foot high rebound waves that surge and explode unexpectedly. At high water (60,000 cfs), most of the rapids turn into migrating whirlpools, and Jaws becomes a huge surging wave with a build-and-break cycle that can last half-a-minute. After Jaws, the river eases up for its final descent to the Fraser River confluence.

LOGISTICS: The take-out is just past the Thompson River Bridge at the Fraser River confluence in Lytton. This is on private land so you must request access to this property first. This can obtained from the Lytton band manager at the Lytton Band office, PO Box 20, Lytton, B.C. V0K 1ZO. Their phone number is (604) 455-2304 or (604) 455-2353. You must pull hard to river right to reach the take-out since it is actually about 50 yards up the Fraser in a massive backeddy. The put-in is 9.4 miles upstream along Hwy 1 at the Nicoamen River confluence. (Hwy 1 follows the river upstream from Lytton.) (Best Guidebook: Rafting In British Columbia; Whitewater Trips for Kayakers, Canoeists and Rafters in British Columbia)

TRINITY RIVER, California

SECTION: "Burnt Ranch Gorge," Cedar Flat to Hawkins Bar
REGION: Trinity County
CLASS: V
MILES: 8.5
GRADIENT: 45 avg; 100 in gorge
WATER LEVELS: 500 to 3,000 optimum; rafts prefer 800-900+
SEASON: Summer (after high water) or anytime flow is good
GAUGE: 90% of Trinity at Hoopa; (916) 653-9647 or
       (707) 443-9305
USGS MAPS: Ironside Mtn., Willow Creek

DESCRIPTION: Burnt Ranch Gorge offers a unique world-class experience to the expert paddler. It is a pool-drop river, with big pools separating all of the biggest rapids. Each rapid has a distinct personality and unique features.

The whitewater begins 1.8 miles below Cedar Flat at China Slide. This is a tight Class IV boulder garden that leads through shallow boulder fields and ends with a few sharp dips through small curling waves. Just downstream, the river disappears over a horizon line and into Box Canyon. Scout this rapid, Class IV+ Pearly Gates, for a clean line down an eight-foot slide. The next rapid, Class IV+ Tight Squeeze, is a mile downstream. Tight Squeeze calls for some quickzig-zag maneuvers amidst big boulders. Below Tight Squeeze, the river gets progressively tougher until it finally hits the falls section 4.2 miles below the put-in.

Middle Burnt Ranch Falls on California's Trinity River.

The first big drop in the falls section is Upper Burnt Ranch Falls, a steep Class V ten-foot sliding falls flanked by mammoth boulders. The second drop is Class V Middle Burnt Ranch Falls, a twenty-foot descent over a series of sharp ledges and around car-sized boulders. The final rapid in the falls series is Class V Lower Burnt Ranch Falls. A massive landslide rearranged this rapid in 1991, turning it into a pulse raising fifteen-foot high slide down a white chute toward the right cliff. A quarter-mile downstream from Lower Burnt Ranch Falls, the river dips another twelve feet through boulders at Hennessy Falls. A quarter-mile downstream, the river tears through a long boulder garden at Origami, which ends with a pickett fence of boulders and no obvious exit route. A third of a mile past Origami is Table Rock. Though this Class V-VI rapid looks very innocent, strong currents can suck and pin boaters under a severely undercut rock. Portage on the left. The last big rapid is 2.2 miles after Table Rock at Gray's Falls. Here, the river plunges five feet into a hole against the left wall, requiring some unique battle plans to emerge upright. The remaining 2.5 miles of river rarely exceed Class II.

LOGISTICS: The put-in is at Cedar Flat, a wide turn-out just short of the Hwy 299 bridge over the Trinity River, about 40 miles west of Weaverville (2.5 miles east of the little town of Burnt Ranch). The take-out is down a steep dirt road that turns north off of Hwy 299 from Hawkins Bar. Hawkins Bar is another small hamlet 8.5 miles west of Cedar Flat along Hwy 299. (Best Guidebooks: California Whitewater; A Guide to the Best Whitewater in the State of California; Western Whitewater)

TUOLUMNE RIVER, California ▬▬▬▬▬▬

SECTION: "Cherry Creek," Holm Powerhouse to Meral's Pool
REGION: Tuolumne County
CLASS: V
MILES: 9
GRADIENT: 105 avg; 200 in the Miracle Mile
WATER LEVELS: 600-2,000
SEASON: March to mid-May and July through October (don't try
        it during peak runoff!)
GAUGE: Get the flow at Meral's Pool by calling (916) 653-9647,
        then figure that most of that is coming from the Holm
        Powerhouse into Cherry Creek. The dam usually
        releases more water during weekdays than on weekends,
        and releases the least water on Sundays.
USGS MAPS: Lake Eleanor NW, Duckwall Mtn, Jawbone Ridge,
        Lake Eleanor, Tuolumne City

DESCRIPTION: This is where all California Class V stud-boaters go to prove their machismo to their buddies. The run starts on Cherry Creek below the Holm Powerhouse, dives through some Class III+ and IV boulder gardens, then joins the main Tuolumne one mile into the trip. Another mile downstream, things begin to get serious with Corkscrew, the first Class V rapid. Here, big granite boulders and sharp drops present obvious, albeit difficult, routes. A half-mile downstream is Class V Jawbone. Again, big boulders appear everywhere in the main current, whipping up a myriad of complex hydraulics and boat crunching drops.

Mushroom and Toadstool (both Class V) start 3.2 miles below the put-in. In the first 50 yards of the rapid, the river drops 30 feet through sharp ledges and big holes, then plunges toward a huge, undercut flake of rock that could seriously damage an inattentive paddler's forehead. After the flake, the river twists, then drops another six feet around a big rock and into another foamy hole. The next drop, Catapult, is a half-mile downstream of Mushroom, and contains an awesome slalom route that ends with a sharp plunge into a right-hand chute.

The Miracle Mile (Class V) begins just after Catapult, and drops over 200 feet through a myriad of complex, boulder-choked rapids. Airplane Turn (Class V) at mile 6.1 ends with a big hole that can be a nasty keeper at some flows. At mile 6.4, one of the river's worst rapids, Class V Lewis' Leap, dives sharply over a series of big ledges that terminate in a big hole. Paddle hard! Less than a half-mile below Lewis' Leap is a Clas V-VI rapid, Flat Rock Falls, that is usually portaged due to a severe undercut in the main channel.

About a quarter-mile below Flat Rock, the entire river plunges 30 feet down giant steps at Lumsden Falls. Yeah, it's been run, but that doesn't mean you ought to do it. Portage on the left. Just beyond the bridge at Lumsden Falls is a possible take-out at Lumsden Campground. If you continue toward Meral's Pool you'll have three more outstanding Class IV rapids... Against the Wall, Horseshoe Falls, and Meral's Pool Table.

LOGISTICS: To reach the put-in, take Hwy 120 toward Yosemite then turn north onto Cherry Lake Road 14 miles east of Groveland. Then, go seven miles to a bridge across the Tuolumne. A mile-and-a-half later, turn right and follow the road to the put-in. To find the take-out, head back to Hwy 120 and turn back toward Groveland. Turn right off of Hwy 120, 6.5 miles from the Cherry Lake Road intersection, onto Ferretti Road and go about a mile. When you cross the second cattle guard, turn right onto Lumsden road and follow it five bone-rattling miles to the put-in. (Best Guidebooks: A Guide to the Best Whitewater In the State of California; California Whitewater; Western Whitewater)

WENATCHEE RIVER, Washington ▬▬▬▬▬

SECTION: "Tumwater Canyon," Tumwater Canyon to Exit Rapid
REGION: Chelan County
CLASS: IV-VI
MILES: 7.5
GRADIENT: 64
WATER LEVELS: 1,500 to 2,800 recommended for first time;
    becomes exponentially tougher as water level
    increases; has been run much higher by experts
SEASON: Before or after snowmelt; best around the end of July
GAUGE: Take about 70% of the Wenatchee gauge at Peshastin
    (206) 526-8530
USGS MAPS: Winton, Leavenworth

DESCRIPTION: Tumwater can be one inti-ti-ti-timidating chunk of wh-wh-wh-whitewater! I've paddled it at *sane* flows of 1,500 to 2,800 cfs with no problem, and have been stomped by its massive hydraulics at higher levels. Though the gradient isn't all that severe in the canyon, much of the river is flat. When it finally decides to go downhill, it does so in a hurry.

The first huge rapid, The Wall, is adjacent to milepost 94, which parallels the entire run and affords some easy scouting opportunities. This rapid is a 200 yard long series of Class IV-IV+ ledge-holes at low water, but gets worse with each additional cfs that comes down the river. At 10,000 cfs, it's a cool rapid just to stare at and tremble before you leave to find another river to paddle. There's a 10 to 12-foot high dam at milepost 95 that has been run by 14 to 17-foot rafts. More pool-drop Class III to IV rapids (depending on water levels) start just below the dam, and build to another climax at milepost 97. Here, the river smashes into a huge midstream hole that has to be avoided on the left, then bucks through more ledges before petering out in long Class III rock gardens.

The last rapid, Exit, is a huge Class VI disaster area that has killed some unwary boaters, and has kept smart paddlers away. Scout this one out from Hwy 2 by hiking over a small hill 0.5 miles west of the Leavenworth city limits.

The Tumwater Canyon section of Washington's Wenatchee River contains some huge holes.

LOGISTICS: Easy shuttle! From Leavenworth, head 0.5 miles east to the wide shoulder and scout out Exit Rapid. The take-out is on river left above the top of the rapid. The lower put-in is 5.6 miles above the take-out at another shoulder. The upper put-in is at the bridge near Tumwater Campground at the top end of Tumwater Canyon. (Best Guidebook: A Guide to the Whitewater Rivers of Washington)

YOUGHIOGHENY RIVER, Maryland ▬▬▬▬▬▬

SECTION: "The Upper Yough," Sang Run Bridge to Friendsville
REGION: Garrett County
CLASS: IV-V
MILES: 9.5
GRADIENT: 53; 3.5 at 116
WATER LEVELS: 1.6 on Sang Run Gauge or 2.9 on Friendsville
Gauge minimum, 2.5 on Sang Run Gauge and
3.8 on Friendsville Gauge maximum
SEASON: Winter or Spring after heavy rains or snowmelt, or
during the rest of the year during the week when Hoyes
Run Hydroelectric Station releases water. (NOTE:
this river goes up and comes down fast! Be ready to go
when releases start!)
GAUGE: Get the Friendsville Gauge at (412) 644-2890; otherwise,
call a local outfitter like Precision Rafting Expeditions
at (301) 746-5290
USGS QUADS: Sang Run, Friendsville

DESCRIPTION: The "Upper Yough" begins easy, with three
miles of river barely jumping around Class II. After Warm Up
Riffle, a Class II, get ready for Gap Falls, a big slide through
waves and holes. After another mile of mellow stuff, the river
really springs to life as it heads for three miles of intense
whitewater action.

The first rapids are Bastard, Charlie's Choice and Triple Drop.
The right side of the third part of Triple Drop contains National
Falls, a big Class V drop. If it makes you weak just looking at it,
go left. After the next few exciting rapids (Tommy's Hole and
Zinger) comes Heinzerling (Class IV-V). The "easy" route starts
right, then works left to a big finale that involves riding off the
pillow of a big rock into or around a hole. The next rapid, Meat
Cleaver (Class V), is the most notorious rapid on the Upper
Yough. This rapid starts with a weave among some big boulders
then ends with a sharp ledge packed with two sharp rocks that
threaten to broach anything not pointed in the right direction. After
the next rapid, Powerful Popper, paddlers come to Lost and Found
(Class V), a complex boulder garden with an assortment of routes.

The significant Class III-IV rapids after Lost and Found are called Cheeseburger Falls, Wright's Hole, and Double Pencil Sharpener. After that, the river gets easy again for the last three or four miles to the take-out.

LOGISTICS: The shuttle issue is pretty hot in this area so check about the legal ramifications surrounding these access points *before* you use them. The put-in at the Sang Run bridge is found by taking Route 42 south out of Friendsville down to Bishof Road. Turn right on Bishof Road and go to Sang Road. Turn right on Sang Road and head to the bridge. The take-out is in the town of Friendsville. (Best Guidebooks: Appalachian Whitewater, Vol II; Wildwater West Virginia Volume I)

SELECTED BIBLIOGRAPHY

BOOKS

The Adventures of Huckleberry Finn, Mark Twain. Harper (1884)

Appalachian Whitewater Guide, Volume I, the Southern Mountains, Bob Sehlinger, Don Otey, Bob Benner, William Nealy, and Bob Lantz. Menasha Ridge Press (19??)

Appalachian Whitewater Guide, Volume II, The Central Mountains, Ed Grove, Bill Kirby, Charles Walbridge, Ward Eister, Paul Davidson, and Dirk Davidson. Menasha Ridge Press (1987)

Beyond the Wall, Edward Abbey. Holt, Rinehart and Winston (1984)

The Big Drops, Ten Legendary Rapids of the American West, Roderick Nash. Johnson Books (1989)

California Whitewater, A Guide To The Rivers, Jim Cassady and Fryar Calhoun. North Fork Press (1990)

Canoeing and Kayaking Guide to the Rivers of Kentucky, Bob Sehlinger. Menasha Ridge Press (19??)

Canyonlands River Guide, Bill and Buzz Belknap. Westwater Books (1974)

Colorado Whitewater, Jim Stohlquist, Colorado Kayak Supply (1982)

Down the River, Edward Abbey. E.P. Dutton (1982)

Exciting River Running in the U.S., Elizabeth Medes. Contemporary Books, Inc. (1979)

The Exploration of the Colorado River and its Canyons, John Wesley Powell. Dover Publications, Inc. (1961)

A Fine and Pleasant Misery, Patrick F. McManus. Henry Holt and Company (1978)

The Floater's Guide to Colorado, Doug Wheat. Falcon Press Publishing Co., Inc., (1983)

A Guide to the Best Whitewater in the State of California, Lars Holbek and Chuck Stanley. Friends of the River (1988)

A Guide to the Whitewater Rivers of Washington, Jeff Bennett. Swiftwater Publishing Company (1991)

Idaho, the Whitewater State, Grant Amaral. Watershed Books (1990)

Idaho River Tours, John Garren. Garren Publishing (1987)

Idaho Whitewater, the Complete River Guide for Canoeists, Rafters and Kayakers, Greg Moore and Don McClaran. Class VI Whitewater (1989)

The Log of the Panthon, George Flavell. Pruett Publishing (1987)

Rafting in British Columbia, Doug VanDine and Bernard Fandrich. Hancock House Publishers Ltd (1984)

River Days, Travels on Western Rivers, Jeff Rennicke. Fulcrum, Inc., (1988)

River Reflections, A Collection of River Writings, Edited by Verne Huser. Globe Pequot (1988)

River Rescue, Les Bechdel and Slim Ray. Appalachian Mountain Club (1985)

River Runners' Guide to Utah and Adjacent Areas, Gary C. Nichols. University of Utah Press (1986)

Rivers of America, Paul Vasey. Gallery Books (1990)

The Rivers of Costa Rica, A Canoeing, Kayaking, and Rafting Guide, Michael W. Mayfield and Rafael E. Gallo. Menasha Ridge Press (1988)

Rivers of the Southwest: A Boaters Guide to the Rivers of Colorado, New Mexico, Utah and Arizona, Fletcher Anderson and Ann Hopkinson. Pruett Publishing Company (1982)

Run, River, Run, A Naturalist's Journey Down One of the Great Rivers of the West, Ann Zwinger. Harper and Row (1975)

Running the Amazon, Joe Kane. Vantage Books (1989)

Sierra Whitewater, A Paddlers Guide to the Rivers of California's Sierra Nevada, Charles Martin (1974)

Sierra Whitewater, A Paddler's Guide to the Rivers of California's Sierra Nevada, Charles Marting. (1974)

Soggy Sneakers, A Guide to Oregon Rivers, Second Edition, Willamette Kayak and Canoe Club (1986) (3rd edition published by The Mountaineers)

Soggy Sneakers, A Guide to Oregon Rivers, Third Edition, The Mountaineers (199?)

Stanislaus, The Struggle for a River, Tim Palmer. University of California Press (1982)

Virginia Whitewater, H. Roger Corbett. Seneca Press (1988)

Washington Whitewater I, Douglas A. North. The Mountaineers (1988)

Washington's Wild Rivers, The Unfinished Work, Tim McNulty and Pat O'Hara. The Mountaineers (1990)

We Swam the Grand Canyon, The True Story of a Cheap Vacation That Got a Little Out of Hand, Bill Beer. the Mountaineers (1988)

A Week on the Concord and Merrimack Rivers, Henry David Thoreau. Notes by Dudley C. Lunt. Bramhall House (1950)

West Coast River Touring, Rogue River Canyon and South, Dick Schwind. the Touchstone Press (1974)

Western Whitewater, From the Rockies to the Pacific, Jim Cassady, Fryar Calhoun, and Bill Cross. North Fork Press (1992)

Whitewater Adventure: Running America's Great Scenic Rivers, Richard Bangs. Thunder Bay Press (1990)

Whitewater Boatman, The Making of a River Guide, Robert S. Wood. Ten Speed Press (1984)

Whitewater Home Companion, Southeastern Rivers, Volume I, William Nealy. Menasha Ridge Press (1981)

Whitewater Rafting in Eastern North America, A Guide to Rivers and Professional Outfitters. Lloyd D. Armstead (1989)

Whitewater Rafting in Western North America, A Guide to Rivers and Professional Outfitters. Lloyd D. Armstead (1990)

The Whitewater Sourcebook, A Sourcebook of Information on American Whitewater Rivers, Richard Penny. Menasha Ridge Press (1989)

Wildwater: The Sierra Club Guide to Kayaking and Whitewater Boating, Lito Tejadas-Flores. Sierra Club Books (1978)

Wildwater West Virginia, Volume I, The Northern Streams, Paul Davidson, Ward Eister and Dirk Davidson. Menasha Ridge Press (1985)

Wildwater West Virginia, Volume II, The Southern Streams, Paul Davidson, Ward Eister and Dirk Davidson. Menasha Ridge Press (1985)

A Wolverine Is Eating My Leg, Tim Cahill. Random House, Inc. (1989)

MAGAZINES, CALENDARS AND VIDEOS

American Whitewater, the Journal of the American Whitewater Affiliation, PO Box 85, Phoenicia, NY 12464

Blazing Paddles, an incredible Class V whitewater film by Camera One, PO Box 75556, Seattle, WA 98103 (write Camera One for a complete list of their whitewater videos)

California Whitewater, an extraordinary glimpse of California rivers by Camera One, PO Box 75556, Seattle, WA 98103

Canoe Magazine, 10526 NE 68th, Suite 3, Kirkland, WA 98033

Classic Images, a breathtaking whitewater calendar produced yearly by Rapid Shooters, 7221 Hwy 49, Lotus, CA 95651

Great White Hunters, Photographic Expeditions, 7500 East Arapahoe Road, #355, Englewood, CO 80112

Paddler Magazine, PO Box 697, Fallbrook, CA 92028

"Slammin Salmon", an entertaining bloopers video by Gayle Wilson Productions, 265 Alta, Ashland, OR 97520

"Whitewater Bloopers II: The Carnage Continues", part two of Gayle Wilson's blooper series; Gayle Wilson Productions, 265 Alta, Ashland, OR 97520

ABOUT THE AUTHORS

JEFF BENNETT: After three years of flatwater canoeing, Jeff got his first taste of whitewater on the Snake River in 1978 just outside of Jackson Hole, Wyoming. Then, after spending a few years paddling the rivers of the Eastern United States, he picked up his gear and headed West. Jeff has now spent many years guiding on the rivers of California, Oregon, and Washington, and has paddled hundreds of rivers throughout the United States, Canada, and Costa Rica. In 1991, he came out with his first book, A Guide to the Whitewater Rivers of Washington, which has gone on to become Washington State's leading guidebook. Jeff also appears in The Inflatable Kayak Handbook, has contributed to Soggy Sneakers Guide to Oregon Rivers, 3rd Edition, appears in a Rapid Shooters Classic Images Calendar, and even lurks beneath a wall of whitewater on the video sleeve of Blazing Paddles. Jeff also has a number of first descents to his name and has appeared in magazines and on TV. When not paddling, he spends his spare writing, playing guitar, or perusing topo maps for new adventures.

BOB CARLSON: Though Bob started rafting in 1969 with ARTA, his passion for whitewater didn't launch until 1974. While working toward his Ph.D. in mathematics, Bob quit school, left his girlfriend, and spent his federally insured student loan on a new raft. Too cheap to buy a new pump, he built one from scratch. That same pump is sold today through *Carlson Designs,* together with Carlson River Boards and other specialized whitewater equipment. Over the years, Bob has also worked for Lockheed's space program, as a math teacher, as an architectural draftsman for Bank of America, and appeared in the January 1986 issue of Scientific American with Carlson's Icosahedron, a complex puzzle. Many have seen him at his most famous moment, flying out of a raft at "That's Dumb" on California's Upper Kings River in the early video edition of "California Whitewater."

JIM CASSADY: Jim began paddling whitewater in an open canoe in his native homeland of Maryland before migrating westward to Long Beach, California. There, he taught social science in a local high school, learned to kayak, and became a professional river guide. He now lives in the San Francisco Bay area and is the founder and co-owner of Pacific River Supply in El Sobrante. He also co-authored California Whitewater and Western Whitewater, From the Rockies to the Pacific, and designed the SOTAR self-bailing raft, produced by Whitewater Manufacturing of Grants Pass, Oregon. Cassady led the first raft trips down some of the West's toughest rivers, including the Upper Kings, the South Fork of the Salmon, and Washington's Cascade River. His latest accomplishments include co-designing the Carlson River Board with Bob Carlson, and contributing river flow columns to Headwaters, Paddler Magazine, and the San Francisco Chronicle.

MIKE DOYLE: Mike's love of whitewater began in 1970 when he was only 11 years old. He spent eight years paddling the whitewater streams of New York's Adirondack Mountains before heading west in 1978 to attend the University of California Berkeley on a full swimming scholarship. His competitive spirit took him and the U.C. Berkeley team to the top in 1979 and 1980, becoming NCAA Division I Champions both years. Mike started rafting in 1979 on California's Kings and Stanislaus Rivers, and has logged many incredible first descents. In 1985 he founded *Beyond Limits Adventures* and runs first class rafting trips down the North Fork Stanislaus and the Lower Stanislaus through Goodwin Canyon. By 1991, Beyond Limits Adventures had moved its headquarters to Riverbank and became one of California's premier outfitters with trips conducted on 15 California rivers. In the off-season, Mike attends to his business as a general contractor in Modesto and catches up on time with his beautiful wife Bonnie and their two daughters, Elizabeth and Emily.

DAVE HAMMOND: Dave—affectionately known as "Indian Dave" to his East Coast paddling friends—has been boating whitewater rivers since 1980. He started in West Virginia, where he spent six years guiding the state's hottest commercial runs. When not guiding, he was out making some extraordinary first raft descents and exploring many of the East Coast's obscure steep creek runs. In 1987 Dave moved to California in order to expand his boating horizons. In less than a year he became the co-owner of *Beyond Limits Adventures,* one of California's premier Class V outfitters. Some of his California first raft descents include the Middle and South Fork of the Kings Rivers, two extreme runs that have yet to be duplicated. In his spare time Dave squirt boats, river boards, and looks for more uncharted water.

TIMOTHY HILLMER: Tim worked for ten years as a whitewater guide on rivers in California, Oregon and Colorado. His fiction, poetry, and articles have appeared in numerous publications. In 1987 he won first prize in the Westword magazine fiction contest, and in 1988 was named Teacher of the Year by the Colorado Language Arts Society. After completing his Masters degree at the University of New Hampshire in 1991, he is currently finishing a novel about rafting, and teaching at an alternative junior high school. He lives with his wife, Nancy, and their two daughters, Rachel and Carly, in Louisville, Colorado.

TIM KEGGERMAN: Tim started paddling whitewater rivers in the Southeast, where he owned a North Carolina rafting company based on the Nolichucky River. Next, he headed for West Virginia and spent his Summers guiding on the Appalachian's hottest runs, then ducked out at the end of each season for a Winter of skiing in Colorado. After marrying his wife, Terri, they moved permanently to Colorado, where they went on to found *Crested Butte Rafting* in 1983. Crested Butte Rafting is now a high adventure outfitting specialist, with high octane rafting adventures on the Upper Slate, Taylor, and Upper Arkansas Rivers. In the Winter, Crested Butte Rafting offers more seasonal activities in the heart of Colorado's Rockies. In his spare time, Tim picks guitar and plots future descents on the Rocky Mountain's toughest rivers.

DOC LOOMIS: Doc is known throughout the Pacific Northwest for his numerous first raft descents, amiable demeanor, and great sense of humor. His motto that "if it can be kayaked it can be rafted" has allowed him to see many rivers few rafters will ever explore. Doc participated in all three of the early raft rallies, in Russia, North Carolina, and Costa Rica, and has been a frequent first place finisher in western rafting competitions. Doc's stunning photography has appeared in A Guide to the Whitewater Rivers of Washington and delights scores of fellow boaters during his frequent slide shows. Off the river, Doc is a maniacal mountain biker who can peddle circles around friends half his age.

KEVIN O'BRIEN: Kevin is a free lance photographer, writer, and adventure filmmaker. A veteran kayaker and raft guide of 18 years, he has made first descents of remote rivers in the U.S. and the Himalayas, including the Seti Khola in western Nepal. With adventure sports and travel central to his work, his photography and stories have appeared in many popular magazines and catalogs, including Canoe, Paddler, Outside, Time, Sports Illustrated and Patagonia ads. He currently lives at Hidden Valley, a ski area southeast of Pittsburgh, Pennsylvania. His wife, Chara started paddling at the age of four, is a veteran raft guide, and is the daughter of pioneering West Virginia paddler Bob Burrell.

JAMES SNYDER: Jim starting rafting over two decades ago in an attempt to prolong adolescence. For the last 17 years he's been manufacturing *Rivr Styx Paddles* and designs kayaks under the logo *Preferred Modes*. Jim is probably best known as one of squirt boating's pioneers. He invented many of the moves kayakers try to emulate today, wrote the leading book on the sport, The Squirt Book, and appeared in the hot video Certain Squirtin'. Jim's kayaks, such as the Bigfoot, Shred and Maestro, are world-renown for their leading edge designs. He now designs kayaks for New Wave Kayaks. Jim makes his home on the banks of West Virginia's Cheat River with his wife Doris and his children Nathan and Amelia. Jim's goal in life is to be "whitewater rich," which he defines as "...when the weather and river level say go, *you go!*"

INDEX